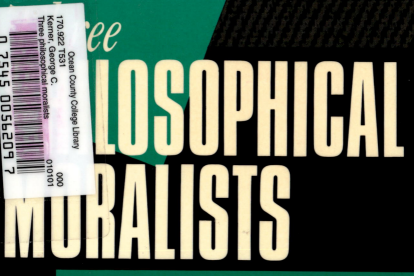

Three PHILOSOPHICAL MORALISTS

Mill, Kant, and Sartre

An Introduction to Ethics

GEORGE C. KERNER

THREE PHILOSOPHICAL MORALISTS

Mill, Kant, and Sartre

THREE PHILOSOPHICAL MORALISTS

Mill, Kant, and Sartre

An Introduction to Ethics

George C. Kerner

CLARENDON PRESS · OXFORD
1990

Oxford University Press, Walton Street, Oxford OX2 6DP
Oxford New York Toronto
Delhi Bombay Calcutta Madras Karachi
Petaling Jaya Singapore Hong Kong Tokyo
Nairobi Dar es Salaam Cape Town
Melbourne Auckland
and associated companies in
Berlin Ibadan

Oxford is a trade mark of Oxford University Press

Published in the United States
by Oxford University Press, New York

© George C. Kerner 1990

British Library Cataloguing in Publication Data
Kerner, George C.
Three philosophical moralists: Mill, Kant, and Sartre:
an introduction to Ethics.
1. Ethics. Theories I. Title 170'.1
ISBN 0-19-824228-X
ISBN 0-19-824227-1 (pbk)

Library of Congress Cataloging in Publication Data
Three philosophical moralists: Mill, Kant, and Sartre: an
introduction to ethics/George C. Kerner.
Includes bibliographical references.
1. Ethics. 2. Ethics, Modern. 3. Kant, Immanuel, 1724–1804—
Ethics. 4. Mill, John Stuart, 1806–1873—Ethics. 5. Sartre, Jean
Paul, 1905–1984—Ethics. I. Title. II. Title: 3 philosophical moralists.
BJ1012.K47 1990   170'.92'2—dc20   89-27213
ISBN 0-19-824228-X
ISBN 0-19-824227-1 (pbk)

Photoset by Rowland Phototypesetting Ltd,
Bury St Edmunds, Suffolk
Printed in Great Britain by
Biddles Ltd, Guildford and King's Lynn

For my daughter Irene

PREFACE

UTILITARIANISM, Kantianism, and existentialism are the main alternatives in moral philosophy today. Of course there are other 'isms' in the market place. But none of them, I believe, is as worthy of scrutiny as those three. What, if anything, makes life worth living and gives it meaning? This is the question of ethics. Mill, Kant, and Sartre have offered the answers which are the most intriguing.

The reader should not look in this book for a full-scale commentary on the ethical writings of these three authors. I have not tried to explore every facet of what each of them has ever said about ethics. Instead, I have focused on what is central in Mill (the hedonist and consequentialist), in Kant (the formalist and deontologist), and in Sartre (the existentialist). Although I have tried to avoid over-simplification in presenting their views, some aspects of their writings are emphasized more than others, and some things each of them have said, even if important in their own right, are ignored altogether. By assessing and comparing the central views of these three philosophers I have sought to determine which of the lines of thought they represent is the most incisive. This has led me sometimes to go beyond exegesis and critique and to develop, to some degree, my own views, particularly on the topics of pleasure, rules, and emotions. Few of those views are totally new. Many of them have been, in one form or another, voiced before, although not in the same overall context.

This book is not a foray into some uncharted territory in ethics, but an up-to-date introduction to moral philosophy and, in some measure, a contribution to the advancement of that subject. While it cannot be said that Sartre's existentialism is quite the final word in ethics—probably nothing ever will be—we shall see that progressing from Mill to Kant (chronology in this instance not corresponding to progress), and from Kant to Sartre, there is an increasing radicalness with which the problem of ethics is posed. This should teach us at least to ask the right questions. My overall thesis is that the objectivist doctrines of both Mill and Kant (for different reasons, to be sure)—together with the revisions that have or may be made to them—are to be rejected and that the truth lies closer to the subjectivism of Sartre. He makes us realize that in morality there are no objective answers, but only questions directed at our deep subjectivity.

After the virtual disappearance of meta-ethics—that is, the analytic and logical study of moral language—there has developed, for the past twenty years or so, an avid interest in the study of substantive moral issues. A great deal of work has been done in applied ethics. However, such discussions proceed on the assumption that objective solutions are capable of being found to them. By and large, the meta-ethical questions which were raised and discussed in such works as C. L. Stevenson's *Ethics and Language* (New Haven, 1944), and R. M. Hare's *The Language of Morals* (Oxford, 1952) have been forgotten or ignored. For a considerable period, the most hotly debated issue in ethics was whether there is such a thing as objective moral knowledge at all. The practitioners of applied ethics have, in a way, turned the clock back. The philosophical underpinnings of their discussions have been, broadly speaking, either Millian or Kantian or a mixture of the two. And the same kind of backwardness characterizes a great deal of the more general and fundamental present-day discussions of normative ethics. One takes up positions along the battle lines which were drawn up by Mill and Kant. Or one makes refinements and revisions designed to effect a compromise between the two. In either case, the objectivist dogma of both Mill and Kant is not questioned. One of my aims has been to counteract this trend. Both Mill and Kant were fundamentally mistaken, even though, on the level of objectivism, diametrically opposed to one another. Conciliatory manœuvres between the two are futile. The thing to do is to scrap objectivism.

'Subjectivism' has been a scare-word among academic philosophers. It has been, you might say, a club with which to beat your opponent over the head. If a philosophical view could be shown to have subjectivist consequences, it was presumed to have been reduced to absurdity. To some extent this has changed. There are now voices which say that ethics cannot be completely objective and that one must pay attention to the 'agent-centred' considerations in arriving at moral conclusions. This kind of syncretism is as fruitless as the effort to combine Millian consequentialism with Kantian deontology. One says that straight utilitarianism must be tempered by due regard for the 'interests' of the agent, such as his personal relations with others and his 'commitments' and 'projects'. These sound like echoes from Sartre, but Sartre imperfectly understood. The basic source of misunderstanding Sartre is perhaps a failure to distinguish clearly enough between subjectivism and relativism. We must appreciate Sartre not for bringing to our attention certain subjective 'aspects' of morality, but for putting forth an entire philosophy of man and of the worth of his life which is radically opposed to the whole objectivist tradition. He aimed at a total reorientation of moral philosophy. According to him, the moral philosopher must not ask 'How, or to what extent, objective answers to moral problems are possible?' but devote himself to the exploration and illumination of human subjectivity.

This book is intended to be a stimulus, rather than a substitute, for studying the ethical writings of Mill, Kant, and Sartre. In fact, it is best read as a companion to Mill's *Utilitarianism*, Kant's *Groundwork of the Metaphysic of Morals*, and Sartre's *Existentialism and Humanism*. The list of abbreviations gives details of editions and translations which I shall use to give page references to these as well as to other works by my three authors. All other references will be given in the footnotes.

I have made use, in a largely modified form, of some material in the following articles of mine: 'Passions and the Cognitive Foundation of Ethics', *Philosophy and Phenomenological Research*, 31/2 (1970), 177–92; 'The Immortality of Utilitarianism and the Escapism of Rule-Utilitarianism', *Philosophical Quarterly*, 21/82 (1971), 36–50; 'Urteil und Gefühl; Glaube und Absicht', in R. Haller (ed.), *Jenseits von Sein and Nichtsein* (Graz, 1972), 229–44; and 'Emotions are Judgments of Value', *Topoi*, 1/1–2 (1982), 52–6. I am grateful to the publishers of those articles for permission to do so.

George C. Kerner

East Lansing
March 1989

CONTENTS

ABBREVIATIONS

BN   J.-P. Sartre, *Being and Nothingness*, trans. H. E. Barnes (New York, 1966).

CJ   I. Kant, *Critique of Judgment*, trans. J. H. Bernard (New York, 1951).

CM   J.-P. Sartre, *Cahiers pour une morale* (Paris, 1983).

CPrR   I. Kant, *Critique of Practical Reason and Other Writings in Moral Philosophy*, trans. L. White Beck (Chicago, 1949).

CPuR   I. Kant, *Critique of Pure Reason*, trans. N. Kemp Smith (New York, 1965).

CW   J. S. Mill, *Collected Works* (Toronto, 1981).

EH   J.-P. Sartre, *Existentialism and Humanism*, trans. P. Mairet (Brooklyn, n.d., London, 1948).

GR   I. Kant, *Groundwork of the Metaphysic of Morals*, trans. H. J. Paton (New York, 1964).

LE   I. Kant, *Lectures on Ethics*, trans. L. Infield (New York, 1963).

MM   I. Kant, *The Doctrine of Virtue: Part II of The Metaphysic of Morals*, trans. M. J. Gregor (New York, 1964).

OS   I. Kant, *On the Old Saw: That may be Right in Theory but it Won't Work in Practice*, trans. E. B. Ashton (Philadelphia, 1974).

RE   I. Kant, *Religion within the Limits of Reason Alone*, trans. T. M. Greene and H. H. Hudson (New York, 1960).

TE   J.-P. Sartre, *Sketch for a Theory of Emotions*, trans. P. Mairet (London, 1971).

UT   J. S. Mill, *Utilitarianism* (Indianapolis, 1979).

INTRODUCTION

The Question of Ethics

WHAT is ethics? A look in the dictionary tells us that it is the study of what is good and bad in our conduct and how we ought to live. But it is more illuminating to say that in ethics we try to discover what is really important in life, what gives it meaning and makes it worth living. For by putting it in this way we make it clear that in ethics we are concerned with the right way of living in the ultimate sense.

Medicine, for example, is also concerned with how we ought to live. But no one would say that it is ethics. The reason is that it tells us what to do, or what not to do, only in order to preserve or to regain our health; it never raises the question of whether or not health is itself a thing worth aiming at. The same is to be said about all the other practical disciplines such as law, engineering, agriculture, and what have you. The lawyer, in his professional capacity, never asks whether or not it is a good thing that his client gets acquitted. The engineer never asks whether or not it is a good thing that the bridge will hold or the agricultural expert whether or not the soya beans should prosper. The physician, the lawyer, the engineer, the architect, the financial consultant, the pest exterminator, and so on, take the desirability of certain things for granted. Moreover, the practitioners of such arts operate within more-or-less established rules, regulations, and procedures. For the lawyer there are the rules of law, for the builder the building codes, for the broker the rules of brokerage, and so on. In ethics, on the other hand, there are no presupposed goals and no previously codified and sanctioned rules.

But in that case ethics may well appear to be a totally free-wheeling affair. It would seem that we can reasonably hope to find out what ought to be done in order to decrease our chances of getting cancer of the lung, or how to build a sturdy bridge, or how to seed a lawn. We can also hope to get to know how to do well the job of a nurse, or a bank clerk, or the commander of a company of soldiers. With regard to tasks such as these it is clear enough what are the criteria of success and how to decide whether or not someone has done his job well. But how are we to determine what is the right way of conducting ourselves just in general, that is, without any antecedently given goals or procedures to guide us? The ethical question as we have formulated it seems altogether too indeterminate.

For this reason, some philosophers have given ethics a more restricted definition. We must ask, they say, 'What is the point or object of morality?' and then they go on to say that that point or object is 'the harmonization of human interests' or 'the amelioration of the human predicament'.[1] 'What is the good life, the life worth living?' is, for them, a question which falls outside ethics and belongs to religion(s) or imaginative literature or the private recesses of individual souls. Ethics as a rational enterprise must deal solely with how humans, since they have to live together on this planet and since they have to cope not only with the scarcity of goods but also with the imperfection of their own nature, can get along with one another with the least possible degree of friction and open antagonism and how they can engage in the pursuit of their wants and desires—whatever these wants and desires happen to be—with the greatest possible degree of co-operation.

The first trouble with this kind of definition is that it smacks of circularity and emptiness. 'Harmony', 'amelioration', even 'co-operation', are themselves laudatory terms. When people live in harmony and when they co-operate, then, in a sense, it goes without saying that they behave as they ought to behave; and 'amelioration' just means betterment. The second is that a definition of this kind, if it does not automatically usher in the doctrine of utilitarianism, strongly favours it; this is unfair. When you define ethics you define a problem and your definition is not to suppose, in advance, that it is solvable only in one direction. The promotion of peace and harmony may be one of our moral concerns, but ethics is not defined by it. Someone's moral aim may quite intelligibly be a revolution. He may feel that what is needed is not the smooth co-operation of men as

---

[1] See, for example, S. E. Toulmin, *An Examination of the Place of Reason in Ethics* (Cambridge, 1953), and G. J. Warnock, *The Object of Morality* (London, 1971).

they are, but a radical conversion of them and society. Further-more, Kant, as we shall see, argued that ethics has no purpose or object beyond itself at all.

Another attempt to make the ethical question more manage-able, although no longer very popular, is to say that ethics is concerned with our duties—and our duties, so it is adjured, go with and are relative to the customs and mores of our society and the place we occupy in it. To know the answer to the ethical question is to know one's societal station and its duties.[2] But this way of bringing decidability into ethics is even more arbitrary. For the behavioural norms which exist in a given society need not be beyond moral reproach. Nor need they constitute a coherent whole. It may easily happen that they exhibit internal conflicts. It follows that, by relying on existing moral norms, the problem of choice would not always be capable of solution. This problem is particularly acute in contemporary Western societies in which different 'life-styles' clamour for recognition. More-over, while which moral norms are actually adhered to is relative to societies and cultures, the world is becoming a 'global village'. Therefore, it is becoming increasingly difficult among societies and cultures to agree to disagree. What 'we' do has increasingly an impact on 'them' and vice versa. So, even if I lived in a morally homogenous society, reliance on accepted moral norms would not solve my moral problems as a citizen of the world. For it would be quite quixotic to take the position that the moral norms and values of my society and culture are superior simply because they are the norms and values of *my* society and culture and that therefore inter-societal and cross-cultural disagree-ments should be settled on the basis of *them*.

If ethics is to take into account the full extent of man's moral consciousness, it must pose the question of how we should live in its unrestricted sense and face the fact that it is not a run-of-the-mill question. And, whatever may be said about its oddity, it is one which we do ask. Moreover, when we ask it, we are not

---

[2] This kind of view has been held by many sociologists and anthropologists. One of the best philosophical discussions of it is F. H. Bradley, *Ethical Studies* (Oxford, 1927). But, abhorring relativism, Bradley did not say that 'My Station and its Duties' (the title of the central essay) is the *ultimate* word in ethics. And neither did Kant. Although he advocated an ethics of duty, Kant by no means thought that our moral duties are simply what our society expects from us.

indulging in superficial, fancy, or idle musing. It is a question deep-seated in us. Nor should philosophers hide from it under their academic mantles. What is human life all about? This question springs from our most basic disquietudes. It has a way of forcing itself upon us. Sometimes we even feel that we have found an answer to it. We then feel absolutely safe and that nothing can harm us. We are then at peace with ourselves and the world; all anxieties have vanished. We then experience also a sense of total commitment; we are filled with a single-minded purpose and seem to have found our true calling.

Perhaps not many people have experiences of this kind and it is unlikely that any of us have them with any permanence. In day-to-day life our attention and our will are divided. Our satisfactions are limited and fragile and our commitments inconstant. We just gather the nosegays. But this state of mind may also fill us with a deep sense of dissatisfaction and we may yearn to stop floundering. To some extent we are all familiar with experiences which in their depth and intensity carry us beyond the fragmentariness of our day-to-day existence. Occasionally, the meaning of our whole life seems to be in our grasp.

However, the objection that there can be no answer to the question of what, in the ultimate and absolute sense, is the right way of living and that therefore ethics, as we have conceived it, would have to be an unprofitable business, is of course not answered by simply pointing out that that question is related to deep human experiences. For those experiences might point to nothing and there might be nothing that justifies them. The feelings of absolute safety and peace or a total single-mindedness of purpose might signify nothing. They may be like a 'high' induced by drugs. We could be lulled into a feeling of immense peace and security and excited into having a profound sense of purpose, but there might be nothing, or at least nothing we can put our finger on and make evident to others, that could make those feelings sensible and justified. However deeply we may feel satisfied with our lives or however committed we are in our purpose, it might all be a grand illusion. The fact that we persist in our ethical quest, and at times even appear to consummate it, proves nothing. In reality there might not be an answer—not an objective one anyhow—to the question of ethics in spite of the fact that we keep asking it and sometimes feel that we have found the answer.

Moral philosophy, when pursued resolutely, takes this possibility seriously. It does not take it for granted that there is an answer to the question of ethics. It is flattering and comforting to think that our powers are constantly growing, that we are steadily becoming capable of ever greater achievements; and we are inclined to include in this idea moral growth. But to do so is entirely gratuitous. Science and technology perform greater and greater feats, but it does not follow from this that we are becoming better equipped to discover and to live the good life. We may be falling into greater and greater moral darkness. Ordinarily we do not worry about this. We assume that, if we can do something, it is worth doing. For example, we believe that, if we can put men on the moon or Mars, we ought to do it, or, so long as we are in the position to fight a war and to win it, we ought to fight it. Our moral sense is stirred only when our enterprises have been checked or frustrated, when there is an impasse. We then stop and ask whether or not the things we find ourselves doing, or capable of doing, are really worth doing. We are then struck with the immense difficulty, perhaps even the impossibility, of giving an answer.

There is a further reason why ethics can be approached only with trepidation. There is something odd and suspicious about the very idea of ethics as a specialized enquiry. It would seem that the question of the meaning of our lives is one with which all of us equally are, in fact, must be, concerned. We raise this question simply because we are beings who are conscious of our own lives and not as specialists who choose to study a certain limited subject. Only the mathematician has to be concerned with the problems of mathematics and being a mathematician is only one among many alternatives. But there is no alternative to being a human and being concerned with the right way of living. You do not *choose* to be concerned with the question of what makes life worth living as you choose to be concerned with, say, geology. Furthermore, the mathematician, the geologist, the lawyer, the physician can take a holiday and stop being concerned with the problems of his speciality. He may even retire or change his profession. But, apart from suicide, there is no such thing as quitting being human. Nor is there such a thing as taking a moral holiday. I may get a reprieve—be able to put off the sticky decisions for a while—but I can hardly create it through my own will and I can never prolong it indefinitely. Things have a way of breaking in on us. There is the young woman confronted with an unwanted pregnancy, the executive who has to choose between success on the corporate ladder and his integrity, the revolutionary who has to suppress his feelings of compassion and decency. People in situations like these cannot beg off and say that they are occupied with something else or not in the right mood for dealing with ethics. An attempt to withdraw and to suspend morality may always end in immorality. Life goes on and your withdrawal is as good as having made an active decision.

Let us make another comparison. In playing games there is a difference between the right and the wrong. But all this is in a way arbitrary. Standards of excellence in playing games apply to us only if we choose to try to play a game well to begin with, if we take it seriously. Suppose you go to the golf course with a Sunday golfer and after a while you can no longer contain yourself and say, 'Well, you play pretty badly.'[3] And suppose also that he answers, 'I know I play badly, but I don't want to play any better, I just want to have fun.' All you would say then is, 'Oh, then it's all right.' But suppose that you witness someone telling an atrocious lie or betraying a friend. You say to him, 'You behave badly.' Were this man to reply, 'I know I behave badly, but I don't want to behave any better,' would you say to *him* that then it is all right? You would not. You would say, 'Well, you *ought* to want to behave better.' We cannot escape moral demands as we can escape the demands of sportsmanship. Ethics knows no tolerance. While we do not have to be concerned with ourselves or others being good at golf or tennis, we do have to care about whether or not our own lives, as well as the lives of others, are good lives.

But what about the amoralist, someone may ask? There are people who murder, rape, deceive, betray, and so on, and who, after we have told them 'You behave like a beast', say, 'I do not care.' Well, there is, presumably, a mental illness such that

---

[3] This example is adapted from Wittgenstein 'Lecture on Ethics', *Philosophical Review*, 74 (Jan. 1965), 3–12.

whoever suffers from it is incapable of caring about anything
—himself, others, the world. A person who is afflicted in this
way would, however, not be one for whom there is an alternative
to being ethical, but one for whom there would be no true
alternatives at all. He would not be like the 'amoralist', or 'moral
sceptic', as some perfectly normal people are sometimes called.
Imagine a young woman who has been brought up with very
strict notions concerning chastity. As she is growing up—going
to college, meeting new and more sophisticated friends—she
may well feel at one point like saying, 'To hell with that!',
meaning chastity. Is she then rejecting ethics as we have defined
it? Of course not. She is likely very far from saying, as the true
amoralist would have to say, 'To hell with it *all*.' To go against
and to scorn conventional morality is something a person may
do just because his ethical concerns run deep. A person may well
reach the conclusion that the morality handed down to him does
not provide a way of life really worth living. But the true
amoralist would have to say that nothing whatever is really
important. And such a person is, I believe, a very rare aberrant.

What I have just said may create a wrong impression. The
boundary between being either moral or amoral is not clear-cut.
Someone who cares about absolutely nothing is a limiting case.
Being an amoralist is a matter of degree. Amoralism is a
diminution of humanity. The life of an amoralist becomes
mechanical. He just goes through the motions; his heart is not in
it. He may keep a pet, but his care of it is neglectful. He may find
his girlfriend's dress fetching, but shies away from any lasting
involvement with the person in it. He shows no constancy, no
true passion, no fidelity. His life is fragmentary and episodic.

Is the egoist amoral? Yes, if he is also inconsistent, that is, a
coward and a parasite. He then resents self-seeking in others,
wishes to be the only egoist in the world and to take advantage of
the social virtues of others. He then makes an arbitrary exception for himself; as Kant would say, he is unwilling to universal-
ize his own attitude. Actually, we may want to say that such a
person is not amoral but immoral, for it is not that he does not
care about anything, he just does not care about others. Still, he
is different from the consistent egoist who says that seeking
one's own advantage is right for everyone and is willing to take
his chances in an egoistic world. The 'rugged individualist'

has a morality, although, as most of us would say, a wrong morality.

The consistent egoist is a kind of fanatic, and there are others: for example, the scientist who in the name of his research is willing to perform crippling experiments on human subjects, the religious zealot who burns heretics, the collector who robs and murders for the possession of a rare piece. There is the story of a painter of ancient Greece who had one of his slaves chained on to a rock and poked with a red-hot iron so as to be able to capture on canvas the suffering of Prometheus. Keeping in mind our definition of ethics, it would seem that we would have to regard such people as not amoral, for they evidently care very deeply about certain things—scientific truth, art, salvation—and see the meaning of their lives in promoting them. In order to say that they are nevertheless amoral, we would have to think of their single-mindedness as due to the stunting of their human sensibilities.

So it remains true that, unless you are a lessened human, you are concerned with morality. By the same token, if being concerned with ethics is just being human, it appears curious that ethics should take the form of an intellectual discipline, that it should figure along with such things as mathematics, geology, law, and medicine in a college curriculum. If all of us are concerned with ethics, what is the place of experts in it? In such things as medicine, engineering, or golf, the opinions of the specialist take precedence over those of the layman. But when it comes to determining what ultimately matters in life, it does not seem that any special training, education, or talent can make some of us superior to others. At any rate, even if we were to believe that there is something to be learnt in ethics, we should not think that we can acquire that knowledge from some sort of coach or scientist or college professor. For instance, when it comes to my health, I accept the word of the physician. But I do not look for someone to tell me what will make my life worth living. Ethics belongs to everyone and there is a sense in which, in that regard, no one can tell anyone anything. The reason is actually not that there are no people who are more experienced and wiser than others. It is rather that, by just taking someone else's word for it, we would be relinquishing the responsibility for our own lives, in other words, our autonomy.

So where does the moral philosopher come in? This question becomes even more pressing since, from another angle, it may be urged that ethical problems are not problems of knowing at all, but of doing. They are not intellectual problems, but problems of the will. We always *know* what is right and what we ought to do—it is all spelt out in the Scripture or told by our conscience. The trouble is that we do not always adhere to that knowledge. Our lives have a meaning simply if we do not slide back and are not of two minds. Moral development is not intellectual discovery and theoretical learning but becoming more mature and more responsible. It consists of our will and character becoming stronger. The answer to the ethical question lies not in the study of books, in scholarly and scientific investigations and reasoning, but in growing up. The point is to become a better and not a cleverer or more knowledgeable person. Moral teaching, it may therefore be said, would have to be teaching of a special kind. It would have to consist of such things as persuading, kindling, and inspiring. But moral philosophy, presumably, is not exhortation and preaching.

Being impressed by the last point, some philosophers—notably the meta-ethicists referred to in the Preface—have gone so far as to say that moral philosophy is itself morally neutral. They distinguish sharply between ethical theory and normative ethics. The moral theorist does not take sides. He does not raise and attempt to answer moral questions. In a disinterested spirit he just wants to discover and to clarify the meaning and the 'logic' of raising and answering such questions. He merely wants to determine what goes on when we think and talk about what is the ultimately right way of living. He himself makes no proposals concerning what such a life is.

This view is exaggerated, which is not to say that the job of the meta-ethicist is needless. It is just that the presumed choice between being either a theorist of morality or a moralist is an unreal one. Many philosophers, including the three whose views we shall examine, have been both. They have endeavoured to analyse the concepts which operate in our moral consciousness and discourse, but they have also tried to find the answer to the substantive question of what is the ultimately right way of living. Being a moralist does not entail mere moralizing. The dogmatic moralizer wants us to accept his gospel uncritically.

He, like the typical physician, gives us a prescription without bothering to convince us that he has prescribed the right medicine. Consequently, moralizing may usurp our freedom to make up our own minds. But moral philosophy does not interfere with our freedom of conscience. Instead it challenges it. In fact, moral philosophy constitutes in a very real sense the foundation of genuine morality. It need not make us morally better: more steadfast or kind and charitable. But it schools our moral thinking and frees us from mere custom and authority. When our motives are social conformity or the pronouncements of an ayatollah, our actions really lack the ethical dimension. Such things can produce outwardly exemplary behaviour in us. But without reflecting on the ultimate worth of our lives and actions—in fact, without ourselves being moral philosophers —we would be, at best, like well-behaved robots.

Moreover, the moral philosopher, as opposed to the zealous moralizer, does not presume that people are apt to live in moral darkness and ignorance from which they are to be rescued. He believes that, deep down, ordinary men are cognizant of the answer to the ethical question. It is always there in man's consciousness although perhaps only darkly. He conceives his own task as being merely the uncovering and the reminding us of it. He thinks of himself chiefly as one who describes, analyses, and clarifies truths already known instead of proposing totally new ones. In a sense, he does not try to tell us anything which we do not already know.

Still, there is a great deal of controversy in philosophical ethics. Why, if it is largely just description and analysis, is this so? The ingredients of our moral consciousness are complex and convoluted; they derive from a long cultural history in which various strands are interwoven. While the moral philosopher tries to achieve a unified answer to the ethical question, our moral consciousness is not necessarily coherent. Therefore, there may easily be disagreements concerning where to put the emphasis and which principle of organization to choose. Quite often, when a person is confronted with a moral choice, he is confused because there are several considerations, motives, and norms which clamour for attention. They constitute, we may say, the data of ethics. They are the ground-level, unreflected, and ostensible reasons for choosing or rejecting a course of action. The world is not a panorama—to be aesthetically enjoyed or scientifically investigated; it is full of implications with regard to conduct. It is made up of ills to be remedied, demands to be met, dangers and failures to be overcome or avoided, opportunities to be used, and challenges to be lived up to. These forces may not all pull in the same direction. It is the multiplicity and possible incoherence of ethical data that make moral philosophy both difficult and necessary. In life, not everything falls naturally into place. Not only our instinctual reactions to what is round us, but also our socially and culturally conditioned sentiments and attitudes are products of blind forces rather than of an intelligent design. Our customs, mores, and traditions are just handed down. Many of our preferences result from the brute exigencies and limitations of our lives. They come from economic stress and group interests. Myths, prejudices, fears, and selfishness are at least as prominent in our moral consciousness as is our reflective intelligence.

It is here that moral philosophy comes to the rescue. Out of the multiplicity of moral data, out of their buzzing and blooming confusion, the moral philosopher, traditionally at least, tries to construct, one might say, a unifying theory or system. Consequently, he must go beyond pure description and analysis; he must interpret and be selective, even creative; and that provides plenty of room for controversy.

Another source of controversy in ethics is what may be called moral psychology. What can make our lives cohere and make them into meaningful wholes must derive from something deep in us. The ultimate meaning of man's life must reflect the ultimate truth about him. Moral philosophy must therefore delve into the question of what man is, what basically motivates him, what makes him tick. As we shall see, it is exactly the differences in answering that question which are responsible for the differences in the normative views of our three authors. According to Mill, humans are pleasure seekers. To say that man is rational, is merely to say that he is an intelligent pleasure seeker, that he seeks pleasure and happiness with intelligence and foresight. From these premises follow Mill's hedonism and utilitarianism. According to Kant, on the other hand, reason has a loftier purpose. Quite independently of any considerations of happiness, it gives us the moral law or what he called the

'Categorical Imperative'. However, both Mill and Kant held that there is such a thing as human nature and consequently objective knowledge of what makes life worth living. Disagreeing with both, Sartre held that humans have no nature, at least not in the way in which things or objects have natures or essential properties. Man is a subject and not an object. It follows, for Sartre, that in morality there are no objective answers, but only questions directed at our subjectivity. The meaning of life is constantly being created, not discovered. All ethics is subjective. What does this mean? This entire book is meant to give the answer, but a few remarks about the terms 'subjective' and 'subjectivism' may clear the air.

(*a*) Subjectivism is not relativism; it contrasts with objectivism and not with absolutism or universalism. 'Detroit is 90 miles away' is relative; its truth depends on the geographical location of the speaker. It is, you might say, systematically ambiguous. On the other hand, 'Detroit is 90 miles from East Lansing' is absolute; it is true no matter where it is uttered. Another pair of utterances illustrates the quite different distinction, that between the subjective and the objective. 'I feel pain', said calmly and collectedly, although relative (its truth depends on how *I* feel) is objective—I either am or am not in pain. 'Ouch!', on the other hand, is subjective. Whether or not, in fact, I am in pain makes no difference to its truth or falsity—simply because it does not even profess to be anything either true or false. If I feel no pain while saying 'Ouch!', I have not uttered a falsehood, although I am then faking and insincere.

(*b*) Sartre himself never puts it in these terms, but subjectivism may be looked upon as the thesis that moral judgements are neither true nor false and that in this respect they are like 'Ouch!', 'Fie!', 'Wow!', and what have you. Of course, a moral judgement, like 'It is morally wrong to abuse children', is not very much like 'Abusing children, fie!' It is more like an imperative. The force of 'It is morally wrong to abuse children' boils down to 'Do not abuse children'. And imperatives, like exclamations, are neither true nor false either, although, like exclamations, they are capable of being insincere. According to Sartre, in morality there is no truth or falsity, only honesty and candour and their opposites.

(*c*) We can now reinforce the point that subjectivism is not relativism. 'Relative' contrasts with 'absolute' or 'universal', but 'subjective' does not. A statement is relative if its truth-conditions are dependent on the location, condition, or viewpoint of the person who makes that statement; it is absolute if they do not. Thus there is a clear sense in which what is subjective is neither relative nor absolute. For a subjective utterance has no truth-conditions at all. In *this sense* only what is objective can be either relative or absolute.

(*d*) We can, however, speak of the contrast between the relative and the absolute or universal in an *altogether different sense*. In *that* sense, as we shall see in a second, that contrast is applicable also to what is subjective. We pointed out that an utterance is relative if its truth depends on who is its *author* and *his* viewpoint. But, in a *different* sense, we can make the distinction between the relative and the absolute with regard to who is the *addressee* of an utterance and *his* viewpoint. When looked at in this way, the onus of what is said is not its truth, but its point. An utterance, apart from being untrue, may be unhappy when it fails to have relevance to the hearer. Sometimes when I say something, I draw a blank. Suppose that, out of the blue, I call up a man in Africa and say to him, 'The weather promises to be fine tomorrow in East Lansing.' Or suppose I tell a legless man, 'Buy yourself some new shoes.' An imperative, although neither true nor false, has its appropriate scope. If its scope is restricted, it is relative; if it is unrestricted, it is absolute and universal. If there is anything Kant and Sartre agreed on, it is that moral imperatives are unrestricted in scope, they are properly addressed to everyone, they are, in this sense, absolute and universal.

(*e*) The disagreement between Sartre and Kant is this. Kant held that moral imperatives are objective. How is this possible, since, as we have pointed out, imperatives are neither true nor false? Well, they can still be either right or wrong. For example, if I say to a man with high cholesterol, 'Eat more fatty foods,' I do not say anything false but wrong just the same. For Kant, moral judgements, although they, as imperatives, are neither true nor false, are nevertheless capable of objective validation. Sartre, as a subjectivist, denies this. For him, just as for Kant, moral judgements are absolute and universal in scope, but, perhaps for this very reason, no objective justification can be given for them. His position can thus be characterized as subjectivistic universalism which is very different from individualistic relativism. For Sartre, moral judgements are, or are like, imperatives which are addressed to everyone; for the individualistic relativist, they are just introspective reports. In Sartre's view, when I say 'Child abuse is morally wrong', I address everyone with the imperative 'Do not abuse children'. For the individualistic relativist, when I make that moral judgement, all I do is to state how I feel; I just say '*I* disapprove of child abuse'.

(*f*) What is subjective is not identical with what is illusory. The contrast between the subjective and the objective is not that between (mere) appearance and reality. Reality is neither subjective nor objective, it just *is*. The contrast between illusion and reality can be drawn within both the subjective and the objective. To say that, for the subjectivist in ethics, there is no difference between what seems morally right and what really is morally right is just a confusion. What is *objectively* right is not identical with what *is* right. The challenge for a subjectivist like Sartre is to show that what really is subjectively right is distinct from what merely seems subjectively right, that is, merely arbitrary.

PART ONE

Mill and the Ethics of Happiness

JOHN STUART MILL (1806–73) never attended school but, under the tutelage of his father, became a highly educated man. For thirty-five years he served as an administrator in the East India Company, an arm of the Victorian empire, but his life was really dedicated to promoting progress in scientific knowledge, individual freedom, and happiness for all. He wrote numerous works spanning all fields of philosophy as well as economics and politics. His influence has been greater than perhaps any other English-speaking philosopher. From his middle twenties he shared both his intellectual and emotional life with Mrs Harriet Taylor, and after some years, when she became a widow, they married. He possessed a keen analytic mind but was also a man of great passion. This did not always enable him to enjoy to the fullest the human happiness of which he was such a great advocate.

1

A First Look at Mill's Hedonism

ONE famous attempt to bring unity and consistency into our moral thinking is Mill's Principle of Utility. Mill formulated it as follows: 'actions are right in proportion as they tend to promote pleasure or happiness' (*UT* 7). This terse formula is really a combination of two, or even three, subsidiary principles. It says, first, that the moral rightness of actions depends on the value of their consequences. This is the principle of consequentialism or teleology. Second, it says that the only consequences of actions which are of intrinsic value are pleasure or happiness. This is the principle of hedonism. Mill's doctrine is thus a combination of consequentialism and hedonism. And this is not a necessary conjunction. It is possible to hold that the ultimate value of the consequences of what we do does not lie in their being pleasant, but in some other thing such as self-realization or knowledge or the classless society, or some good altogether indefinable.[1] Moreover, it is possible to claim that what determines the moral rightness of actions is not the value of their consequences at all, but, as it is often put rather vaguely, the 'nature of the act itself'. Kant did just that and his view of morality is therefore called non-consequentialist or deontological. Third, once it is claimed that what really counts are the valuable consequences of actions, we want to know to whom these consequences should accrue. Egoism and altruism give diametrically opposed answers. Mill shied away from both of those extremes; for him everyone's pleasure or suffering is to count equally, including that of the agent. Our moral duty is to promote the total happiness of all of mankind or, as Mill actually put it, of the 'whole sentient universe'. This may be labelled the principle of universalism. So

---

[1] Such was the view of G. E. Moore, sometimes called 'ideal' utilitarianism. See his *Principia ethica* (Cambridge, 1903). With the same kind of aloofness and vagueness some contemporary utilitarians designate the good as that which serves the (unspecified) interest of humans.

Mill's doctrine as a whole is to be called universalistic hedonistic consequentialism. It is important to keep these different aspects of Mill's doctrine separate, for, as we shall see, the problems connected with each one of them are different from one another.

Let us first take a look at Mill's hedonism. He is anxious to defuse the instinctive negative reaction which people may have to the idea that pleasure is the goal of life. In his own words, that idea may strike one as a 'mean and grovelling doctrine', a view 'worthy only of swine' (*UT* 7). Mill's reply to those who crave for what is 'higher' in life is that, when he says that pleasure is the ultimate end of life, he includes *all* the pleasures that humans are capable of having and that hedonism is therefore capable of accommodating all that is refined and elevated. The worth of a pleasure, he urges, depends not only on its quantity (as his predecessor Bentham had held and to whom is attributed the aphorism 'quantity of pleasure being equal, push-pin is as good as poetry')[2] but also, or perhaps primarily, on what he called its quality. Some pleasures, Mill held, are just better and more worthy of being aimed at than others apart from how intense they are and how long they last (*UT* 8).

Assuming for the time being that the quantity of a pleasure is an intelligible notion, what exactly can be meant by the quality of a pleasure, and how is it to be determined? The quality of something is usually a matter of standards and the question whether or not it comes up to a given standard, a matter of quantitative measurements of one sort or another. A high-quality car tyre is one that is resistant to punctures, lasts at least 40,000 miles without its tread wearing down, and so on. Sometimes the standards of quality are even codified and officially laid down. The Department of Agriculture, for example, says that Grade AA eggs are those of a certain freshness, of a certain firmness of their shells, and so on. Mill, however, could not have been thinking along these lines, for, in that case, the quality of a pleasure would be reduced to its quantity or the quantity of

[2] Jeremy Bentham actually said in his *Rationale of Reward* (London, 1825):
Prejudice apart, the game of push-pin is of equal value with the arts and sciences of music and poetry. If the game of push-pin furnish more pleasure, it is more valuable than either. Everybody can play at push-pin; poetry and music are relished only by a few. The game of push-pin is always innocent: it were well could the same be always asserted of poetry. (206)

something related to it. He had an entirely different idea in mind.

For some readers it has seemed that Mill's idea was that the standard of quality of pleasures lies in the hierarchy of human nature much as it had been conceived by the classical humanists. Classical humanism goes back to Plato and Aristotle[3] and it has been a commonplace among high-minded educators. Human nature, or the human soul, has different parts or faculties and these form a rank-order. The lowest are our appetites (for drink, food, sex) and these we share with other animals. Next higher is our faculty of complex emotions as well as of imagination. Highest of all is our reason or intellect. Reason, above all else, is what makes us specifically human. The good life—the life worth living—according to the classical humanist, is life in accordance with nature. But since human nature constitutes a hierarchy, the good life for men consists in denying, or at least curbing, the lower in us and promoting the higher. Enjoyments are good but only in degrees in which they are derived from the exercise of what is higher in us. The good life is, ultimately, the life of the intellect.

Indeed Mill does say that the higher pleasures go with the higher human faculties. Therefore, there is something to the claim that Mill was not really a hedonist at all but a humanist. If we introduce the notion of quality into pleasure, the purity of the hedonism of a Bentham or of the ancient Aristippus[4] seems to be lost. If the higher degrees of quality of pleasures were constituted by being derived from the higher human faculties, then what is ultimately good would not be pleasure, but the exercise of the higher human faculties. Or, if what makes a pleasure a pleasure of high quality were the fact that it is a pleasure of a certain kind, pleasure derived from a certain kind of object or activity—for example, from reading Shakespeare as opposed to playing tiddly-winks—then it would be Shakespeare's poetry which is intrinsically more valuable than tiddly-winks and not one pleasure as such over another.

---

[3] See Plato, *The Republic*, especially Books IV and IX, and Aristotle, *Nicomachean Ethics*, especially Book I.

[4] Aristippus of Cyrene (4th cent. BC) and the other Cyrenaics advocated a hedonism which emphasized the pursuit of physical pleasures for they are the most immediate, intense, and secure.

Such criticisms of Mill's professed hedonism are, I believe, misdirected even though it is unquestionably true that the idea of human development played an important role in his thought. I wish to argue that, in spite of his insistence on the qualitative differences among pleasures, he was a consistent hedonist and stuck to the view that it is pleasure and pleasure alone that is intrinsically good. Pleasure is good simply because it is pleasure, and one pleasure, apart from quantity, is better than another simply because it is *felt* to be preferable.

When Mill refers to the hierarchy of the human faculties he is merely giving us an informal hint. His serious attempt to define the qualitative differences between pleasures is his theory of the 'qualified judges'. He remains a consistent hedonist since he, in effect, says that pleasures provide their own standard. The degrees of quality of pleasures are not just *revealed* to us in our experiences of them; our preferential experiences *make up* these qualitative degrees. The quality of pleasures is thus more like the quality of wines than of tyres or yard goods.

An analogy will make this clearer. When it is getting cold outside, we shall feel it. We do not need some other standard —such as a thermometer reading—to find this out. Similarly, when one pleasure is higher than another, we shall feel that too. We need not think of the temperature of the air as being really where the mercury stands or what is the rate of the movement of its molecules; and we do not have to think of the qualitative degrees of pleasures as being really the qualitative degrees of humanity. The gist of what Mill is saying is that the pleasures which are higher in quality are just those which are *felt* as higher.

Of course, it is not quite as simple as that. How can what any Tom, Dick, or Harriet happens to prefer determine what all humans should prefer? It is likely that the intuitively promising candidates for high-quality pleasures are sought after only by a few. Mill therefore proposed that those whose preferences determine the matter (much in the same way as those whose preferences determine the quality of wines or perfumes) are the experts. What he offers is in effect the following definition. Given two pleasures which are equal in quantity, then if all, or most, 'qualified or competent judges', as he called them (*UT* 11), prefer one of them to the other, the one preferred by them is the higher in quality. In this way, rather than by reference to an unverifiable conception of the hierarchy of man's nature, objectivity is to be preserved. From what some people—people with certain credentials—*do* prefer, we can derive what, objectively speaking, all of us *ought* to prefer.

The next question is, of course, how do we tell who is a qualified judge? Do we not here already need evaluative criteria? And does not then the whole Millian scheme become circular? This query has a lot in it. But, we shall see, it is also liable to hide from us a kernel of truth in what Mill is saying.

According to Mill, a qualified judge must meet three qualifications (*UT* 8–10):

(a) *The first requirement is familiarity with the pleasures in question*. This seems eminently reasonable. Who can judge what he is not familiar with? Still, right off, the spectre of circularity appears. For familiarity, just as the lack of it, may lead to both underestimation and overestimation. Some pleasures will have to grow on us; they cannot be fully appreciated at first. But equally, familiarity may be excessive and result in our becoming jaded. Or, in the opposite direction, it may lead to habituation or addiction. If you indulge in a pleasure too often and to the exclusion of others, you might no longer be able to do without it, or see beyond it, and you might lose your perspective.

The situation threatens to be embarrassing. The qualified judges must have the *right* degree of familiarity. That, must we not say, can only be the degree of familiarity which allows them to enjoy a pleasure exactly as much as they should—no more, no less. But then, before we can be sure that our prospective judges satisfy the requirement of familiarity, we must already have made up our own minds concerning the qualitative rank-order of pleasures. In other words, we must already have the answer to the question which we wanted to put to *them*.

(b) *The second requirement is capacity*. A person is not a qualified informant concerning the qualities of pleasures if he does not have the capacity to experience a wide enough range of pleasures. If, for example, he has a tin ear, it stands to reason that we do not want to pay any attention to him in trying to determine whether Beethoven's Ninth or 'Jingle Bells' provides the higher quality pleasure or, for that matter, whether the pleasure of listening to music is superior or inferior to the pleasure of, say, fishing. But here the danger of circularity is even more evident. A person is capable of enjoying a pleasure, must we not say, if he can get out of it what there really is to be got out of it. In order to know whether or not someone has the capacity truly to enjoy something, we must thus already know the quality of enjoyment it can afford. So again, to try to refer the matter to a panel of judges will be useless. If we are not to make any mistakes in selecting them, we must already possess the knowledge we hope to gain from them.

(c) *The third requirement is 'a sense of dignity'.* We must exclude from the ranks of the qualified judges those who, says Mill, lack a 'sense of dignity', who, due to their faulty character, will choose what they themselves recognize as the lower of two pleasures. This, it would seem, shows beyond any doubt that the theory is bankrupt. For he who lacks a 'sense of dignity' must be one who chooses wrongly, that is, chooses what is a lower pleasure over one that is higher. And in order to know that a given person is one who does that, we would then already have to know which are the higher and which are the lower pleasures.

Having made these points, we must not lose sight of what is well taken in Mill's idea of a qualified judge, even if this is to go beyond his actual words. When someone is familiar with a given pleasure in the right degree does indeed call for a decision. But making such a decision does not have to be arbitrary. In our growing acquaintance with a thing or activity we may detect that we have reached the optimal point. To be sure, we cannot define that point. Still, there are signs of when it has been reached. We then experience a certain ease and sure-footedness; our doubts and confusions are left behind and our orientation is clear. When a person has reached that peak, he can be helpful and convincing to others. What he says and does will then possess a kind of lucidity and infectiousness. Similarly, although we cannot give a non-circular definition of the capacity to enjoy the things worth enjoying, the fact is that there are people who, either innately or through experience and training, are capable of more varied, fuller, and deeper enjoyments than others, and these people can genuinely impress and help us. What they say and do may lead us to see, on our own part, that they are on to something worth emulating. A person who possesses a 'sense of dignity', let us say, is simply a person who cares. It is not that he first uses an inner light which tells him the 'intrinsic superiority' (*UT* 10) of one pleasure over another and then, as a matter of a further mental operation, translates this knowledge into action. He simply is the kind of person who is deeply into what he does and enjoys. It is this involvement on his part that may engage us as well and make us believe that he is a person of good judgement, and therefore one who is worth taking as an example.

The consequence of what we have just said is, however, this. To have a sense of dignity—we may also call it possessing a sense of integrity—is to have the strength of *one's own* convictions. Therefore, having this quality does not make someone into a qualified judge in Mill's own sense, that is, into someone whose preferences constitute an *objective* standard for others to follow. We respect a person who resolutely lives on a 'higher plane'. But, at the same time, *his* integrity and sense of dignity may be an intrusion and imposition on *my* integrity and sense of dignity. When he puts poetry ahead of push-pin, it might be obtuse for me to take no notice and to go on in my own merry way. Nevertheless, *his* preference of poetry over push-pin is not an objective reason to follow suit. For me, it can be nothing more than an impressive example. The same conclusion follows from another look at what Mill called familiarity and capacity. One cannot use these presumed advantages that some of us have over others in order to dictate to them. We pointed out in the Introduction that in ethics there are no authorities and specialists and that, in the end, no one can here tell us anything. No doubt there are qualified judges of wines, figure skating, dogs, examination papers, prospective employees, and so on. But we can tell with confidence who the people who serve competently in such roles are because they operate within more or less established traditions and in the service of more or less established goals. In a sense, there are even objectively certifiable competent judges of pleasure, for example, counsellors of holiday travel. However, their job is not to tell us what pleasures we ought to prefer, but to fit the available resources of enjoyment to our already existing tastes and preferences.

Still, in an oblique way, Mill, in his theory of the qualified judges, was pointing to an important truth. In striving for the life worth living we cannot just listen to others, even if they have better credentials. But we can strive for a higher level of discernment in ourselves—for self-development. There are no qualified judges to whom we can hand over the evaluation of our lives. Still, we can endeavour to become qualified judges ourselves and this process does not necessarily preclude looking up to others. In ethics one must find one's own answers. Nevertheless, we *can* benefit from others. But this learning depends on elective affinities. When it comes to the really important questions of our lives, we do not go to the polymaths. We go to those with whom we feel a kinship. Moreover, we do not then just seek information, but a bond.

There are no airtight criteria for being a qualified judge which can be applied, to use Mill's phrase, through a purely 'intellectual operation'. Here there are merely sundry indications which vary from case to case, and are subject to our own experience and judgement. What is valid in the concept of a qualified judge is the sort of thing that is found in a truly good teacher. Such a teacher does not dictate. By saying this and that, he will *lead* us to a sharper and superior awareness. By following his lead we can—if we are patient, diligent, and receptive—come to what we ourselves will realize to be keener and fuller experiences. But whether or not someone is such a teacher is to be judged, in the end, by our own susceptibilities.

Mill was so anxious to maintain the objectivity of the distinction between the higher and the lower pleasures that he sounded almost fanatical. We read:

From this verdict of the only competent judges, I apprehend there can be no appeal. On the question which is the best worth having of two pleasures, or which of the two modes of existence is the most grateful to the feelings . . . the judgment of these who are qualified by knowledge of both, or if they differ, that of the majority among them, must be admitted as final. (*UT* 11).

It is hard to believe that this was written by the author of *On Liberty* (*CW* xviii) in which we find some of the most eloquent arguments against following authority ever put forward. The above passage is even more astounding because two pages back Mill had characterized the 'sense of dignity' as the 'love of liberty and personal independence' (*UT* 9).

In conclusion, we have seen that the 'competent judges' would be infallible only at the cost of the whole theory becoming circular. I have argued that, therefore, the distinction between the higher and the lower pleasures can only be a subjective, although not an arbitrary one.

2

Mill's Arguments for Hedonism

EVEN if the notion that pleasures are of higher and of lower quality is at least subjectively viable, why should I put credence into hedonism to begin with? Well, here is Mill's argument. That something is visible is proved by someone seeing it and that something is desirable is proved by someone desiring it. If we see something, then it is visible. Similarly, if we desire something, then it is desirable (*UT* 34). The completion of the argument seems to be, since it is beyond dispute that humans do desire pleasure, it follows that pleasure is desirable.

Now the analogy on which this argument is supposed to rest clearly does not hold. 'Visible' means 'capable of being seen'. From '*x* is (was, will be) seen' it therefore does follow that '*x* is visible'. But the dictionary truth is that desirable does not mean 'capable of being desired'. It means instead 'worthy of being desired' or 'ought to be desired'. Consequently, there is no analytically valid inference from '*x* is (was, will be) desired' to '*x* is desirable'. Mill, it seems, is just guilty of the fallacy of deriving value from fact: you cannot get what *ought to be* desired out of what merely *is* desired any more than you can get blood out of a rock. There is, of course, another sense of the word 'desirable'. It also means 'pleasing' or 'agreeable'. But this is obviously not the relevant sense. When the question arises whether or not something is desirable in *that* sense, we may indeed resort to direct experience. Were someone to ask, for example, whether or not Preska is a desirable brand of coffee, we may answer 'Try it, we think you will enjoy it'. But we should never say anything like that in answer to the question 'Is pleasure desirable?' It is unintelligible to wonder, and to put to empirical test, whether or not pleasure is agreeable or pleasing.

But if we interpret Mill's argument in this way, its faultiness becomes too blatant. Mill himself denied that there is a logically tight proof that pleasure is desirable or good as an end (*UT* 34). It is therefore silly to maintain, as in effect G. E. Moore did, that Mill tried to do what he himself said is incapable of being done and then accuse him of having miserably failed.[1] It is better, I believe, to say that Mill, in the argument that we have sketched, was appealing to our subjectivity and engaging in psychological persuasion. If a person says that he desires something for its own sake, then he has to admit that he considers it desirable or good as an end. It is true that a person may *sometimes* say that, although he wants something, he does not consider it desirable or good. He may say that a certain desire of his is a weakness which he would be glad to be without. But his self-criticism must have limits. He may deprecate and regret having some of his desires, but not all of them and particularly not those which he feels deeply and steadily and around which he may be building his life and which are not just his whims or momentary yens or spasmodic cravings. Were he to continue in his self-effacing mood indefinitely, we would eventually regard what he professes rather hollow and a mere pose.

I wish to suggest that it is this psychological relationship between the desired and the desirable, and not analytic and logical entailment, that lies behind Mill's argument. From '*x* is desired' it does not analytically follow that '*x* is desirable or good as an end'. But when a person says 'I desire *x* for its own sake', he implies, and cannot deny, that he believes that *x* is good or desirable as an end. To this extent Mill's reading of human subjectivity is correct. But when he goes on to claim that we all desire *pleasure* with a kind of inevitableness which amounts to being part of our very nature, he is off the track. It is by no means true that an antihedonist must always be either confused or less than candid. He can quite honestly claim that desire for pleasure is not in the repertoire of his desires.

Mill as a hedonist does not of course claim merely that pleasure is *a* thing which is desirable or good as an end. He claims that pleasure is the only such thing, and, he reasons, this is so because pleasure alone is what people in fact do desire as an end. This looks again like an attempt to derive value from fact. It looks as though Mill believed that there is an analytic derivation of ethical hedonism from psychological hedonism. Looking at it

---

[1] MOORE *Principia ethica*, pp. 64 ff.

in this way again does not do justice to Mill's intentions. He, I suggest, was here too presenting a piece of reasoning which draws on the psychological or subjective connection between the desired and the desirable. 'Human beings desire for its own sake pleasure and nothing but pleasure' was for him not a premiss from which it analytically follows that pleasure is the only thing which is good or desirable as an end. Instead, he was saying that *since*, as was his view, humans desire pleasure and pleasure alone as an end, it is only with regard to pleasure that they can truthfully say that it is desirable or good as an end. The life dedicated to the pursuit of pleasure is the only life free of illusions and self-deception.

If I say that I desire something for its own sake, I imply—give it to be understood—that I consider it good as an end. This is just part of our shared understanding of each other. With regard to Mill's hedonism, the converse of this connection is perhaps even more to the point. On occasion a person may well claim that he considers something desirable or good as an end but that he does not really desire it. He may say that he happens to be too strongly tempted by something else. But were he chronically neglectful of his professed values and never to experience regret and remorse for not being true to them, we would not take him seriously. We would then suspect that he is paying mere lip-service to his ideals. There are also people who seem to pursue their goals with a cold, emotionless, and automaton-like determination. But in order to avoid looking at them as inhuman monsters, we must assume that they hide their feelings from us. So, if it is indeed the case that, basically we truly desire and are emotionally attracted to nothing but pleasure, it is with regard to pleasure alone that we can truthfully claim that it is desirable or good as an end. If *psychological* hedonism is true, humans—if they are not confused, unreasonable, stubborn, unforthright, uncandid, or subject to self-deception—must admit that they are *ethical* hedonists. Anyone who calls anything but pleasure good as an end must then be either muddled or a hypocrite.

But is psychological hedonism true? Do humans want nothing but pleasure? As already indicated, it is here, I wish to argue, rather than in the lack of a valid inference licence, that the weakness of Mill's position lies.

Is psychological hedonism true? Is all desire ultimately desire for pleasure? Of course there are a multitude of recalcitrant cases. However, Mill argues, none of them constitute genuine counterexamples. Money, for instance, is often desired but only, he points out, as a *means* to procuring some pleasurable thing. When we do desire as an end something which at least in name is other than pleasure—such as health, or power, or knowledge, or even money—Mill says that he can explain that. Take what may seem to be one of the most stubborn cases—wanting to be virtuous just for virtue's sake. Mill's contention is that a person who has such a passion, and Mill believed that we all do, nevertheless initially sought virtue only because of its pleasurable consequences, such as a favourable reputation. It is true that, through a process of conditioning, a person comes to desire virtue as an end in itself. But, in that event—so Mill was in effect arguing—the process through which this came to be so was a process of pleasure-transference. At the end of this process, while virtue was then no longer sought for its pleasurable *rewards*, it had itself become a pleasure.

By using the jargon of many psychologists, we can recast Mill's argument like this. The initial or 'natural' reinforcers of our behaviour are reinforcers because they give us crude and primitive pleasures. But there is the process of conditioning or association through which each initial source of pleasure is replaced by other sources of pleasure of untold complexity and refinement. Although we 'in the beginning' seek the pleasure of food, drink, and crude amatory engagements, when we seek knowledge, beauty, power, virtue, and the like, we seek them for the same reason—pleasure.

Psychological hedonism may thus be looked upon as a reformulation of the essentials of behaviourist psychology in more colourful terms. Where the behaviourist says 'reinforcing stimulus', the hedonist says 'pleasure', and where the behaviourist says 'conditioning', the hedonist says 'pleasure transference'. In this way psychological hedonism seems to acquire a solid scientific basis.

Now the behaviourist, as a scientist, may have better things to do than to argue that he can explain *all* motives of human conduct through patterns of reinforcing stimuli and the rest. He just wants to get on with developing the details of his science: the specifics of functional dependencies. But for the psychological hedonist as a moral philosopher the whole point has to be whether or not he has succeeded in specifying the overall and exclusive motivational sources of human conduct. Consequently, to the extent to which he wishes to couple his own theory with behaviourism, he must regard the latter as an exhaustive theory of human behaviour. But is behaviourism such a theory? Let us consider.

A man wolfs down a large quantity of food. Can we from his past history and the occurrent stimulus tell whether his present behaviour is due to his being very hungry or to his being a glutton? Well, gluttony leads a person to eat a large quantity of food without a history of food deprivation, while hunger does not. Nevertheless, this is not conclusive. A person may eat massively even though not deprived of food for a long time without doing it from gluttony. He may have other reasons for stuffing himself. Perhaps there was a bet or he just wants to show off or whatever. Neither is food deprivation a sure-fire proof of hunger. In extreme depression a man may be wasting away but still not be, or at least not feel, hungry. It is true that such cases are not the rule. Food deprivation *is* a clue for hunger. Hunger does not come and go with the clouds. But rough-and-ready clues are not enough for a science of behaviour. Here one needs 'covering laws' which specify operationally defined necessary and sufficient conditions. But it is impossible to see how we can arrive at these even in what should be a relatively simple case of hunger versus gluttony.

There are more intriguing, although perhaps more tendentious, examples. Kant, as we shall see, drew a distinction —which he thought was absolutely essential to morality— between acting purely from the motive of duty and doing what is one's duty from calculating self-interest or for the sake of the anticipated pleasure of having done one's duty. To be sure there are again clues for telling that someone did his duty from 'impure' motives—he tells everybody about his deed, glows when he is admired and praised for having done it, but will neglect doing it again when people take no notice. Still, when these signs are absent, we cannot be sure that a given act was due to pure conscientiousness. There simply are no conditions which are both necessary and sufficient for attributing the motive of duty to someone. No amount of hardship and deprivation to himself or others which a person is willing to accept will prove that he did not act for the sake of some reward which might just have been his own inner satisfaction or the fulfilment of some compulsive need. The reason why behaviourism cannot capture all the aspects of human conduct is that human conduct does not merely exhibit regularities. A piece of human behaviour may come about *because* the agent *aims at* fitting it into a regular pattern. The idea in his mind that his act would be an act of a certain kind—say, honest, kind, or vengeful—may be exactly what moves him to perform it. In other words, his conduct may be due to his obedience to rules, principles, laws, norms, standards, ideals, and the like.[2] A bare uniformity of conduct is not a rule or a principle of it. I cannot reject the former, but I can reject the latter. I cannot reject the laws *of* my behaviour, but I can reject the laws *for* my behaviour.

When talking about human conduct we may be interested not in predicting and explaining but in evaluating. When we ask about a person's motives, we need not be wanting merely to find out whether or not what he did was to be expected. We may be asking instead what was his reason for acting in the way he did. In other words, we may be interested in what, in his view, made his action right. When we say that an action was done from gratitude, remorse, friendship, curiosity, vanity, kindness, avarice, one-upmanship, honesty, cruelty, chastity, philanthropy, bigotry, ambition, reverence, duty, and so on, we are not stating for the sake of stilling our curiosity that the action was of the kind that humans often do perform in certain circumstances and that therefore it could have been predicted. Instead, our interest lies in pointing out that the agent saw things in a certain light and regarded certain things as good reasons for acting in the way in which he did and that because of this his action, in his eyes, was justified.

For that matter, not just predicting, but evaluating human conduct is a form of understanding it. Making someone's action intelligible may involve passing an evaluative judgement on it as opposed to just subsuming it under a factual generalization. We may, to begin with, be interested in the coherence of his conduct. Here the question is not yet whether, in our own view, his

---

[2] Cf. Anthony Kenny, *Action, Emotion and Will* (London and New York, 1963), 97.

reasons are good reasons. Still, we are making an assessment. We are gauging the agent's lucidity and resoluteness. To call someone's conduct coherent is to imply that one understands it and that one, in a sense, commends it. Extreme lackadaisicalness prompts both puzzlement and criticism. Further, if someone's conduct goes considerably beyond what we ourselves are inclined to regard as justifiable, knowing his motives might not help us to understand it. Suppose someone chops off his finger because he is obsessed with cleanliness and cannot remove the inkstain from it; or burns down the garage, because there are spiders there; or suppose a soldier kills the entire population of an enemy village, because he suspects that there is a spy in it. Even if we are to grant that such actions could be 'explained' in the sense that, when enough investigating was done and enough psychological theory applied, it could be shown that they were to be expected, there would be a sense in which we could not understand them. Understanding someone's conduct is, in one respect, feeling some affinity with it. In order to comprehend others, we must feel that there is some foundation to engage in common undertakings with them, some measure of reciprocity, some congruity between their aims and motives and ours. I do not wish to suggest that we can understand only those actions of others of which we ourselves fully approve. Within limits, we can understand a person's actions even if we could not imagine them as ours. But total outrage with a person's conduct will also lend a measure of unintelligibility to it.

3

Pleasure as Reason for Action

PSYCHOLOGICAL hedonism as an ethically relevant doctrine has to be the view that pleasure is the only ultimate *reason* for action, for *ethical* hedonism is the view that pleasure is, in the end, the only *good* reason for action. The ethical relevance of psychological hedonism requires therefore that we take 'desire' in the sense of deliberate desire in contrast to mere impulse. Can the psychological hedonist show that deliberate or reflective desire is always desire for pleasure?

Well, when someone is asked why he did something and he says that he did it for pleasure, there is a kind of finality about his answer; further questioning would be otiose. However, this is so not necessarily because the agent has then given the decisive *reason* for his action. 'I did it for pleasure' may come to the same thing as saying 'I did it because I liked doing it' or 'I just wanted to do it'. In other words, it may imply that what was done was done for no reason at all. So the kind of finality there is in the answer 'I did it for pleasure' does not show that pleasure is even *one* ultimate reason for action.

It is true that *sometimes* pleasure or the avoidance of pain is our final goal. When someone is asked why he did something, he may say 'I knew it was going to give me pleasure' or 'I had had no real fun for months'. Indeed, there are situations in which the final reason for why one did something is a hedonistic reason. But any number of things can be a person's ultimate reason for acting. There is an indefinite variety of final answers. 'Because I was afraid', 'Because that evened the score', 'Because I promised', 'Because it was the only decent thing to do', 'Because it was my duty', 'Because I was ordered to'—these and countless other replies to the question 'Why did you do it?' imply that, as far as the speaker is concerned, the matter is closed.

Now, of course, we might find any attempt of the agent to clinch the issue too cryptic and ask him to expand on how he perceived the situation in which he was acting. We may ask him to explain what exactly he thought constituted the danger or the insult or why he thought he was confronted with a legitimate authority, or how he came to believe that he had incurred an obligation, and so on. But the point is that this is equally so when his answer is that he did what he did for the sake of pleasure. In that event too we may want to press him further, to ask him what exactly constituted that particular pleasure he anticipated, what exactly he thought was going to be the fun.[1]

Here is another point. To act from a reason is not just to be galvanized into action, or to act on an impulse. It is to choose to act in a certain way by reflecting on it. It therefore involves a commitment to a personal policy, or a 'maxim' as Kant will call it. Hence, the hedonist's position must come to this: the only ultimately intelligible personal policy is to maximize one's pleasure. When someone says that he acted in a certain way because it was approved by his mother or by his peers, or because it was the only honest thing to do, and so on, the hedonist is not satisfied. He would say that that person either acted blindly or was hiding the truth from us. Kant discussed psychological hedonism in an answer to his friend and critic Garve, whom he quotes: '[all] motives presuppose a previously perceived difference between a condition that is worse and one that is better. This perceived difference is the element of . . . happiness . . .' (*OS* 48). Kant rejects the second part of this definition of having a motive because it would have made a shambles of his own conception of morality which, as we shall see, is that of acting from duty as a purely rational concept and not for the sake of happiness as a concept of our 'lower nature'. But there is no need to contrast our conscious desire for pleasure and happiness solely with our dedication to duty. To be motivated, or to act from a reason, is indeed to view a past or present state of affairs as worse and a possible future state of affairs as better. But to say that the only thing that makes that difference in the eyes of the agent is the contrast between his pleasure and his displeasure is totally arbitrary. For example, for the person who acts from charity, the 'worse' is someone else's misery and the 'better' is when that person's misery has been alleviated; for a person who acts from

[1] Cf. J. C. B. Gosling, *Pleasure and Desire* (Oxford, 1969), ch. 8.

vengeance, the 'worse' is not having inflicted reciprocal injury and the 'better' is having done so. Let us admit that *one* possible maxim of humans is the maxim to seek pleasure in one form or another. But it is clearly not the only one. Any number of other personal policies are equally intelligible—being fair and just, never forgetting an injury, letting bygones be bygones, doing one's duty, and so on. Wanting something with thought and intelligence entails considering it desirable or good as an end —and it *is* possible to want pleasure in this way, although it is rare, I suspect, to do so. If we just look, and are not in the sway of a preconceived theory, we see that on innumerable occasions in innumerable lives pleasure is not of any concern at all.

Mill says that when we ask whether pleasure is the only thing desired as an end—and hence the only ultimate reason for action—'we have evidently arrived at a question of fact and experience' which is to be settled by 'self-observation, assisted by observation of others' (*UT* 38). But almost immediately after this we read that desiring something and finding it pleasant are 'parts of the same phenomenon—in strictness of language, two different modes of naming the same psychological fact' and that 'to desire anything except in proportion as the idea of it is pleasant is a physical and metaphysical impossibility' (*UT* 38). Mill thus wavers between putting forth an empirical hypothesis and making a conceptual claim. This shiftiness has its reason, for it is not difficult to build a case against psychological hedonism as an empirical hypothesis. If we approach the matter with an open mind, we can easily find exceptions to the supposed psychological law that we only desire pleasure as an ultimate end. It is then plain that we also seek as ends such things as having loyal children, respect from our peers, success in our career, and so on. Consequently, Mill sought to find a way to bypass these evident facts. He could not afford to let a critique of psychological hedonism even to get off the ground and tried to make that doctrine into a kind of self-evident truth.

But what *is* intuitive plausibility of psychological hedonism? The issue is not really how much objective evidence there is for it, but what is our subjective attitude towards it. In certain of our moods it seems irresistible. It seems then as something that we must consent to if we are to be clear-headed, honest, and candid, free of illusions, self-deceptions, and hypocrisy. On the other hand, the ready acceptance of psychological hedonism might also come from resignation, resentment, and bitterness. The wish to be without illusions may stem from disillusionments. Therefore, to urge that, in the end, we always seek pleasure alone may originate from the suspicion and fear that humans never quite are as they could or ought to be. 'You desire nothing but pleasure' is normally a reproach, and that presupposes that it is possible to desire things other than one's own pleasure as an ultimate end. In our self-deprecating moods we may think that we *never* manage to be beyond that reproach. In our more sanguine moments, on the other hand, psychological hedonism will appear to us quite gratuitous. Should we all be branded as incorrigible voluptuaries? The psychological hedonist seems to be bent on wholesale denigration of humanity. Being loyal to friends, honour, mastering skills and arts, developing one's talents, maintaining one's integrity, contributing to the welfare of one's great-grandchildren, working for a distant political or social cause—all these and countless other things will then look to us plainly as not cases of desiring pleasure. 'Gandhi, in working for the liberation of India, was aiming at his own pleasure'—what a ridiculous thing to say!

'Self-observation, assisted by the observation of others' (*UT* 38) is therefore far from being a conclusive method of arriving at psychological hedonism. So Mill resorts to another strategy. Psychological hedonism is to be borne out by language itself. 'Desiring a thing and finding it pleasant' are 'in strictness of language, two different modes of naming the same psychological fact', he says (*UT* 38). However, in that case, psychological hedonism would be merely a doctrine about words. It would be invulnerable but also vacuous. 'Desiring something as an end' and 'finding it pleasant', Mill would then be telling us, simply *mean* one and the same thing. Should someone claim that he desires something without any thought of pleasure, the psychological hedonist will then simply point out that he is contradicting himself. But in that case the assertion that we desire the things we find pleasant and nothing else will have become like the assertion, say, that alligators eat edible things and nothing else. It will be empty. Suppose that one of those creatures chews and swallows a rotting piece of wood. Does this show that sometimes alligators eat non-edible things? Of course not. All it proves is that their eating habits are unusual. The result of making psychological hedonism conceptually invulnerable is that it says that we desire what we desire; in other words, it says nothing at all.

The fact of the matter is that there is no necessary relation between desiring something and finding it pleasant. Moreover, this relation is not simple and embeds an ambiguity. The claim that we desire pleasure and pleasure alone may mean that the final spring of human actions is always a desire for a pleasure which the agent believes he will have as a consequence of what he is contemplating doing. It is, by and large, this form of psychological hedonism that we have been discussing. Mill himself, at least in his more judicious mood, rejects this form of it. In his 'Remarks on Bentham's Moral Philosophy' he says that the notion that 'all our acts are determined by pains and pleasure *in prospect*, pains and pleasures to which we look forward as the *consequence* of our acts . . . can in no way be maintained' (*CW* x. 12). Psychological hedonism of this kind is a form of egoism.

But many human motives patently seem to involve anything but expectations of the agent's own future pains or pleasures. Now the hedonist whom even Mill himself condemns will say that of course pity, compassion, friendship, sense of duty, and the like are not forms of *direct* concern with our own happiness or unhappiness. When motives like these are present, we *are* concerned with others. But he will insist that this concern is nevertheless there only as an *indirect* concern with ourselves. We act in these ways only because we know or suspect that doing so makes *us* feel pleased, or prevents *us* from feeling rotten.

But this idea is contorted and involves a confusion. It is one thing to say that we always get pleasure from having managed to do what we wanted to do; it is another to say that we want to do everything only for the sake of getting that pleasure. Being kind to others, for example, may be followed by self-congratulatory feelings. But it is contrived to say that our kindness to others is always done only in order to be able to get such feelings. The egoistic hedonist confuses the pleasure of the fulfilment of a desire with the desire for that pleasure. If the two were the same, we should have sorely few pleasures. If I deliberately aim at a pleasure, that itself may make it impossible for me to get it. This points up the futility of the corresponding form of ethical hedonism. To say that pleasure always *ought* to be the end of human action is self-defeating, since, in some cases anyhow, in order to get a pleasure, I must not seek it. For example, there is the pleasure of having done an unselfish thing. But I can get that pleasure only if I did not aim at it. If I discover, or so much as suspect, that I did not act purely for the sake of the good of someone else, but instead for the sake of the satisfaction which I anticipated from having so acted, that anticipated satisfaction will not materialize. In order to have the pleasure of unselfishness, I must first *be* unselfish. This is similar to the fact that, in order to have the pleasure of eating, one must first be hungry, that is, desire food. No matter how much one might desire the pleasure of eating, one shall not get it if appetite is lacking.

We *may* desire the pleasure of satisfying a desire, but that is a derivative and sophisticated thing. Once we find that doing something gives us pleasure, we may come to want to do it for the sake of that pleasure. But we cannot start with that. We could never come to desire the pleasure of eating if we were never hungry. Similarly, we may discover that helping others brings us pleasure and as a consequence shall be more keen on helping them. But we can make that discovery only after having helped others spontaneously, just from our kind heart. To say that such things as acting from kindness, doing our duty for duty's sake, acting from friendship, as well as seeking power or vengeance are always engaged in for the sake of the pleasure they may provide for us, is to put the cart before the horse. In order to receive genuine pleasure from helping others, we must first want to help them, period. In order to reap the pleasure of righteousness, it is necessary that we first just want to do what is right. Before we can have the pleasure of friendship, we must first just want to be someone's friend. For that matter, there is sweetness in our revenge only if we first just thirst for someone's blood.

We said that Mill himself rejected the egoistic form of psychological hedonism. His own considered view was that what governs human behaviour is not necessarily pleasures and pains in prospect but also pleasant or painful prospects. In the essay from which I cited a few pages ago, he continues: 'The pain or pleasure which determines our conduct is as frequently one which *precedes* the moment of action as one that follows it' (*CW*

x. 12). For Mill, to have a motive is always to find the idea of acting in a certain way pleasant, but not necessarily because we expect that, after having accomplished the action, we shall reap pleasure as a reward. But in the light of the first part of Herr Garve's definition of a motive or reason for an action, which we referred to a while ago, this will not do either. To have a motive or reason for acting is to think of the future—or of the passage from the past, through the present, to the future. Therefore, my present pleasure cannot be my reason for action, except for the prolongation of it, or for trying to have it again.

At any rate, I may have a reason for acting in a certain way, may want to do a certain thing—and would do it voluntarily —without pleasure entering into the picture in any form or fashion. Here is an example. The weather is fine, so I am about to make off for the beach. I am reminded that I promised to visit my sick aunt. With a sigh, I leave for my aunt's house. When asked, I shall say that what was behind my decision to go to see her was simply that I had promised. I shall say also that there was no pleasure, not even of self-congratulation, involved in my decision. In spite of the annoyance, I just thought that I ought to go. Moreover, I went voluntarily. I was not forced. Nor did I act from an irrational obsession. I went because I wanted to go.

There is no one thing that constitutes wanting to do something, or doing it voluntarily. Actually, 'He wanted to do x', just as 'He did x intentionally', may add very little to 'He did x'. It may merely serve to disclaim that the agent was coerced, or under a severe threat, that it was all a mistake or an accident, or a sheer habit, and so on. We cannot bring all wanting under a common denominator. In a way, a person's wanting to do something is not even incompatible with his not thinking that doing it will realize or promote a good. His wanting may be a mere yen or craving. I may want to roll in the mud, or put flowers in my hair. A man with a stomach-wound just desperately wants to drink. In another way, however, what we want to do *is* what we believe will realize or promote a good. Full-blooded wanting is not just an impulse but the having of a more or less settled purpose. Which is not to say that momentary impulses are just illusions. What counts as a genuine case of wanting something depends on what is wanted. A momentary urge may count as really wanting to go and see the cherry blossoms, but not as truly wanting to have and to raise children. Moreover, the psychological hedonist of the kind we are now discussing assumes that, when I want to do something, I must always have an inner stirring, an enthusiasm, for doing it. But, as the above example shows, wanting to do a certain thing may be nothing more nor less than the reflective or deliberate decision to do it without having in the slightest degree an urge to do it.

Mill seems to have been cognizant of this point in his discussion of the will. The will, he says, although originally an 'offshoot' of desire, can detach itself from desire 'so much that . . . instead of willing the thing because we desire it, we often desire it only because we will it' (*UT* 38–9). A little later he states, 'we may will . . . what we no longer desire'. Will becomes separated from desire through 'habit', says Mill (*UT* 39). But will cannot be habit. The more habitual an action is, the less voluntary will it be. The will may indeed lead to actions not prompted by pleasure—present or future—but not because it is habit. In order to comprehend a voluntary action, we must know the relevant normative beliefs of the agent—his convictions, ideals, goals, and the like. If none of his ideas of good and evil entered the picture, and the action was wholly due to habit, we shall dismiss it as not having been a voluntary action at all.

4

What is Pleasure?

WE must now ask what, after all, *is* pleasure? Only if we can unravel that question can we definitely settle the issue of hedonism, both psychological and ethical. It seems clear enough that Mill thought of pleasure as a feeling. He said that hedonism is proved by introspection, considered pleasure the opposite of pain, and spoke of it as something we 'get' from our experiences and actions.

Is pleasure a feeling? Well, feelings are of different kinds and it will make a difference whether we think of pleasure as a feeling of emotion such as fear and anger or as a sensation such as the feeling of warmth or a tickle. Were pleasure a sensation, it would be something that exists in our consciousness in its own right. When I relate a sensation of mine to the world I merely entertain a causal hypothesis. For example, to say that the ache I feel is a toothache is to imply that it is the condition of a tooth of mine that is behind it—and I am then conceivably mistaken. If my teeth are thoroughly sound, I shall have to admit that what I feel is not a toothache, as least not a normal toothache. This contrasts, for example, with the pleasure of listening to music. When I say that I am enjoying a piece of music, I am not putting forth a causal hypothesis. If there is no music, I have not made a mistake concerning causal connections; what I have said will then occasion total puzzlement. Pleasure, in other words, is often related to its origin not in the way a sensation is related to its cause. If what I enjoy is a piece of music, it is my experience of that piece of music that gives my pleasure its identity. Sensations, on the other hand, are separable from what is responsible for them. While it may, for example, be quite evident that my sensation of warmth comes from the fire in the fireplace, I can still be aware of that sensation, focus my attention on it, without thinking of the fire in the fireplace. This is not to deny that our sensations may be rich with associations. A sensation may set off all kinds of reverberations. Proust's madeleine evoked the whole world of Combray, and, for Gide, to drink cinnamon-flavoured chocolate was to drink Spain. Nevertheless all such associations are still pure immanence, they are immediately present *in* the sensation and are not what is perceived through those sensations.

So it is clear that pleasure cannot be a sensation. Stings, tickles, aches, and the like are just brute experiences. They may be complete in virtual isolation from the trail of our thoughts. Pleasures, on the other hand, are often internally connected with other contents of our consciousness; they may be savourings of our perceptions, ideas, beliefs, expectations, intentions, memories, and the like.

This is not to say that sensations cannot be enjoyed. It is sometimes argued that pleasure cannot be a sensation because it makes sense to ask where in our bodies a sensation is located, but it does not make sense to ask where in our bodies our enjoyments are located. But it clearly does make sense to ask where in our bodies the pleasure of the coolness of a drink or of the melting induced by a massage is located. Pleasure is chameleon-like: its colour changes with its environment. If what is enjoyed is a sensation, the pleasure has the character of a sensation. If what I enjoy is a tickle, my pleasure, just as that tickle, stands out in its own right. I am aware of it as long or short, as steady or intermittent, as having such and such a degree of intensity, and as being located in my body or this or that part of it. The thing to realize, however, is that, since also ideas, thoughts, emotions, moods, images, fantasies, as well as actions can be pleasurable, many pleasures are very different from sensations.

On the ethical side of the issue, in the sensationalist view of pleasure, hedonism would become virtually unintelligible. How could we think that all we ever do we ought to do for the sake of amassing certain sensations? How could a certain glow, or a variety of glows, throbs, and tickles, however much enjoyed, and however rich in associations, be what makes life worth living and give it meaning? Moreover, as many philosophers have pointed out, the sensationalist view of pleasure makes a hedonistic life into a life of constant frustration. Episodes of sensation do not add up. The life of a person is not a storehouse of sensations. Pleasurable sensations do not accumulate as spoonfuls of honey.

The pleasurable sensation I had yesterday, just as the physical pain I suffered when I had my tonsils out, is gone and gone forever. I may retain the memory of it, but that is quite a different matter. In fact, the memory of a sensuous pleasure may not even be pleasant but painful, for I may be pained by the thought that I might never have it again. All this was known to Aristippus as well as to Horace with his famous advice, *carpe diem*, ('enjoy the moment').[1] The life of sensuous pleasure excludes both memories and anticipations. But the aim to live purely in the moment is as chimerical as the aim to live in eternity. Timeless existence is not a viable option for humans. As Simone de Beauvoir said, if I were just a body having a place in the sun and my 'breath would measure the instant', I would be delivered from all cares, fears, as well as regrets, but it would all eventually become insipid and boring; the world of sensuous contentment becomes cloying and 'I should want to refresh myself by departing and seeking new horizons'.[2]

Earlier, when we discussed the possibility of there being different qualities of pleasure, we assumed that the idea that pleasures differ in *quantity* is intelligible enough. We now see that to speak of the quantity of a pleasure makes sense only with regard to the pleasures of sensation. Sensations do have various intensities and durations. But, by the same token, we see that the quantity of pleasure is an ethically useless notion.

Could pleasure, instead of a sensation, be an emotion such as anger or joy? Emotions are different from sensations, although, particularly when an emotion is intense, there are sensations associated with it. Pleasures are often pleasures of, at, about, with something. And such object-directedness is a characteristic of the emotions as well. My anger, jealousy, and so on, have, so to speak, a subject-matter. Just as many pleasures, emotions presuppose other forms of consciousness. We cannot be angry, or envious, or elated without having certain thoughts, expectations, memories. The emotions build on other mental contents. The same is often true of pleasures. A thought, an idea, an

---

[1] I have referred to Aristippus earlier (see ch. 1 n. 4). Horace was a Roman poet (1st cent. BC) who popularized the ideas of the Cyrenaics for the Romans.
[2] Simone de Beauvoir, *Pyrrhus et Cineas* (Paris, 1944), 21. The free translation is mine.

expectation, a hope, a sight, a sound, an emotion, all these can be what I take pleasure in.

Just the same, pleasure itself cannot be an emotion. Unlike particular emotions such as anger or remorse or gratitude, feeling pleasure has no specific occasions. When I feel anger at someone, for example, I must believe that I or someone else has suffered an injury, and I must have some intentions, even if suppressed, of retaliation and of causing destruction and harm. On the other hand, there are no conceptual limits on what one may feel pleased about. The dimensions of pleasure are unfathomable. What gives me pleasure may be sunshine or rain, light or dark, success or even failure. Nor is there any kind of conduct which is characteristic of pleasure. The behavioural description of one pleasure may differ totally from that of another. Even such things as smiles and laughter do not provide a sure-fire criterion—for they may be ironic—and moans and groans, although they often go with pain, may be moans and groans of pleasure. When someone is in the grip of an emotion, he characteristically wants or hopes for something. But when all we can say about a man is that he is enjoying himself, we shall not have the slightest idea of what he may want or hope for (except, perhaps, that the thing he is enjoying should continue and not be interfered with).

A sensation may be a pleasure, we said, but pleasure itself is not a sensation. Similarly, although an emotion may be a pleasure, pleasure itself is not an emotion. In fact, there is no single thing to be called pleasure. There are only pleasures, that is, the various sorts of sensations, emotions, moods, cogitations, and, as we shall see shortly, activities which are enjoyed. Pleasure becomes tangible only in other things.

From the ethical point of view, we saw that, if we confine pleasure to the realm of sensations, pleasure could not constitute an intelligible goal of life. Would it be more plausible to think of pleasurable emotions as being the goal of life? Emotions, unlike sensations, *are* intrinsically connected with the rest of our lives. In them, my past, present, and future appear in a certain light. Fear points to a danger, anger to an injury, nostalgia exults the past, joy celebrates the future.

Still, the having of as many, or as varied and as intense, enjoyable emotions as possible cannot be what makes our lives worth living. For *any* emotion, just as any sensation, may be enjoyed. I may be partial to wallowing in a hot bath, while another man's delight may be to feel raindrops falling on his head. Similarly, I may be keen on love, compassion, kindness, and gratitude, but equally well on vengeance, hatred, envy, and lust. Thus, while a life dedicated to getting certain sensations would be silly, chimerical, and capricious, a life dedicated to experiencing certain emotions can be deemed positively condemnable. It is true that, since our emotions connect up with the whole gamut of consciousness, they can make up a rich life. A keenly emotional life is therefore more intelligible than the life dedicated to just getting certain sensations. Still, pleasures as enjoyed emotions cannot provide an objective *norm* for the good life any more than pleasures as enjoyed sensations can.

Finally, not only sensations and emotions but also activities can be pleasant. When we enjoy an activity, what sensations or emotions, if any, are present is irrelevant. When I say, for example, that a tennis match I played was a pleasure, I need not be referring to any sensations or emotions that I might have had while playing it. The pleasure of the game was in the playing of it. It was there, not as a kind of accompanying thrill during the course of it, nor did it surge forth all at once when it was over. What we do and the pleasure of doing it are so intimately connected that, said Aristotle, 'it admits of dispute whether the activity is not the same as the pleasure'.[3] If what I enjoy is carpentry, it is not that two separate things are happening: my carpentering and my enjoyment of it. When we get pleasure from doing something, it is not that the doing of it is one thing and the enjoyment of it totally another. Of course, playing tennis or planting the begonias may cause me to have certain emotions or put me into a certain mood or give me sensations of one sort or another. But these sensations, emotions, and moods are not what make up my enjoyment of those activities. As a matter of fact, they may be distracting and interfere with my enjoyment of what I am doing.

The pleasure of my doing something is not a separate thing from my doing it. It lies essentially in the manner in which I do

[3] *Nicomachean Ethics*, 1175b. These, and some other Aristotelian points in this chapter, can be found also in Gilbert Ryle, *The Concept of Mind* (London, 1949), especially pp. 107 ff.

it. It consists of my doing it with interest and attention, of my being absorbed in it, and of my wanting to go on with it. An activity is a pleasure when both my head and my heart are in it and when I am not interfered with while engaging in it. Of course, enjoying doing something is not just and not even necessarily being absorbed in it. I may enjoy listening to the lapping of the waves even though I am only half aware of them. Moreover, there are plenty of things we do with great attentiveness which we hate doing. I may, for example, concentrate on doing something because I just want to see if I can do it, or because of a reward, or because there is a great deal at stake. An activity is a pleasure only when the attention given to it is given for its own sake: I must engage in it not as a means for gaining or avoiding something else. And it must not be carried out simply as a matter of habit, not to mention compulsion: the cigarettes of a chain-smoker might afford very little pleasure. Finally, an activity is a pleasure only if I am, or at any rate think I am, at least to some degree, successful in performing it. A serious tennis player cannot enjoy his game if many of his overhead shots are duds.

The fact that some pleasures are enjoyed activities creates the possibility of non-consequentialist hedonism. Mill thought of pleasures as consequences or as antecedents of actions. For him, actions themselves had no intrinsic value. But perhaps pleasures as enjoyed activities, the consummation of activities themselves, constitute the ultimate goal of life. My actions, more profoundly than my sensations, and even more profoundly than my emotions, *are* my life. Still, the conclusion must be that enjoyable activities cannot, objectively speaking, be the end of life any more than enjoyable sensations or enjoyable emotions can be. For the regrettable truth is that humans, just as they can enjoy any sensations and any emotions, can also enjoy or consummate any activities: it is possible to enjoy and be absorbed in pulling the wings off flies and watching them run around in circles, or to be keen on working for the establishment of a tyrannical, jingoistic, and murderous government.

5

Universalistic Consequentialism

LET us now turn to Mill's utilitarianism proper, which we labelled universalistic hedonistic consequentialism. What are his arguments? Here Mill is often accused of having committed not only the fact-value fallacy again, but the fallacy of composition as well. He said, 'each person's happiness is a good to that person, and the general happiness, therefore, a good to the aggregate of all persons' (*UT* 34). This, it is easy to point out, is as invalid as the argument that, since each bee has a pinched-in waist, a swarm of bees also has a pinched-in waist. However, I do not think that by 'the aggregate of all persons' Mill meant all men collectively—a kind of mystical body. I believe that what Mill intended to say was that, since to each and every one of us our own happiness is a good, general happiness, that is, the happiness not only of ourselves but of all others as well, is a good to each and every one of us.

But, in that case, too, it may be objected that the argument is not valid. Assuming that his own happiness *is* a good to each and every person, it does not follow without further ado that the happiness of all others is a good to each and every person. It may be said that there is a hidden premiss in Mill's argument—namely, that caring for the happiness of not just ourselves, but of all others as well, is part of our (socialized) nature. Now it is true that Mill held that utilitarianism accords with human nature. He said that, although the tendency to look at our conduct in the light of its consequences to general happiness is not totally inborn, as, for example, our faculty of vision is, it involves only the development of an inborn sympathetic instinct. It is, you may say, our second nature. But he did not wish to derive the Principle of Utility as a normative ethical principle from what he took human nature to be. In his essay on 'Nature' he said that that term 'is a collective name for all facts, actual and possible' (*CW* x. 374) and those who take it to imply 'commendation, approval, and even obligation' believe erroneously that 'what is constitutes the rule and standard of what ought to be' (*CW* x. 377). In *Utilitarianism* (*UT* 34) as well as in his 'Remarks on Bentham's Philosophy' (*CW* x. 6), he said that there can be no proof that we ought to follow the Principle of Utility.

I wish to suggest that, just as in the case of individualistic hedonism, Mill was again engaged not in logically valid argument but in psychological persuasion. We must ask, what does it mean to say that each person's happiness is a good to that person? The phrase '*x* is a good to *A*' is ambiguous. It can mean that *x* is beneficial to *A*, given the peculiarities of *A*. For example, getting insulin injections is a good to Jones since he has diabetes. But, of course, it does not follow that insulin injections are good for everyone. So it is clear that we cannot argue that, since happiness is a good to some given person, it is a good to people in general. However, '*x* is a good to *A*' may also mean '*A* regards *x* as a good'. As we pointed out earlier, when a person says that he regards a certain thing as good, he implies that he desires it. Consequently, I wish to maintain that, when Mill said, 'each person's happiness is a good to that person, and general happiness, therefore, a good to the aggregate of all persons', he meant that, since each and every person desires his own happiness, each and every person has to admit that he also desires the happiness of all other persons as well.

What I am proposing then is that Mill, instead of offering an analytic argument for universalistic hedonism, believed that he can address each and every one of us as follows: 'You desire your own happiness as an end, so you must admit that you desire, and therefore regard as desirable or good as an end, the happiness of all persons in general.'

When discussing Mill's arguments for *individualistic* hedonism I said that there was, psychologically speaking, nothing wrong with this method of argumentation: were you to admit that pleasure and pleasure alone *is* what you desire, you must also, in candour, admit that pleasure and pleasure alone is desirable or good as an end. I said also that what was wrong with Mill's argument was that its starting-point—namely, psychological hedonism—is untenable. With regard to his argumentation for *universalistic* hedonism, the situation is different: the very principle of his attempted persuasion and not just his premiss is ineffectual; it rests on a misreading of our subjectivity.

Mill's psychological hypothesis concerning the connection between private and public happiness is nothing more than a gratuitous credo. It is doubtful, to say the least, that humans believe that their own happiness is dependent on, or even in harmony with, the happiness of humans in general. Here, it seems, Mill has not hit on an ingrained feature of the human mind as he had when he discussed individual hedonism. There is, for one thing, *Schadenfreude*—when one of my fellow creatures is miserable, that, in comparison, may make me feel happy. I may also feel that there is just so much happiness to go around and consequently that, if others are happy, I have less of a chance for happiness. Or consider a rare book or a secluded beach —sharing such things with others would ruin my pleasure.

Was Mill then a wide-eyed and naïve optimist? I wish to suggest that, in his theory of the 'sanctions' of (utilitarian) morality, he attempted to support his view of human subjectivity as being essentially social. If Mill had been intending to offer his sanctions as a kind of justification of utilitarianism, he would have been on the wrong track. For if utilitarianism is *morality*, it can and need have no justification. It is not meaningful to ask 'Why should I be moral?', for morality is exactly what tells me what I should be and do. Or, in the light of what I said in the Introduction, the question 'Why should I be moral?' is the same as asking 'Why should I live a life that is meaningful and worth living?' To harbour a doubt of this sort, as I pointed out earlier, is a rare aberration. We can only entreat, or treat, such a peculiar person; we cannot give him reasons in order to dispel his scepticism. But Mill never raised the question 'Why should I be a utilitarian?'—and then tried to answer it. In his doctrine of the sanctions of morality he was not trying to show that there is an *advantage* in being a utilitarian, that by being a utilitarian I shall profit and by being an anti-utilitarian I shall lose. Instead, he was trying to point out that there is a natural psychological passage from individualistic to universalistic ethical hedonism. The word 'sanctions' that he uses is actually a misnomer. His concern was not with the question 'why *should* we be utilitarians?' but with the question 'Why, in candour, must we be utilitarians?'; and his doctrine of the sanctions of morality was designed to show that

being a utilitarian is just being honest with oneself (*UT*, ch. iii).
There are four 'external' sanctions, as Mill called them:

(*a*) We follow the Principle of Utility because we hope that
others will reward us for doing so and fear their coun-
termeasures if we do not.

(*b*) Since 'most people assume' that God takes an interest in
the welfare of all His creatures, we, or most of us, have the
same hope and fear with regard to him.

(*c*) Due to our 'disinterested devotion' to our fellow man, it
simply pleases us to please others.

(*d*) Since we believe that God desires the welfare of His
creatures, the natural expression of our 'disinterested
devotion' to Him is doing what serves the welfare of our
fellow man.

Now only the first two of these sanctions can conceivably be
looked upon as objective justifications of utilitarianism—
justifications by appeal to our self-interest. We may think that
what Mill is saying is that there are rewards and punishments
which will come not only from society, but also from God,
depending on whether or not we are utilitarians. The other two
external sanctions, on the other hand, are direct inclinations;
they involve no thought of rewards or punishments, and thus no
appeal to our calculating self-interest. Actually, we should not
see in *any* part of Mill's doctrine of the sanctions of morality an
objective justification of utilitarian practice to our self-love. The
sanctions of utilitarianism are just certain hopes, fears, and
inclinations which we as humans living in a society happen to
have; whether or not these feelings are objectively justified is
beside the point.

This becomes quite clear when we consider that Mill finds no
need to discuss whether or not God in fact exists or what the
actual nature of His will may be. To the extent to which men
believe that God exists and *believe* that He is benevolent, they
have certain fears and hopes; and this is all that matters.
Whether or not these fears and hopes are well-founded is
irrelevant. The second and fourth external sanctions of utilitarian morality are not that there is a God and that He is
benevolent, but merely our *belief*, warranted or not, that He
exists and that He cares about the happiness of His creatures.

The sanctions were not meant by Mill to be objectively justifying reasons for being utilitarians but only so many psychological forces which happen to gear human behaviour towards general utility. A sanction of morality, said Mill, is always something subjective, always something 'in the mind itself'; moral obligation in no way 'has its seat outside the mind' (*UT* 29). Utilitarianism, according to Mill, has a hold on us in the end through our conscience. We first follow the Principle of Utility because of its external sanctions. But Mill is in effect saying that, because of a process of conditioning or internalization, we develop in us a feeling for the 'pure idea of duty' which prompts us to follow the Principle of Utility for its own sake. The origin of this feeling has a long history so that it has become 'encrusted over' with sympathy and love as well as with fear. Furthermore, said Mill, it is a mixture of self-esteem and self-abasement. Due to such complexity and depth, the demands of conscience are *felt* to be objective. Just the same, Mill insisted, they are subjective just as the demands of all feelings are. The utilitarian sense of duty is not an infallible intuition (*UT* 28–30). To feel that a certain form of conduct is right is quite compatible with its actually not being right.

To conclude this chapter, let us take a wider look at what Mill conceived to be the relation between ethics and religion. One of the objections to utilitarianism which he thought was necessary to discuss was that utilitarianism is a godless doctrine. Since for Mill happiness is a this-worldly affair, in order that there be a distinction between, and knowledge of, what is ultimately right and wrong, God and religion are not needed. Nevertheless, he maintained, utilitarianism is not a godless doctrine, since both utilitarianism and religion, he said, agree concerning which actions are the ultimately right ones. Mill argued that, if we admit that it is the nature of the deity to desire the well-being of all His creatures, we must believe that His commandments could never be at odds with the Principle of Utility. Moreover (presumably since the age of Prophets is over) religion could never render the philosophical doctrine of utilitarianism superfluous since, even if the distinction between right and wrong were to depend on God's will, we should need a principle for determining what His will is and for interpreting His commandments. This principle, in Mill's view, has to be the Principle of Utility. Where religion comes in is not in teaching us *what is* right but solely in helping us to *adhere* to what is right. It is to affect our heart, not to instruct our head.

Mill's treatment of religion is too superficial. He who believes that religion is the foundation of morality will counter by saying that, although the pronouncements of utilitarianism and of religion, if 'enlightened', may agree on which actions are morally right, what *constitutes* such rightness is God's will and not their utility. For a genuinely religious person, immorality is a sin and disobedience, and not just a failure to calculate and to act in the light of human advantages. For Mill, God's nonexistence would really be morally indifferent. As far as the knowledge of right and wrong is concerned, if God did not exist, we would still have the Principle of Utility. And we have seen that, even as a sanction of morality, religion is, for Mill, only one among others. What is needed from the moral point of view, for Mill, is religious *belief* and not the truth of it. When a person happens to believe in God, that will reinforce his utilitarian conduct; it does not matter whether or not that belief is true. In the essay 'The Utility of Religion' Mill says that it is 'perfectly conceivable that religion is morally useful without being intellectually sustainable' (*CW* x. 405). It is only the subjective effects of religion that matter—and these effects happen to be, from the utilitarian point of view, by and large, desirable. This is not so much because religion sanctifies the 'received maxims' of morality, for in doing so it may well silence the utilitarian critique of such maxims, but because 'It makes life . . . a far greater thing to the feelings, and gives greater strength as well as greater solemnity to all the sentiments which are awakened in us by our fellow creatures and mankind at large' (*CW* x. 485). Divine benevolence and 'the whole domain of the supernatural' are removed 'from the region of Belief into that of simple Hope'. This has 'the power for increasing the happiness of life and giving elevation to the character'. It is for this reason that Mill concludes that:

. . . the indulgence of hope with regard to the government of the universe and the destiny of man after death, while we recognize as a clear truth that we have no ground for more than a hope, is legitimate and philosophically defensible. (*CW* x. 485)

Mill's discussion of religion culminates in the advocacy of a 'Religion of Humanity' which is freed from all the trappings of supernaturalism. Such a religion, he maintains, is capable of doing everything that ordinary religion might be capable of doing for the moral improvement of man, and more (*CW* x. 486–9). Religion as ordinarily conceived may nevertheless be continued to be believed in as a useful myth. Thus, contrary to Mill's claim, utilitarianism *is* a godless doctrine. His views on religion actually amount to a mockery of it. We shall find a deeper treatment of religion in Kant as well as in Sartre.

To summarize, Mill believed that human egoism is not hidebound; from individual hedonism there is a natural road to universalistic hedonism. But it does not require a great deal of worldly wisdom to realize that the more a man cares about his own happiness and pleasure, the less will he often care for the happiness and pleasure of others. Nor does Mill's theory of the sanctions of utilitarian morality strengthen his case. Societal rewards and punishments are notoriously ineffective and our sympathy is a tender flower often crushed by our bad upbringing and circumstances. As to religion, some of us do not believe in any God at all and some of us think that to believe in a purely utilitarian God is a sacrilege. In some way Mill himself seems to have realized all this, for he adds the 'inner' or 'ultimate' sanction. But he too hastily assumes that 'the pure idea of duty' must be a utilitarian one. We shall see this more clearly when we turn to Kant.

6

Utilitarian Revisionism

MILL himself pointed out that utilitarianism may prompt the objection that it puts 'expediency' in the place of morality, that in the name of utility anything goes (*UT* 22). It is sometimes argued that, in order to answer this objection, Mill modified his view so that it became what is now often called 'rule-utilitarianism'—the doctrine that not acts but rules are to be judged by their utility. Indeed he did make an attempt to do justice to the apparent role of rules, virtues, and ideals in morality. Although Mill's text is far from clear in this regard, since it is now frequently thought that so called 'rule-utilitarianism' is an improvement over so called 'act-utilitarianism', it will be worthwhile to look at that allegedly distinct and superior version of utilitarianism.

The act-utilitarian says that, in determining whether a course of action is morally right or wrong, we must ask straightaway whether the consequences of that course of action are good or bad. Rule-utilitarianism tells us something presumably quite different—namely, that we must proceed indirectly, that in determining the moral rightness of an action we must ask, in the first instance anyhow, whether or not it conforms to a moral rule or exemplifies a moral virtue. Act-utilitarianism seems to entail that what, in the ordinary view, is a virtuous action, one done in obedience to a moral rule, may be a morally wrong action. It is possible that an action done, say, from the spirit of self-sacrifice will misfire and have bad consequences. This is paradoxical, since the most we would ordinarily be willing to say then is that the action was unfortunate or foolish, but not that it was morally wrong. In order to mitigate this paradox Mill urges that the utilitarian by no means neglects moral rules. In the seemingly rule-utilitarian spirit he suggests that, in deciding whether an act is morally right or wrong, we should not ask right off what is the value of *its* consequences; instead we should first ask what is the rule which that act exemplifies. The question 'Is this act right?' thus becomes the question 'Is this an act that conforms to a moral rule?' The threatening paradoxes are thus, it would seem, avoided. An act of self-sacrifice, for example, we then seem to be able to say, is right simply because it is a virtuous act—one done in obedience to the right rule. Or, when contemplating telling a lie, it is enough for me to know that there is a moral rule which says 'Do not lie'.

But what is then left of utilitarianism? In our list of moral rules, the rule-utilitarian will say, we must include only those rules which, on the whole, tend to promote general happiness. Where the question of utility is to make its impact is not in the particular acts but in selecting the moral rules. We should subscribe only to those moral principles which, on the whole, serve general utility.

However, the crucial question is, are the justification of particular acts, and the appraisal of the rules of conduct, two logically distinct things? The rule-utilitarian is confronted with a dilemma. If the moral assessment of particular acts is to be totally shielded off from the consideration of their consequences, how is this still utilitarianism? For then we should have to say that there are rules of conduct which ought to be obeyed regardless of the value of the consequences of doing so. On the other hand, if we say that the value of the consequences of particular acts still remains ultimately decisive, rule-utilitarianism is not really different from act-utilitarianism.

I am inclined to believe that Mill was and remained a steadfast act-utilitarian. He never really abandoned the notion that what matters in the end is always the value of the consequences of particular acts. I further believe that he did this because he realized that no utilitarian worth his salt can really do otherwise. Mill's point about using accepted rules was merely that, for one thing, they alert us to the fact that the assessment of the value of the consequences of particular acts on universal happiness is often difficult and chancy. Our acts are likely to have remote and hidden consequences. If we take the short view—the view of 'expediency'—it may seem to us, for example, that a given self-sacrifice brings more suffering than it prevents. But in the long run this might not be so, for an act of self-sacrifice may strengthen the spirit of self-sacrifice in general—and *that* consequence would be highly desirable for the utilitarian, for, on the whole, that spirit serves general happiness. Or, take lying. Sometimes it may be expedient to tell a lie. But it is still possible to be an act-utilitarian without having to say therefore that lying, on such occasions, is morally right. For *some* of the consequences of an expedient lie are almost invariably bad. Any lie, says Mill, 'tends to destroy the trustworthiness of human assertions' (*UT* 22). Since to be able to put our trust in what people say to one another possesses significant utility, there is always a prima-facie utilitarian case against every lie.

G. E. Moore, although he was not a *hedonistic* utilitarian, was so impressed by the difficulty of assessing the value of the consequences of particular actions that he claimed that we always ought to follow traditional moral rules, even though we know that there are cases where following them is not useful, for we cannot know what those cases are.[1] Some have even maintained that only God knows the value of the consequences of our acts, so that, as utilitarians, we should just follow God's commandments, and not worry about utility on our own at all. Mill himself never went as far as that. His argument in favour of following, by and large, moral rules and not worrying about the value of the consequences of particular acts, relies more on common sense. He says that, while the Principle of Utility is the final criterion with regard to the moral rightness of our acts, it is *only* the final criterion. In the garden variety of cases we do not have to try to apply it right off. Tradition has given us aids. There are 'secondary' rules. The situation is similar, says Mill, to that of the navigator following the nautical almanac. An accepted moral code consists of many utilitarian 'signposts'. By and large, a society sanctions over the long run only those rules which are conducive to its welfare. So it is advisable to make use of recognized moral rules and ideals. It is likely that acts which go against them will defy the wisdom of the ages to our detriment.

So the revisionist efforts on the part of the utilitarian are, in a way, just so much ado about nothing. The act-utilitarian is by no means helpless in the face of the charge that utilitarianism puts 'expediency in the place of morality'. He does not have to say

---

[1] Moore, *Principia ethica*, 162.

any such paradoxical things as that self-sacrifice may well be morally wrong and punishing the innocent morally right. He is quite in the position to maintain that self-sacrifice is morally right and lying and punishing the innocent morally wrong, except perhaps in only a few, indeed very few, instances.

The act-utilitarian is by no means barred from making use of moral rules. He must just consider such rules as instrumental rules. An instrumental rule is a directive or device of management, and its binding force derives solely from the degree in which it renders its service. It is *conceivable* that I shall do better in a particular instance by ignoring a rule of this kind. In bridge the third hand should play high, but obviously there are exceptions to that rule. An instrumental rule may also save me time and trouble, but whether or not I ought to follow it in a particular instance is ultimately a question of whether or not using it leads to the desired goal. With regard to such rules there is therefore no irreducible difference between justifying a rule and justifying particular actions coming under it. An instrumental rule is a good rule only to the extent to which it works. But if, in a particular instance, it does not, it must be ignored, and if it ceases to work in general, it must be discarded altogether or revised. It is because of these features of instrumental rules that utilitarianism remains paradoxical. It still runs into trouble with those of us who, along with Kant, believe that *moral* rules are stronger than instrumental rules, that to them no exceptions may be made.

Apart from what Mill himself might have thought, can the utilitarian strengthen his conception of rules? Well, he might wish to say that moral rules are rules for engaging in a practice and not mere rules of thumb. There are rules which define tasks, roles, rights, and responsibilities. Such rules are laid down and put in force on the basis of some authority or by custom. Consequently, they ought to be followed not because and to the extent to which following them is likely to get the desired result. We are to follow them simply because they are rules for doing or holding a job as opposed to rules for getting a job done.[2]

If the utilitarian were to say that moral rules are rules of this

---

[2] This subtle but important distinction is made by B. J. Diggs in his 'Rules and Utilitarianism', *American Philosophical Quarterly*, 1/1 (1964), 32–44.

kind, he could argue that, in so far as particular actions are
concerned, we must justify them in terms of the moral rules
which are in force in a given society or culture and not in terms of
their utility. Or can he? Not if utility is to remain the ultimate
rationale for engaging in a rule-governed practice. In that case
particular actions which are justified by the rules may still be
criticized on the ground that, everything considered, they nevertheless lack utility. So the utilitarian who, like Mill, is worried
about the charge of putting expediency in the place of morality is
still confronted with a dilemma. If he says that the rightness of
particular actions is to be determined *solely* by the moral rules
which are backed by society or some other authority, he would
cease to be a utilitarian. For then he would consider the rules
final and would not permit any utilitarian criticism of them. He
would then be committed to the position that the thing to do is to
follow the rules, whatever they may be, rather than to maximize
utility. Never mind, he would have to say, that 'going by the
book' may have disastrous consequences. The second horn of the
dilemma is that the utilitarian after all ought to search for the
best utilitarian rules—those which really do promote utility
—and regard only *them* as obligatory. But then the utility of
particular actions retains its decisiveness. For the test of the
utility of a rule must, after all, lie in the cumulative utility of the
actions enjoined by it. Thus the second horn of the dilemma
again leads to the eradication of the distinction between justifying rules and justifying particular actions and consequently to a
collapse of rule-utilitarianism back into act-utilitarianism, and
to the cancelling of the supposed advantage of the former over
the latter.

Mill's treatment of justice also tempts us to say that he was a
latent rule-utilitarian (*UT* ch. v). Justice and utility seem quite
distinct and even conflicting concepts. Mill maintains that they
are not. Justice is justice only because of its special and vital kind
of utility. For justice concerns rights and without the recognition
of rights the utilitarian programme has not even got a chance.
Duties, Mill explains, are of two kinds. Some are correlated with
rights, some are not. For example, I have the duty to be
charitable, but no one has the right to my charity. On the other
hand, the duty to keep a promise, for instance, does go together
with a right—the right of the person to whom the promise was

given to expect or demand that what was promised be done. And, Mill says, justice is that part of morality which involves rights.

But this is not all smooth sailing. Equality, Mill himself admits, is also essential to justice. That concept, together with the concepts of fairness, basic rights, and liberties, breeds trouble for the utilitarian. For Mill, equality means equal recognition of everyone's rights; it does not mean the equality of rights. Before there can be any rights there must be a society organized through laws defining the rights and powers of its members. Utility demands that these be not the same for all. A flat, unstructured egalitarianism is not conducive to the greatest general welfare.

Still, justice, in the eyes of many, involves a demand for an absolute and universal equality of certain *minimum* rights —such as the right to life and livelihood and, to a certain degree, to personal freedom. This demand can come into conflict with the Principle of Utility. To deprive anyone of *all* his rights is *always* and *necessarily* unjust; so at any rate many have urged. But the utilitarian can say nothing more than that to deprive someone of his rights is not justified unless doing so increases the greatest sum total of happiness. To be dramatic, the utilitarian cannot say that slavery is *always* and *necessarily* wrong since it is at least conceivable that by enslaving some we can increase the sum of happiness realizable throughout a society. The unhappiness of the slaves may be outweighed by the increased happiness of the masters. Of course it is very unlikely that the overall happiness of humans *is* promoted, at least in the long run, by keeping a portion of them in slavery. There will be bitterness, resentment, and eventual revolts. However, the point of the criticism is merely that the utilitarian cannot admit that enslaving anyone is necessarily always wrong.

There is also the matter of just punishment. Punishment, to be just, must be deserved. But it is at least conceivable that on some particular occasion judicially inflicting harm on an innocent does have utility. Rule-utilitarianism may again appear to be a way to appease our intuitions. It *may* be the case that punishment meted out on a given occasion on considerations of utility runs counter to such principles as that it must follow guilt and that it must be proportional to the crime. But, Mill may say,

if we consider a whole punitive system in its continued operation, we see that punishment can have favourable utilitarian
results only if it does *not* go against those principles. For if it did,
it would cause feelings of insecurity and alarm and hence damage
the underpinnings of society.

Still, the traditional principles of just punishment can, in the
utilitarian's eye, again be nothing more than instruments of
utility. He must admit that there *may* be cases in which
constraints such as the innocence of the accused would have to be
discarded. Indeed it is more than just conceivable that a whole
system of punitive practices which is intuitively unjust could
become justifiable on utilitarian grounds. There is a tendency in
any society to condone in the name of the public good what we
should intuitively consider to be injustices against particular
persons and groups. Society, in the name of utility, often offends
against equality and fairness not only through the acts of
violence of mobs but through the practices of the officials, the
courts, and even legislative bodies.

Could the rule-utilitarian look at principles of justice and
other moral rules as stronger than any kind of instrumental
rules? There are rules—let us call them 'constitutive rules'
—which *define* forms of conduct. In a practice governed by such
rules, there *are* acts of a certain kind only because there are such
rules. Take the rules of a game. You can strike out or steal a base,
for example, only because there are the rules of baseball. Since
such rules determine what is to count as an act of a certain sort to
begin with, you cannot, logically, ask whether you should follow
them in every particular case. If you wish to play a game, you
must follow its rules, period.

Could the rule-utilitarian adopt this conception of rules? Only
if he were to maintain that utilitarian morality is a kind of
self-contained practice or 'game', and this he palpably cannot do.
It is of the essence of utilitarianism that morality is a means for
furthering a goal which stands over and above all rules. The
rule-utilitarian wishes to say that utilitarian considerations
determine the rightness of the rules of our conduct, but it is just
conformity to the right rules that determines the rightness of
particular actions. In other words, he wishes to say that utility is
the ultimate guideline, so to speak, for the legislator, but not for
the judge or the magistrate. He wishes to maintain, for example,

that the rule forbidding punishing the innocent must always be followed although the ultimate reason for having that rule is that punishing the innocent has disutility. For, he will say, the risks of that sort of thing becoming counter-productive are too great. For one thing, the officials administering such a practice might misuse it. He might also say that the public promulgation of the rule that the innocent may be punished will always cause great terror and alarm and hence have grave anti-utilitarian results. Now all this may well be so. But the point is that there may nevertheless be other and stronger utilitarian considerations that weigh in favour of, at least occasionally, 'punishing' the innocent just the same. We can make sure that the officials are not careless or corrupt. Promulgating the policy that the 'innocent' may be punished may in fact have its own utility. Suppose that a powerful and unruly class—some greedy captains of industry, for example—have been regularly perpetrating acts which go crassly against public utility but which are not punishable under existing laws. It may then be in the general interest to strike fear into their hearts by announcing that the 'innocent' may be punished. Nor can it be asserted flatly that such things as the broad exercise of judicial prerogatives or even just plain terrorism of a group of vigilantes can never have any positive utility.

The rule-utilitarian is apt to cite another 'institution' of morality—that of promising—in order to give credence to his view. Following the sort of reasoning which, as we shall see, really belongs to Kant, he may say that, in order that promises can be given at all, there must be the recognition of the rule that promises are to be kept and that the promisee has the right to demand that what is promised be done. The rule-utilitarian will argue, therefore, that you cannot use utilitarian considerations to justify a particular act of breaking (or, for that matter, keeping) a promise. He who has made a promise can refer to utility no more than, say, a chess player in trouble can say that he should be allowed to move a particular pawn three squares because this would make the match more even and challenging.

But, we must ask, how is this view of the obligation to keep a promise still a utilitarian one? Are we not saying now that promises just ought to be kept and that is the end of the matter? The professed rule-utilitarian will say that, through the practice of promising, the intercourse with others becomes more regulated, the future more secure and predictable. But of course this is not necessarily so. In giving a promise, a person gives it to be understood that he intends to behave in a certain way. When a promise is made, a certain piece of future behaviour has become in order. But whether that behaviour has become more *likely* than it would otherwise have been is another matter. The promiser might not have taken his promise seriously, or be a backslider. The rules that define promising make our reliance on promises intelligible; they do not necessarily make it wise. Whether or not promising as a social practice does have utilitarian advantages is not a question concerning the rules of promising; it concerns actual behavioural tendencies.

Let us, for the sake of the argument, concede that the practice of promising is, from the point of view of utility, a good thing. But this does not preclude exceptions. It will still be possible that in a particular case it is better—from the point of view of utility—to break rather than to keep a promise. It cannot, in itself, make any difference from the utilitarian viewpoint whether a given act is classifiable as promise-keeping or as promise-breaking. It is true that breaking a promise may, by weakening mutual trust among people, have an adverse effect on the total value realizable through promising as a practice. Still this possible effect must be for the utilitarian just one thing to reckon with. There may be other utilitarian considerations which make breaking a particular promise nevertheless justifiable. In order to deny this, the utilitarian would have to argue that broken promises are wrong simply because they are broken promises, that they do not just fit into the 'promising game'. But if he does that, he ceases to be a utilitarian.

The practice or game conception of rules is antithetical to utilitarianism. Constitutive rules define goals, but these are *internal* to a given game, practice, or ritual. They are achieved simply by getting things right, by doing them properly. The spirit of utilitarianism is very different. It demands to know why one should bother to do things properly, that is, in accordance with the rules.

Now, one may make still another attempt to reconcile utilitarianism with reverence for moral rules. One may say that, opposed to a free-wheeling pursuance of utility, pursuance of utility through rules will yield a surplus value. For example, given two actions, x and y, which are equal with regard to their impact on human happiness, you ought to perform x and not y, if x is an act that exemplifies, say, honesty and y dishonesty, because honesty, as well as candour, fairness, chivalry, fellowship, solidarity, and what have you, are themselves things of value. In other words, as a utilitarian, you should shoot for a bonus. If you, as a utilitarian agent, do as much for human happiness as another, you are ahead of him if your contribution is made, say, with honesty while his is made with dishonesty. Similar to this revisionist idea is the suggestion that, although, basically, utilitarianism is right in how to judge the moral rightness and wrongness of actions, it needs side-constraints. Utilitarianism must be tempered. General happiness is the thing to be pursued, but not without regard to such matters as human dignity, honesty, integrity, fairness, and candour. We are to seek the greatest happiness of the greatest number, but we should do this without doing such hideous things as framing an innocent or telling lies.

This last-ditch effort to shore up utilitarianism is sometimes called mixed utilitarianism. It is popular today. It advocates combining the pursuit of general happiness with the recognition of the intrinsic value of actions which accord with the mainstays of accepted, or intuitively believed-in, morality. But it too represents the tendency on the part of the revisionist utilitarian to try to have it both ways. Mixed utilitarianism is mixed-up utilitarianism. For how, for example, are we to assign comparable weights to the fact that an action avoids mental suffering to the agent and to others, on the one hand, and to the fact that it is an act of resolute and uncompromising honesty? Or, how are we to balance the value of saving a town from bloody riots and the disvalue of the framing of an innocent bystander? While it is unquestionably true that, in trying to live the right life, we are more often than not confronted with the choice between such things as honesty, human dignity, and loyalty on the one hand, and human welfare on the other, there is no objective way to decide in which way the choice ought to go. We are here confronted with incommensurables, and the decision can only be an unaided subjective one, one made, to use Sartre's phrase, with unalleviated 'rending of conscience'.

7

Utilitarianism and Freedom

In the preceding chapter we discussed the widely shared view that utilitarianism grants too little importance to what may be called the 'moral world'—the commonly recognized rules, principles, ideals, and virtues. And, we argued, revisions of utilitarianism prompted by the need to do justice to the moral world make it incoherent. In this, the final chapter in our discussion of Mill, I shall argue that utilitarianism does violence also to our individual moral consciousness.

We may begin by pointing out that utilitarianism as a conscious policy is self-defeating. The will of the utilitarian, to use Kant's phrase, is 'in conflict with itself'. If I know that you are a dedicated utilitarian, I shall have a reason to mistrust you. I shall then know that you will tell me the truth or that you will keep your promise only if you believe that doing so will, on the whole, promote the general good. Moreover, if I myself am a dedicated utilitarian, I cannot object to your thinking in that way. In fact, if I know that you know that I know that you are a utilitarian, my relying on your word will become unintelligible. For then I know that you know that I know that you will always let utility override honesty. This, from the utilitarian point of view itself, would be very unfortunate, for I should then be filled with anxiety and would not be able to make plans with the same assurance as I would be able to do if you were not a utilitarian. It is of advantage all around to be able to count on one another's word. In a world in which utilitarianism is openly and universally practised, there will be no such thing as mutual trust. This the utilitarian must himself find very regrettable.

But the real cutting edge of the questions which we have raised earlier about the utilitarian conception of such things as fairness and honesty is not merely that they are part of common morality and that utilitarians, to their own detriment to boot, come into conflict with them. It is rather that utilitarianism endangers our own personal integrity. It entails, in practice, hypocrisy and even self-deceit. It might not be conducive to general welfare to avow that the recognized moral rules and ideals are mere instruments which ought to be ignored if utility so demands. The utilitarian, contrary to expectations, may have to condemn Robin Hood, just as does the anti-utilitarian who says that robbery is wrong, period, because the idea of taking from the rich and giving to the poor—if preached openly—will endanger security, law, and order. For the sake of utility, laws—any laws, customs, and rules—believed in without reservation are better than none. I, as a utilitarian, do not want to preach my doctrine to the masses. They may lack the ability to make the necessary calculations concerning the universal value of the consequences of their actions or misuse the utilitarian idea that no moral rules are sacrosanct as an excuse for their selfishness. As a utilitarian, I may well have to work behind the scenes to further unquestioned dedication to self-sacrifice, honesty, private property, justice, and the like. In other words, as a utilitarian I may be forced to deceive others. Actually, I, as a utilitarian, may even have to deceive myself. I too may be stupid and biased and need the myth of absolute moral rules and ideals to counteract my selfishness and greed. Consequently, from the belief that what ultimately matters is utility, I may have to engage in what for me—as a utilitarian—would be the dishonesty of urging myself, and not just others, to follow the strict letter of common morality.

Utilitarianism would in practice lead to lack of candour and even self-deception also, because the damaging psychological and social effects follow from our utilitarian but unorthodox actions only if their true nature is openly avowed. If, for example, I manage to keep my benevolent lie a secret, the possibility of damage on the character and expectations of others will be eliminated, and the utility of my lie increased. Since, as a utilitarian, I may well have to appreciate the value of my own non-utilitarian self, I may also want to dupe myself. I may, for example, want to induce in myself the delusion that what I told was not 'really' a lie. As a practising utilitarian I might have to engage in double-dealing not only with regard to others but also with regard to myself. I must either consider all my principles as merely provisional—and that, as a utilitarian, I may find risky

—or delude myself and think that my lies, betrayals, and cruelties are not really to be called by those names.

Utilitarianism appeals to optimistic, positivistic, and progressive minds. Its adherents may retort that there would be no need for hypocrisy, manipulation, and self-deceit in a world in which utilitarianism is triumphant. In a world free of ignorance, prejudice, and myth and in which there is available a highly developed body of human sciences and a reliable utilitarian calculus, utilitarians may readily avow their own doctrine and people will be free to develop new and purified moral identities, consciences, and selves. Still, even if such a world were to come, in the meanwhile the utilitarians are inviting us to put up with a great deal of double-dealing, in other words, of immorality. Besides, as we shall see shortly, the utilitarian utopia, even if it could be achieved, would have a fatal flaw.

In discussing that part of his doctrine which we have called consequentialism Mill worries about an objection which is the exact opposite of the one which concerned him regarding hedonism. The charge he is anxious to ward off in this case is not that utilitarianism sets its sights too low but that it sets them too high (*UT* 17). You cannot expect people to act from the Principle of Utility as their motive. The welfare of the whole of humanity, not to mention of the 'whole sentient universe', is too intangible an idea. It can never move us. Our actions are inevitably motivated by closer and more parochial loyalties and emotional ties.

Mill's answer is that this objection confuses the standard of the moral rightness of an act with its motive. According to him, the motive of an act has no necessary bearing on whether or not it is morally right. It determines only the moral goodness or praiseworthiness of the agent. Whether a given act was morally right or wrong is one thing; whether the agent is to be praised or blamed for having done it is another. Utilitarianism, says Mill, does not demand that we act from the love of mankind. What makes an act right is purely a question of how in fact it happens to affect the happiness of mankind. If an act happens to promote it, it is morally right no matter what led the agent to do it.

Apparently Mill once became aware of a hitch in this line of thought—for it leads us to say that what someone did might be morally wrong even though it was not his fault. In a footnote (subsequently omitted) in one edition of *Utilitarianism* (*UT* 18) he said that it is not the *actual* consequences of an act that determine its moral rightness; instead, it is determined entirely by the agent's intention. When the cruel potentate has the fugitive who has jumped into the river rescued from drowning, said Mill in that footnote, what the potentate had done is nevertheless morally wrong because the intention of that act was to put the man to death more painfully afterwards. But, Mill continued to insist, motives are irrelevant for the assessment of the moral rightness of actions. The intention, he said, is 'what we will' and therefore 'part of the action' and makes 'the act itself different'. The motive, on the other hand, is not part of an action—it does not affect its identity—it is merely what 'makes' me act in the way I do.

But if we admit that intentions are 'part of an action', can we deny that so are motives? Extenuations can be based on either. If what transpires is bad but contrary to the agent's intentions, we do not blame him or we blame him less. The same is true of motives. That Othello killed Desdemona from jealousy was horrible enough, but it would have been viler still if he had done it from greed—that is, in order to get her inheritance.

Utilitarianism leads to an etiolation of morality. The reason for including intentions in the moral assessment of acts is that acts must be distinguished from mere events. Happenings such as hailstorms and floods may have adverse consequences on human happiness, but we do not call them right or wrong. Those concepts apply only to human *actions* and human actions contain a mental element—not only intentions but also motives —as well as such things as forethought, plan, and deliberation. Mill's footnote is just weaseling. Motives and intentions are conceptually too close to allow the point he was trying to make. An actual performance may be at variance with both intentions and motives. Moreover, asking about a person's intentions is intimately connected with asking about his motives. Suppose Jones makes a remark that embarrasses Smith. Was this Jones's intention? In trying to find out, we shall want to ask if Jones is jealous of Smith or if he hates him; in other words, enquire about his motives. This does not mean that we can never discover the agent's intentions without finding out his motives. There may be behavioural signs, or we can just ask him. Besides, not all intentional acts are motivated. A person may act, and act intentionally, pretty much willy-nilly and on impulse. Still, learning about a person's motives is one way of learning about his intentions. Conversely, the agent's intentions are clues to his motives. If we know that Jones's intention was to harm Smith, this narrows down what we can consider his motive. Both intentions and motives are parts of the rationale of human actions.

In *Utilitarianism* Mill says that a motive is what 'makes' us act in a certain way (*UT* 18 n.). And in his *A System of Logic* he says that motives as well as purposes are causes of actions and volitions (*CW* viii. 836–7). If this were so, the motive would indeed not be 'part of the action' and there would indeed be only a contingent connection between morally good motives and morally right acts. For there is a philosophically often favoured sense—which, to no small measure is due to the influence of Mill—in which *A* is the cause of *B*, only if there is merely, in experience, a constant connection between *A* and *B*, but no conceptual tie between them. If *A* is the cause of *B*, it is merely that we can, with the aid of an appropriate empirical generalization, deduce a degree of probability of *B* from *A*. So, if motives are causes, moral goodness of men is just a good disposition. You can, occasionally, hit a good backhand without being a good tennis player; it is just that if you are a good tennis player then you are likely to hit a good backhand. Similarly, you can, occasionally, do a morally right deed without being a morally good person; it is just that, if you are a morally good person —one with morally good motives—then you are likely to perform morally right actions.

But it is very doubtful that the sort of thing Mill himself mentions as a motive—an emotion—is, as a rule, assignable as the cause of an act. For no empirical generalizations are known —and it is hard to see how they could ever be known—which allow the deduction of the probabilities of specific acts from specific emotions felt on specific occasions. We cannot, for example, imagine how even to start looking for an empirical generalization which would allow the deduction of Jones's smashing of the china from the anger at not having been elected a trustee of his old Alma Mater. The generalizations which connect classes of acts with certain feelings of emotion owe their plausibility to the terms designating these feelings already having conceptual connections with terms used for describing certain acts. For example, we may say that people wish to hurt those whom they hate. But such a statement is not an empirical hypothesis. Jones's wishing harm to Smith is just part of what is meant by Jones hating Smith.

In addition, if motives 'make' us perform our actions, motivated actions would not be voluntary actions. There are indeed mental causes which make or compel us to do things—blind fear or rage, for example. A hideous face in the window may send me cowering in the corner. My neighbour's dog having dug up my young petunias may make me kick it, or its owner. But if my act was a thing of this kind, we do not deem it morally assessable at all. On the other hand, explanation of acts through motives is not incompatible with freedom—it is explanation through the agent's reasons. Motives are not brute agitations. They do not *make* us act. Nor are they mere dispositions or patterns of behaviour. We can decide either to act or not to act from them.

For Mill, it is one thing to assess an action as morally right or wrong, it is another to hold the agent responsible, and either to praise or to blame him for it. According to him, there is only an external connection between my moral consciousness and the moral rightness or wrongness of my acts. What I do may be conducive to general welfare, and therefore morally right, even though promoting general welfare is not my motive. In fact, it is conceivable, in his view, that the utilitarian ideal is realized as well, or even better, if we have never thought or heard of the Principle of Utility. This is the absurdity of consequentialism. For general welfare, or anything else, cannot count as the realization of an ethical ideal if it were a mere fluke or miracle, or just a side-consequence of our intended actions, or just serendipity. Utilitarianism makes morality monstrously impersonal. Suppose mankind wakes up one morning permeated with great euphoria which includes all the subtlety and elevation of Mill's 'higher' pleasures. But, for them, how it all came about is inexplicable; to them their bliss does not connect up with any of their conscious pursuits. Mill would have to say that that state of affairs would nevertheless be morally good, in fact, a utilitarian utopia. But the truth of the matter is, of course, that morality would then not have entered into the picture at all. In a curious passage in his *Autobiography* Mill seems to say that the goal of the hedonist can be realized only, so to speak, absent-mindedly:

I never, indeed, wavered in the conviction that happiness is the test of all rules of conduct, and the end of life. But now I thought that this end was only to be attained by not making it the direct end. Those only are happy . . . who have their minds fixed on some object other than their own happiness; on the happiness of others, on the improvement of mankind, even on some art or pursuit, followed not as a means, but itself an ideal end. Aiming thus at something else, they find happiness by the way. The enjoyments of life . . . are sufficient to make it a pleasant thing, when they are taken *en passant*, without being made a principal object. . . . Ask yourself whether you are happy, and you cease to be so. The only chance is to treat, not happiness, but some end external to it, as the purpose of life. (*CW* i. 145–6)

The point I wish to make can be put in this way. Mill, in his unabashedly consequentialist writings such as *Utilitarianism*, pays attention only to what may be called 'feeling-values' and ignores what may be called 'act-values'. In the light of what I said earlier—namely, that some pleasures are just enjoyed activities—even a hedonist does not have to be a consequentialist. It is possible for the hedonist to say—as Mill does in the above passage—that what makes life worth living is engaging in one's pursuits, whatever they may be, and enjoying oneself into the bargain. We do not have to look at what we do as mere travail for the sake of a pleasure subsequent and external to it. But this is really only a faint-hearted attempt to rest in a poor half-way house. Mill's words are a big equivocation. He seems to say, on the one hand, that we should follow our pursuits as ends in themselves. But then it is inconsistent to say, as Mill also says or implies in that passage, that we should do so, after all, because doing so makes our lives pleasant and happy. Kant, as we shall see, took a resolute step further. For him, consequentialism as well as hedonism are radically misguided.

This leads us to the concept of freedom. If it is our actions that give meaning to our lives, they must be, in some sense, free actions, actions which are our own. It seems that there are two senses in which an action can be free. In one sense, it is free if it is not hindered or stymied. In another, an action is free if it is freely chosen, that is, if the will behind it is free. Mill held that there are free actions only in the former sense. To say that there are also actions which are free in the second sense is, according to him, just an illusion. To anticipate, according to Kant there *are* free actions of the second kind. In fact, he held that, if there were not, there would not be any such thing as morality. Moreover, as we shall see in Part Two, he made the startling claim that it is our free will which, in an important sense, determines what is capable of being accomplished through our own power.

For Mill, freedom is just freedom of achievement or accomplishment. There are some things we can do and others we cannot. It all depends on a person's abilities and opportunities. For example, a man is not free to go skiing if his leg is broken or if there is no snow. The natural order of things as well as the extent of our skills and technology restrict what is humanly possible to achieve. What these restrictions are overall is a matter of speculation. Cracking the atom, space flight, test-tube babies, cloning, and so on are developments which have widened our imagination far and wide. This dimension of our freedom of action is not a philosophical but, on the whole, a scientific subject. It has, to be sure, its philosophical and ethical aspect. What men can do is not always morally right to do. This is, in part, the issue of individual liberty *vis-à-vis* societal restrictions. Mill wrote one of the most influential books on that topic—*On Liberty*. For our purposes it would be beside the point to go into what he said in it. For, in order to understand the nature of morality, the issue is neither what is in fact in man's power to do, nor what he may legitimately do, but whether or not he has the power to choose freely what he wants to do to begin with. Here the question is not what sort of leeway we have, but whether or not we are free to set our own course. Mill's position is that we are not. For him, the idea that not only is it in our power to accomplish, sometimes, what we have set our sights on, but that we are also free to set our sights, is untenable.

In essence, his reasoning to that effect, as set out in his *An Examination of Sir William Hamilton's Philosophy* (CW ix), goes as follows. As far as 'experience' is concerned, Mill says, it is clear that our volitions are not free and undetermined but caused. 'Experience' shows us that there are constant and uniform correlations between any volition of ours and 'some special combination of antecedent conditions' and that we have the 'power of foreseeing actions . . . with a certainty often quite equal to that with which we predict the commonest physical events', at least, as he adds, 'when we have sufficient knowledge of the circumstances' and in 'proportion' to our 'previous experience and knowledge of the agents' (*CW* ix. 446). What are these 'antecedent conditions' which have constant and uniform connections with our volitions and let us predict them? Mill tells us that they are 'desires, aversions, habits, and dispositions, combined with outward circumstances suited to call those internal incentives into action' (ibid.). But, as we have pointed out earlier, experience fails to establish any invariable and uniform connections between specific motives and specific voluntary actions so that reliable predictions can be made. To our earlier example of anger, we may add the example of jealousy. There are any number of different things a jealous man may do. His jealousy and the given 'outward circumstances' (say his wife's adultery) may prompt him to initiate divorce proceedings, to try to patch things up, to leave home and become a drifter, or to kill his wife, or his rival, or himself. The 'constant correlations' between our emotions and our actions are, as we said earlier, really conceptual connections and not anything learnt from experience and observation. Anger and hostile or destructive behaviour go together, but anger is not the cause of such behaviour. Anger is already a volition and hostile and destructive behaviour is the expression of anger and part of the meaning of anger. Equally, while the cigarette habit and the lighting-up of cigarettes also go together, we do not discover this through experience and observation—and an angry man can suppress his anger and even the chain-smoker of ten years can quit.

Mill says further that the uniform connections between volitions and their 'antecedents' can be tested

by the statistical results of the observation of human beings acting in numbers sufficient to eliminate the influences which operate only on a few, and which on a large scale neutralize one another, leaving the total result about the same as if volitions of the whole mass had been affected by such only of the determining causes as were common to them all. (ibid.)

But of course, from the point of view of understanding morality, the question is not whether the volitions of the 'whole mass' of humanity are free, but whether those of individuals are free.

What can be statistically predicted, and what a given individual is free to will, are two separate issues.

Sir William Hamilton's argument for free will was simply this: since we are conscious of our freedom, we are free. But, Mill asked, what *is* the testimony of 'consciousness' with regard to free will? His answer was that we are conscious not of our free will but only of our accountability; and, he continued, that is nothing more nor less than the awareness that we may be subjected to punishment. By way of providing evidence for this view, he wrote the following odd passage:

It is not usually found that Oriental despots, who cannot be called to account by anybody, have much consciousness of being morally accountable. And . . . in societies in which caste and class distinctions are really strong . . . persons may show the strongest sense of accountability as regards their equals, who can make them accountable and not the smallest vestige of a similar feeling towards their inferiors who cannot. (*CW* ix. 455)

Kant would have said that these words display a total misunderstanding of what *moral* accountability is. According to Kant, to have moral consciousness has nothing to do with the fear that others may in fact 'make us accountable', that they may subject us to reprisals and punishments. He would have objected equally to Mill's words which shortly follow:

Suppose that there were two peculiar breeds of human beings,—one of them so constituted from the beginning, that however educated or treated, nothing would prevent them from always feeling and acting so as to be a blessing to all whom they approached; and another, of such original perversity of nature that neither education nor punishment could inspire them with a feeling of duty, or prevent them from being active in evil doing. Neither of the races of human beings would have a free-will; yet the former would be honoured as demigods, while the latter would be regarded and treated as noxious beasts . . . (*CW* ix. 456)

For Kant, neither of these breeds of men would be cognizant of morality. Mill continues:

even under the [above] utmost possible exaggeration of the doctrine of Necessity, the distinction between moral good and evil in conduct would not only subsist, but would stand out in a more marked manner than now, when the good and the wicked, however unlike, are still regarded as of one common nature. (ibid.)

Kant would have said that the good and the wicked *do* possess a common nature; the difference between them is how they go beyond their nature and choose freely to be either wicked or good.

PART TWO

Kant and the Ethics of Duty

IMMANUEL KANT (1724–1804) spent his entire life in what was then Königsberg, East Prussia. After several years as a family tutor, he re-entered the university of his native city and eventually became a professor. In spite of his heavy and wide-ranging teaching duties, he wrote voluminously and some of his works rank among the philosophically most important ever written. He took a keen interest in the intellectual life of eighteenth-century Europe and became himself a noted figure. He never married and his personal life was uneventful. But he was not a recluse. He had a faithful circle of friends and was an immensely popular lecturer. He shared the rising passion of his age for freedom and combined it with a deep appreciation of selflessness and duty instilled in him by his Pietist upbringing.

8

Morality and Religion

I SAID in the Introduction that moral philosophers are not apostles of new moral ideals. Kant was no exception. He maintained that the central concepts of his doctrine—the good will and duty—are 'already present in a sound natural understanding' (*GR* 64). Mill said very much the same thing. He said that men have always believed in utilitarianism, and that 'the youth Socrates' had already propounded it (*UT* 1). Mill apparently believed that all that was really needed in order to make that doctrine accepted by all was to clear away the misunderstandings surrounding it. So both Kant and Mill claimed to be faithful to the facts of our moral consciousness as it already exists. How are we then to explain the radical difference between their views?

I also said in the Introduction that a moral philosopher does not merely describe and analyse. He is also concerned with coherence. And, since our moral thinking in its day-to-day operation is a cultural and historical amalgam which more likely than not is beset with internal conflicts, he must sift and choose. Our ethical consciousness in the West is the product of both religious and secular traditions. While Kant's view is firmly rooted in the former, the reverberations of the latter—which started with the Greeks—are still strongly present in Mill. For the utilitarians, to behave ethically is to try to secure an end deemed valuable in itself unalloyed with prior moral or religious notions. Central to utilitarianism is the thought that morality is a means for reaching an ultimate good which is definable ahead of morality. Morality is just a strategy to secure that good. For Kant, on the other hand, ethics is a matter of obeying principles of which the validity and the binding force is independent of the value of the results of following them. His view was that what matters ultimately is not what our actions lead to but what leads to our actions. This is reminiscent of what is said in the *Old*

Testament: thou shalt follow the Commandments. In teleological ethics, in order to live the good life, we must first arrive at
a conception of what is the highest good. The moral imperatives
merely tell us the means of how it is to be achieved. For example,
for Mill, as we saw, the highest good is to experience as much
pleasure or happiness as possible and morality is there to tell us
how to reach that goal. Kant turns all this around. The thing that
ultimately matters is not reaching a substantive goal, but acting
with a certain quality exhibited in our will, regardless of any
pay-offs. The point for him is to act with a will that is guided by
rules which can be judged to be the right rules apart from the
independent value which may be realized by following them.

The supreme good, for Kant, is made up of the inner structure
of our actions themselves. This is also to say that the highest
value is moral praiseworthiness. In Mill's view, we recall, we can
perform morally right actions from morally bad motives. But for
Kant, it is only what is in us—the nature of our motives and
will—that determines both the moral rightness of our actions
and our moral praiseworthiness. For Mill, as a teleologist, our
conduct is just a means. Moral imperatives are directives to the
individual and the species for living successfully, that is, in a
manner which secures that their wants and desires be satisfied.
Kant, on the other hand, maintains that, although we should be
grateful if our right conduct results in the happiness of ourselves
and others, *that* is not what makes that conduct morally right.

Some of the things Kant says about the relation between
ethics and religion might make it seem that his view of morality
is really teleological also, that for him, too, morality is there for
the sake of an ultimate goal, albeit a supernatural one—our
eternal bliss. In truth, for him morality is not the pursuit of even
that goal. If we are morally righteous we make ourselves worthy
of eternal happiness. But Kant denied that the foundation of
morality is the rewards religion may be taken to promise us.

The whole matter is, however, far from simple. To be sure,
there are in Kant arguments for the irrelevance of religion to
morality. We have no direct intuition of God's will. So, the view
that religion is the foundation of morality would be circular. For
if God's will is to be known at all, it must be known as the
morally perfect will and therefore we must have a conception of
what is morally right before we know what God's will is. If we

deny that God's will must conform to an independent moral principle, we are left with the notion that God is completely capricious, that He is desirous of nothing but power and glory —a conception which is 'directly opposed to morality' (*GR* 110). Essentially the same points are, as we saw, also to be found in Mill. The view that religion is irrelevant to morality is expressed most forcefully in Kant's *Religion within the Limits of Reason Alone*:

> [man] binds himself through his reason to unconditioned laws, [morality] stands in need neither of the idea of another Being over him, for him to apprehend his duty, nor of an incentive other than the law itself, for him to do his duty. . . . Hence . . . morality does not need religion at all . . . by virtue of pure practical reason it is self-sufficient. (*RE* 3)

In another way, however, for Kant, God and religion play a much more important role in ethics than for Mill. We saw that, for Mill, the existence or non-existence of a supernatural Being was, from the moral point of view, largely indifferent. For Kant, on the other hand, morality in a godless universe would become merely a thing to be idly contemplated. In the *Critique of Pure Reason* he wrote: 'without God and without a world invisible to us now but hoped for, the glorious ideas of morality are indeed objects of approval and admiration, but not springs of purpose and action' (*CPuR* 640). And in the *Lectures on Ethics* we read: 'it would seem . . . that God was the obligator of the moral laws. . . . the absence of a supreme judge would make all laws ineffectual. There would be no incentive, no reward, and no punishment' (*LE* 40). In other words, although religion is not the source of moral knowledge, it is nevertheless, contrary to what Kant himself says elsewhere, the incentive of moral conduct. At least an air of consistency is brought into the whole matter through this passage:

> If . . . we do as God has commanded because He has commanded it and because He is so mighty that He can force us to it, we act under orders, from fear and fright, not appreciating the propriety of our actions and not knowing *why* we should do as God has commanded nor *why* we should obey Him. Might cannot constitute a *vis obligandi*. Threats do not impose an obligation, they extort. If then we comply with the moral law from fear of punishment and of the power of God, and for no

other reason than that God has so commanded, we act not from duty and obligation, but from fear and fright. (*LE* 41)

The point is that, although we must consider moral precepts as God's commandments, we must not follow them for the sake of the attached punishments and rewards, but because they are rational principles. Still, if it is reason that is behind it all, why does not God drop out of the picture altogether?

I believe that Kant tried to answer that question in his *Critique of Practical Reason*. Kant said there that, for the sake of morality, we must 'postulate' our own immortality and the existence of God. I shall summarize his arguments. It is the moral law and reason which is the 'determining ground' of the will both in the sense of telling us what is morally right and motivating us to adhere to it. However, the moral law is 'merely formal' (we shall see what that means later) and 'abstracts from all material and thus from every object of volition'. That law nevertheless has an 'object' (purpose or aim); Kant calls it the 'highest good'. While the highest good, as an 'object', is not the 'determining ground of the will . . . the concept of it and the idea of its existence . . . are likewise the determining ground of the pure will' (*CPrR* 214).

What does the last sentence mean? Suppose there is a chain of *haute-cuisine* restaurants called 'Gourmet Heaven'. Tom and Jane know that there is one of these restaurants in their town. So they go there for dinner. In that case, Kant would say, it is that 'object'—the 'Gourmet Heaven' in Bourbon Street—which is the 'determining ground' of their will and action. But suppose that Tom and Jane are stranded in a strange town and are in the mood for delectable food. So they set out in search of a 'Gourmet Heaven'. In that case it is not an 'object' and its 'reality', but merely 'the concept of it and the idea of its reality' which is the 'determining ground' of their will and action. For there may not even be a 'Gourmet Heaven' in that town. While Tom and Jane do not *know* that there is a 'Gourmet Heaven' in that unfamiliar town, they *hope* or *postulate* that there is. The situation is similar to that of the moral person as Kant portrays him.

Kant writes in *Religion*, 'morality required no end for right conduct . . . Yet an end does arise out of morality' (*RE* 4). As we commit ourselves to morality, while we cannot know its reality, we nevertheless hope for or postulate the reality of the highest good. Of course that hope arising out of morality is not prompted by a sensuous desire as the hope of our two epicures is. Morality is, for Kant, a matter of reason, and the hope of the moral person that there is the 'highest good' is a 'rational hope'. While the hope or the postulate of Tom and Jane might be rational in the sense that they might have some empirical evidence that there is a 'Gourmet Heaven' in that unfamiliar town, the hope or the postulate of the moral person that there is the highest good is based on *pure* practical reason. (What pure practical reason is, we shall see later.)

What then is the highest good? In one sense, it is the good will or acting for the sake of duty, in other words, virtue. But virtue is not the total or consummate good. That, says Kant, is virtue combined with happiness (*CPrR* 214–15). However, within the realm of 'nature'—that is, within the world as we experience it and act in it—virtue and happiness are, alas, only contingently connected. The rain falls on both the righteous and the wicked. Still, Kant held, we cannot believe that this kind of cosmic scandal is the last word. Eventually things must be capable of being put to right. The complete good in its ultimate sense —perfect virtue combined with perfect happiness or eternal bliss—must be capable of existing, for otherwise the good will turns out not to be a practical will, but a mere quixotic obsession. Therefore, in order that virtue, as a necessary condition for the highest and total good, be realizable, we must assume that there is a progress of persons through an endless existence toward 'holiness' (*CPrR* 225–6).

Further reasoning along these lines leads to the postulation of the existence of God. The highest good becomes complete only if to perfect virtue there is added what it deserves, that is, perfect happiness. But only an omnipotent and just Being can guarantee such a harmony. 'Therefore,' says Kant, 'it is *morally* [my emphasis] necessary to assume the existence of God.' But, he adds, 'it is well to notice here that this moral necessity is *subjective* [my emphasis] i.e., a need, and not objective, i.e., duty itself . . . it can be called *faith* and even pure *rational* faith' (*CPrR* 228–9). Kant's arguments do not amount to, and were not intended to amount to, an objective proof of immortality and the existence of God. The whole issue for Kant is not theoretical, but practical, that is, one directly affecting the attitude with which we live. His conclusion is not that there is a God, but that, if we are committed to morality, we cannot help but will that there is a God, that is, act as if there were a God. For without God, morality as conceived by Kant—acting purely for the sake of duty—would not make complete sense. Religion is the consummation of ethics. Kant, unlike Mill, felt the need to combine morality with a cosmic order. Being moral is a pilgrimage.

Just the same, our conclusion must be that Kant's ethics remains deontological. Ethical conduct, according to him, must not be aimed at any goal, natural or supernatural. If I am moral I have to hope that my virtue will, in the end, be rewarded. But there is a catch. In order to be virtuous—to have a good will—my will must not be affected by the hope for that reward.

9

The Good Will and the Motive of Duty

ACCORDING to Kant, what is really important in life and makes it worth living is not happiness or pleasure but acting from a good will. In the *Groundwork of the Metaphysic of Morals* he begins by saying that nothing is good 'without qualification' or 'limitation' but a good will. By this he means first that a good will is the supreme or the highest good, and, second, that it is good in itself, that is, good regardless of its tendency to produce results which on independent grounds—hedonistic or otherwise —may be deemed desirable.

His initial arguments for this, perhaps extraordinary, claim go as follows. Our physical, mental, economic, and other resources may be put to either a good or a bad use. Their goodness is therefore not unconditional. Even happiness, he maintains, is not good without qualification, for a person's happiness may be either deserved or undeserved. It is only happiness combined with a good will, says Kant, that will be approved by 'a rational and impartial spectator' (*GR* 61). When a man has an evil will, we are not pleased if he is happy.

What, then, is the good will? Kant says that it is the rational will. What that means we must explore more fully in due course. For the present let us concentrate on Kant's claim that, *in humans*, the good will is the dutiful will, one that wills for the sake of duty. The 'holy' will, as Kant calls it—the will of angels and of God—is wholly good and therefore innocent of the idea of duty. The will of humans, on the other hand, is not wholly good; it is not determined solely by reason and the moral law but is also affected by the passions and appetites and these may always prompt us to act against our duty. In humans the good will must operate against obstacles. Of course it is possible to do what is our duty from motives other than duty. Our inclinations and our self-love *may* co-operate. But we should then still not be acting dutifully and merit moral esteem. An action is dutiful only if it has the idea of duty as its sole motive. Only then is it an action done from the good will and has what Kant calls 'true moral worth'.

Kant says that there are three kinds of actions which are not done from duty and therefore not from a good will and hence lack true moral worth (*GR* 65).

> (1) . . . actions . . . recognized [perceived, known] as contrary to duty . . . about these the question does not even arise whether they could have been done *for the sake of duty* inasmuch as they are directly opposed to it.
>
> (2) . . . actions which in fact accord with duty, yet for which we have *no immediate inclination*, but perform them because impelled to do so by some other inclination.
>
> (3) . . . [actions which] accord with duty and the subject has in addition an *immediate* inclination [to do them].

Now type (1) seems to lump together what are really two different kinds of actions: actions which are *recognized* as contrary to duty, that is, as morally wrong (1a), and actions which actually *are* contrary to duty and morally wrong (1b). With regard to actions under (1a), it is indeed easy to see that they cannot be done from duty. If I have a conviction or belief—correct or incorrect—that a prospective action of mine is morally wrong, I cannot do it from duty unless, *per impossibile*, I were what Kant calls a 'devilish being' who possesses a 'malignant reason' or a 'thoroughly evil will' by which 'opposition to the law would itself be set up as an incentive' (*RE* 30). Only the devil says to himself 'Evil, thou be my good'.

But the situation with regard to actions which come under (1b) is significantly different. Why is it impossible to do from duty what *is* morally wrong and contrary to duty as opposed to what is merely *believed* to be morally wrong and contrary to duty? We saw that, according to Mill, this is quite possible. Well, by the motive of duty Kant did not mean what Mill meant by 'the pure idea of duty'. The latter, you recall, was still just a feeling, although a deep and complex one. For Kant, in contrast, the motive of duty was a matter of reason. Kant did not mean by that motive what is sometimes meant by a 'sense of duty'. It is possible to say that from a sense of duty a soldier tortured his prisoners in order to get vital military intelligence from them. But he would then not have acted from *moral* duty, as Kant understood it. Our moral duties are definable neither in terms of the rules and regulations which go with any institutions nor by any loyalties or devotions which we may have to some organization or to our state and fatherland or even to God. Moreover, and this is the crucial point for Kant, the motive of duty is not a feeling, however compelling, but tied to a rational judgement.

However, we can still press our point. Even a rational conviction that a particular action which is before us is morally right, may be mistaken. Even if it were true, as Kant will argue, that the fundamental moral principle or law itself—the Categorical Imperative—is a priori and necessary, the application of it to particular cases cannot be free of all uncertainty. Our 'pure practical reason'—the foundation of general moral principles—may be infallible, but, Kant himself admits, our 'understanding'—the power to apply general principles—is not. In *Religion* Kant says that one of the tasks of 'conscience' is to warn us against 'probabilism, i.e., the principle that the mere opinion that an action may well be right warrants its being performed' (*RE* 174). Conscience asks reason, says Kant, to judge

as to whether it has really undertaken that appraisal of actions (as to whether they are right or wrong) with all diligence, and it calls the man himself to witness *for or against* himself whether this diligent appraisal did or did not take place. (ibid.)

With great confidence Kant pronounces that, 'It is a basic moral principle, which required no proof, that *one ought to* hazard nothing that may be wrong.' Rather fragmentarily he quotes the Roman author Pliny the Younger (62–113 BC): *quod dubitas, ne feceris!* (*RE* 173). The translator of *Religion* provides a fuller quotation from Pliny in his footnote and translates it: 'if you consider more safe that rule of a certain extremely cautious man: "What you have doubts about, do not do."' Here Kant's philosophy does not strike us as the philosophy of a man of action. The warning Kant sounds is indeed appropriate to, say, a lynch mob or to religious fanatics, as Kant himself meant it to be, but it may also lead to a form of what Sartre will call 'bad faith' or self-deception and what Kant himself calls 'inner lie'. It may lead to a kind of self-righteousness and complacency which may lie in quietism. It may indeed have been possible for a professor of Königsberg to refrain from morally problematic actions. But, as Sartre will emphasize, in the press of circumstances, not to act may be tantamount to acting. We shall return to Kant's concepts of 'conscience' and 'inner lie' in the final chapter of Part Two.

At any rate, we must conclude that Kant was wrong in asserting that actions of the kind (1b)—actions which are, and are not just believed to be, morally wrong—cannot be done from duty. Trying as hard as we may does not guarantee that the moral assessment of an action before us is not mistaken. If we then, nevertheless, with the rending of conscience, go ahead and do it, it seems unfair to deny our actions 'true moral worth'.

Let us now turn to the two other types of actions which, according to Kant, are not done from duty and therefore are not morally meritorious. Nothing much need be said about actions of type (2). If a person does what is morally right but does it only in order to ensure his own interest, we do not say that he has done his duty for the sake of duty and accord him no moral merit. We are all, I think, convinced by Kant's example of the shopkeeper who does not cheat but only because he says to himself, 'Honesty is the best policy' (*GR* 65).

As to actions of type (3), why is acting from an immediate inclination incompatible with acting from duty? Kant himself said that here the 'distinction is far more difficult to perceive'. He was not a bluenosed puritan. Still, while Kant did not claim that dutiful actions must be unpleasant—that they must go, so to speak, against the grain—he made it clear that in performing such actions inclinations must not be, even in part, the moving force. In his *Lectures* he remonstrated against what he called 'coquettish' ethics which adduces sensuous and other pleasing inducements for morality and said that 'to mix moral and non-moral considerations is a terrible perversion' (*LE* 76). In the *Critique of Practical Reason* he exclaimed: 'Duty! Thou sublime and mighty name that dost embrace nothing charming or insinuating but requires submission . . . [and] only holdest forth a law . . . before which all inclinations are dumb . . .' (*CPrR* 193). What concerns Kant is not just that inclinations may lead to actions which are contrary to duty. Inclinations and feelings are as such not necessarily opposed but alien to morality. Duty as a command of reason 'thwarts all our inclinations'

(*CPrR* 181) and 'proudly rejects all kinship with the inclinations' (*CPrR* 193).

The natural tendency of most of us, I presume, is to believe that actions to which we are led by our impulses and inclinations —if they are unspoilt, healthy, beautiful, admirable, and the like—can have a worth which is at least equal to the worth of action which we perform from a cold rational consideration of what is our duty. Some devotees of Kant have therefore maintained that he did not really hold such a rigorous view, which, or a parody of which, does have unpalatable consequences.[1] A cynic once said that, in Kant's view, the moral greatness of Albert Schweitzer lay in the fact that he never stepped on a snail *because* he terribly wanted to. It is true that we find a more relaxed attitude in some of Kant's writings. In various places he says that we can, and even should, do our duty cheerfully; something I do may be both a duty and a pleasure. But Kant still insisted that such cheerfulness must be the effect and not the cause of our doing our duty. In other words, while Kant admitted that a kind of satisfaction or gladness may be felt as a *result* of having acted from duty, he was quite adamant that the prospect of such satisfaction or gladness must not be, even in part, what entices us to do our duty (*CPrR* 220).

Perhaps we can sort things out by distinguishing between acting *with* and acting *from* pleasure or inclination. According to Kant, I may be led to act in a certain way by the pure idea of duty—and therefore do what has 'true moral worth'—and still act gladly and *with* pleasure and in accordance with my inclination. But that pleasure and that inclination must be there only as inoperative concomitants. It is all right, morally, to take pleasure in an action so long as I am not, in any measure, led to that action by that pleasure. But when a pleasure taken in an action, or an inclination towards it, actively functions even as its partial spring or incentive, that action, according to Kant, is no longer morally praiseworthy.

What are we to think of Kant's rigorism—the view that morality, that is, what ultimately makes our lives worth living, lies exclusively in acting purely for the sake of duty. He gives us in the *Groundwork* five illustrations of the distinction between

---

[1] e.g. H. J. Paton, *The Categorical Imperative* (London, 1947), *GR* 89 n.

merely doing what is our duty and, beyond that, doing our duty from duty (*GR* 65–7). These examples are also intended to bring home the truth of his claim that only actions of the latter sort have 'true moral worth'. We have already mentioned the first of these illustrations—that of the honest shopkeeper—and found it convincing. But it does not deal with what is now at issue —namely, duty versus direct or immediate inclinations. The remaining four illustrations do.

The first of these is suicide. Suicide, Kant wants us to assume, is morally wrong. But, he says, if a man who has lost all taste for life does not take his own life simply because he is too terrified to do so—has a direct inclination against it—he reaps no moral merit. Abstaining from suicide has true moral worth only if it involves solely the realization that to take one's own life is a violation of one's duty.

This example does not speak very clearly in favour of Kant's position. Admittedly, if what keeps a person who feels that he can no longer enjoy life from ending it is an animal-like clinging to his bare existence, we do not feel bound to respect him. At the same time, when a prospective suicide really has lost all feeling for life, then the notion that he could still want to preserve it purely from duty becomes rather chimerical. Under those circumstances the idea of doing his duty would also have to be quite indifferent to him. Acting from duty may not be to exhibit the greatest verve for life, but neither is it a mere turgid ritual. It still involves having a kind of positive attitude towards life, even if what is left of it is rather little.

The second example is helping others. We ought to help those in distress. But, Kant points out, we may do so either because we just have a tender heart *or* because we realize that it is our duty to do so. Only in the latter case, he claims, does our conduct have moral merit.

It must be admitted that the distinction Kant is making is genuine enough. I may help a person just because my heart runs over. *Or* I may help him without feeling anything positive for him—I may even be filled with revulsion, disgust, and contempt for him—but help him just the same, purely because I realize that it is my duty to do so. Still, it is certainly an exaggeration, if not worse, to maintain that only in the latter case do I merit moral praise. Admittedly, if I help others out of, say, vanity or in order to fill my otherwise idle days, there is nothing morally admirable in my conduct and my life could then still be hollow. But what Kant maintains is stronger and quite paradoxical. Even if our motive to help another person is to 'rejoice in the happiness of others', he says, we are not morally praiseworthy.

The third example is our own happiness. For Kant, to make ourselves happy is a duty, indirectly, for constant frustration is likely to lead to severe transgressions. However, happiness is, according to Kant, an indeterminate concept and its precepts shaky and full of exceptions. It is for this reason, I think, that he maintains that happiness is sometimes better served by taking an obvious and immediate road to pleasure than by being plagued by anxiety over our future well being. It is morally endorsable occasionally to drink and to be merry and let the future take care of itself. But, Kant insists again, while indulging ourselves is sometimes morally obligatory—it is, you might say a prophy-lactic duty—it is morally praiseworthy only if it is carried out from duty and not just doing what you feel like doing.

Here Kant seems to be lacking in wisdom. There is something absurd about the idea of following our inclinations from the motive of duty. It is impossible, I should think, say, to loiter from duty. To seek a pleasure out of duty will make that pleasure go sour.

Curiously enough, in giving his last illustration, Kant himself seems to have appreciated the point we have just made. He says that the command of Scripture to love our neighbours must be understood as commanding 'practical' love, that is, how we should *act* rather than how we should *feel*. For 'love as a feeling cannot be commanded'. The point, presumably, is that, there-fore, we cannot take moral credit for our love as a feeling or inclination. I can, from duty, do loving, kind, beneficient deeds towards my neighbour, but I cannot, from duty, glow inwardly when I see him.

Kant maintains, then, that an action is morally meritorious only if it is done purely from duty and not, even in part, from some other motive. This is not to say that, according to Kant, acting from the motive of duty is what makes an action morally *right*. It is of course true that, according to him, the value of the actual, or even of the intended, consequences of an action have nothing to do with its being morally right or wrong. Both the moral praiseworthiness and the moral rightness of an action depend instead upon the motive or spirit or attitude behind it. An action is morally right solely because of the inner nature of the agent's consciousness which leads to it. Of course, to will anything is to will certain consequences. But what makes our action right, Kant maintains, is not the value of the willed consequences. An action—that is, the producing of such and such effects—is right if the principle of the will behind it is legitimate. As we shall see in greater detail shortly, what makes such a principle legitimate is its internal and formal structure and not that following it will bring about something which, on some independent and material ground, can be deemed desirable. Nevertheless, it does not follow that it is the motive of duty which makes an action right.

While in Kant's view there is a more intimate connection between the moral rightness of an action and its moral praiseworthiness than Mill's view, he does not say that the two are one and the same. The list of duties which he gives in *The Metaphysic of Morals* does not include the duty to do our duty for the sake of duty. We cannot have the duty to perform a morally meritorious action, for we choose an action and not its motive. It is true that in that work and elsewhere he says that we have the duty to develop our moral goodness in general, that is, our moral strength as the power to act from the motive of duty, but that is a different matter (*MM* 45–6). Not to keep moral rightness and moral praiseworthiness apart would make Kant subject to the charge of pharisaism, for his view would then imply that we should always act for the sake of our own purity and goodness. It would also trap him in a vicious circle. As we pointed out earlier, the motive of duty is, for Kant, the certainty that an action is morally right. Therefore, it cannot be what makes an action right. For my certainty is certainty about the action already *being* right; it is not certainty about my certainty that it is right. While disagreeing with Mill that we can do what is morally praiseworthy or virtuous without doing what is also morally right, Kant agrees with Mill that it is possible to perform a morally right action without doing anything morally praiseworthy. To anticipate, what, according to Kant, makes an action morally right is that its motive or maxim is capable of being adopted by everyone. But it is quite possible that the motive or maxim of a given action is capable of being adopted by everyone without that action being performed *because* its motive or maxim is capable of being adopted by everyone. In that case, the action will be morally right but without what Kant calls 'true moral worth'.

10

The Moral Law and Kant's Formalism

EVERYTHING in nature, said Kant, happens according to laws, but humans can embark on their actions in order to conform to laws (*GR* 80). This is what, according to Kant, is to be meant by man possessing a will. The will is not just desire, but the faculty to act from practical principles or imperatives. Now imperatives, Kant pointed out, are either 'hypothetical' or 'categorical'. The former divide again into two groups. They are either 'technical' or 'pragmatic'. Neither of those are universal or 'valid for all rational beings'. The technical imperatives are rational principles, but they are not principles of *pure* practical reason because they merely spell out the means to ends which, 'due to our sensuous nature', we happen to have. Such ends may vary from person to person and from time to time. The reason why pragmatic imperatives fail to be universally applicable is different. All humans, said Kant in unison with Mill, desire their happiness. However, happiness, he maintained, is a wayward concept. Some, he said, find happiness in abstinence, some in plenty (*LE* 5). Each person must learn what makes him happy from his own experience. Here we can therefore have only rough 'counsels', as Kant called them, mere rules of thumb, and no true principles. Consequently, although for different reasons, neither the 'technical' nor the 'pragmatic' hypothetical imperatives can amount to universal laws. Such imperatives are relative and restricted in scope; they may easily fail to have a point for the addressee.

In contrast, categorical or moral imperatives do not rest on ends resulting from our desires and needs. They themselves specify ends—ends 'valid for all rational beings'. In Kant's view, unlike Mill's, ethics is concerned not with how to realize the ends we happen to have, but with what is to be our ultimate end. Empirical or scientific ethics is therefore impossible. Observation can tell us only what desires humans do have and, combined with science, what they must do in order to satisfy them, but not what they ought to aim at to begin with. Consequently, Kant claimed that *the* Categorical Imperative, or the moral law, must be

sought not in the nature of man, nor in the circumstances of the world in which he is placed, but solely *a priori* in the concepts of pure reason; and . . . every other precept based on principles of mere experience . . . although it can be called a practical rule, can never be called a moral law. (*GR* 57)

What are we to make of this rather startling claim? Today we glibly talk of the relativity of this and the relativity of that. But we must notice that what Kant said about the universality or unrestricted generality of ethics is quite compatible with the ethnic, cultural, historical, and other variations of *actual* moralities, that is, with the relativity of what *in fact* is held to be ultimately right or wrong. There are indeed differences in the moral beliefs of different peoples and of different times. But Kant did not claim that the same moral principles are *in fact* held by all, everywhere and always. What he claimed was that principles of conduct are moral principles only if they are *regarded* as universally applicable, as having an unrestricted scope. Even if you were the only person in the world to hold a particular moral belief, you will *think* of it as valid for everyone. When you say 'One ought never to cheat', or perhaps 'One ought never to forget an injury', or even 'Boiled eggs ought to be cracked at their blunt ends', and *mean* it as a moral judgement, you include everybody. When you claim that something is right merely as a matter of the prevailing mores of a given society, or of positive law, or the rules and regulations of an organization, you do not make a universal normative claim. For example, no one would normally wish to maintain that everyone everywhere and always ought to wear black tie to dinner. There are many kinds of practical rules and precepts and the vast majority of them are not meant to apply universally. They are addressed only to certain professions, nationalities, social groups, ages, or one or other of the two sexes, and so on, and only in certain limited circumstances, such as in polite society, while cooking, driving a car, or building a space ship. The scope of such principles is limited by the roles people play, the jobs they hold, the special causes to which they have dedicated themselves, and the circumstances under which they act. But an imperative like 'You ought not to tell lies' is likely to be issued in an entirely different spirit—without any intended restriction of scope and as binding for absolutely everybody. Of course, the fact that the *intended* scope of a normative judgement or imperative is unrestricted and universal does not determine what its scope really is. That depends, as we said in the Introduction, on the viewpoint not of the speaker but of the audience. Thus, 'Boiled eggs ought to be cracked at their blunt ends' is clearly an unhappy case. How you crack eggs may be of no concern to Jones whatsoever, and no one would brand him an amoralist because of that.

For a deeper understanding of what the universality of morality is, one needs an adequate definition of the moral community of humans. We saw in Part One that Mill's definition of man as an intelligent pleasure seeker will not do. A man is still a man, even if he does not seek pleasure. Kant, on the other hand, defines man in terms of his 'pure practical reason'. In order to understand what this means we must seek to understand Kant's claim that the moral law, or the Categorical Imperative, as the foundation of all moral judgements is known a priori.

I know that all bachelors are unmarried a priori, independently of experience and observation. I do not have to visit even a sample of them in order to know that this is so. On the other hand, I cannot know whether or not all bachelors are unhappy without an empirical investigation. What Kant held was that I know what is morally right just about in the same way as I know that all bachelors are unmarried. I do not have to find out what it is that people actually seek in their lives or what, in actual fact, are the things sanctioned in my society or in any other, or even what, in fact, are the forms of social behaviour that have the greatest utility. The logical law of non-contradiction tells us that we must not say 'Some bachelors are married', for to say that is necessarily false. The moral law, according to Kant, condemns my telling a lie, for example, in a parallel fashion. According to Kant, as we shall see in detail, telling a lie is also, or leads to, a contradiction.

For Mill, morality is universal because all humans are pleasure seekers. Amorality for him is, in effect, not to care for one's happiness or for the happiness of others. For Kant diminished humanity is just illogicality. You are amoral if you are not rational; and being rational, for him, is just not contradicting oneself. The scope of moral judgements, for him, is unrestricted and universal, not because we are all pleasure seekers, but because we all respect logic.

An obvious objection to the claim that the moral law is an a priori law—essentially just the law of non-contradiction—independent of the empirically discoverable human goals and motives, is that in that case that law would not be a practical law; it could not move us to action. This, we recall, was the objection of Herr Garve, who maintained that the only thing that can move a person to do anything is that he thinks that the anticipated state of affairs resulting from the contemplated action promises to give him more happiness. In answering that objection Kant says that, although we cannot change the fact that we all desire happiness, we can refuse to make happiness a condition for following the moral law. We can, he said, 'abstract' from that condition when duty calls and can make our decision as if we did not desire happiness (*OS* 46). Kant flatly opposes Mill's and Garve's view of what can motivate us. A person, he says, knows 'with utmost clarity' that

he *ought to perform* his duty quite unselfishly, and that his desire for happiness *must* be completely divorced from his concept of duty in order to preserve its purity . . . For it is precisely in that purity of the concept of duty that the true worth of morality is found, and *thus one must be capable of it* [my emphasis]. (*OS* 51)

Continuing in the same vein, Kant says that man knows that he can resist all hedonistic motives 'because he ought to'; to deny this 'is the death of all morality' (*OS* 52). So, for the sake of morality, we must presuppose or postulate man's ability to obey the moral law—a law which is not based on man's empirical nature, but is a priori and based on pure reason. But we are now already anticipating our discussion of Kant's concept of freedom, for the ability to act solely for the sake of the purely rational law of morality is exactly what Kant means by freedom of the will.

What then is the moral law? It is, in effect, as we already said, nothing more, nor less, than the law of logical consistency.

Consistency forbids us to believe things that are self-contradictory. What Kant did was to extend the demand of consistency to cover imperatives and volitions as well. When confronted with the decision concerning whether or not a given action is morally right or wrong, we must test what Kant called the 'maxim' or 'subjective principle' of that action by the moral law or the 'Categorical Imperative'. That law or imperative reads, 'Act only on that maxim through which you can at the same time will that it should become a universal law' (*GR* 88), and, this is Kant's essential idea, I *can* will that only if doing so does not involve me in a self-contradiction. The moral law is formal; it is divorced from all content of volition, that is, from *what* is being willed. This is exactly analogous to the way in which the logical law of non-contradiction is formal. That law tells us not to assert a proposition together with its negation, no matter what is the content of that proposition. The moral law, according to Kant, tells us not to will an action, and at the same time, what negates it.

Another analogue may be helpful for understanding Kant's formalism. He says, 'Ethics does not give laws for action, but only for the maxims of action' (*MM* 48). Moral principles do not apply to actions in their total concreteness but only in so far as they already exhibit a principle or form, a shape, if you like. This is similar to the fact that the axioms and theorems of geometry do not apply to physical things in their full concreteness, but only as they already exhibit certain shapes: triangularity, squareness, circularity, and what have you.

It has become customary to call the test of the moral rightness of an action laid down in Kant's Categorical Imperative the universalizability test.[1] The basic notion is this. Before doing something we must ask, 'What if the sort of thing I am contemplating doing were done universally?' Let us make it clear how this differs from utilitarianism. When the utilitarian is concerned with the universal implications of an action, he is concerned with two things. Suppose, I tell a lie. First, this may contribute to others lying as well. Second, as it does so, there will

---

[1] One of the fullest and best discussions of the concept of universalizability and its relevance to ethics is to be found in R. M. Hare, *Freedom and Reason* (Oxford, 1963), where he develops a theory of moral reasoning not unlike Kant's. See *passim* and esp. pp. 86–224.

be deterioration, in Mill's phrase, of the 'trustworthiness of human assertions', and that, as we pointed out earlier, has definite disutility. For Kant, all this is beside the point. For him, universalizability is, first, not a matter of whether or not my conduct is *in fact* likely to increase the frequency of similar conduct in general. According to Kant, we must simply ask, quite hypothetically, 'What *if* everyone were to act in that way?' We are not allowed to rebut that question by saying, 'Well, not everyone will.' We are merely to conduct a thought-experiment. Second, according to Kant, the moral rightness of a form of conduct does not depend on the *material* value of the consequences which would accrue if it were to become universal. It is all a *formal* question, a question of whether or not the universal adherence to my maxim would yield a self-contradiction.

All of our actions have maxims. That is to say, when, in the full sense of that word, I act, there is in my mind, or in the back of my mind, a practical principle however vague and obscure. Through my act, I subscribe, or commit myself, to a general principle of action. The nature of the assessment of such a principle depends, according to Kant, on whether it is 'technical' or 'pragmatic' or 'moral'. If the issue is 'technical', all the resources of science and technology are at our disposal. But if it is 'pragmatic', everything is subjective and just touch-and-go. There is no science of happiness. In either case, however, according to Kant, universal and objective validity is out of reach. The assessment of 'pragmatic' imperatives is purely subjective and, while the assessment of 'technical' imperatives is objective all right, it is relative. For, in so far as they are dictated by our appetites and desires, there is no rational necessity for us to adopt any particular goal.

But, according to Kant, when it comes to the moral assessment of our maxims, both objectivity and universality are achievable. This is so because what is the basis of such assessment—the moral law or the Categorical Imperative—takes into account only the internal and formal structure of our maxims. It says merely that we are morally permitted to act only on those subjective principles which are capable of being adopted by everyone and that it is our duty to abstain from acting on those which are not.

At the beginning of our discussion of Mill I said that Mill is to be called a teleologist or consequentialist because he maintained that the moral rightness of an action results from the value of its consequences, while Kant is a deontologist because he held that the moral rightness of an action depends on the 'nature of the act itself'. This is a very common way of marking the watershed dividing ethical theories. But the expression 'the nature of the act itself' is very imprecise. Perhaps we know well enough, in practice, how to distinguish between acts themselves and their consequences, but it is notoriously difficult, if not impossible, to state the criteria on the basis of which this is done. Since Kant's doctrine is generally taken to be the paradigm of deontological theories, let us ask how, in his terms, is that expression to be understood? Our discussion of Kant so far has already made one thing clear: the nature of an act itself is to be sought in its maxim or subjective principle. A human action which is morally assessable is a unity of the production of an event and of a more or less steady purpose or policy. The deontologist is thus he who says that the moral rightness of an action is determined by its maxim or motive.

But another matter seems to have entered Kant's thinking as well. With regard to many human actions we can distinguish between their real and their formal or conventional consequences.[2] Suppose that, at the appropriate moment of a marriage ceremony, the two principals say 'I do'. The formal consequence of this will be that thenceforth they will be husband and wife; this consequence is logically entailed. The material consequences, on the other hand, may be (here one can speak only of probabilities) that those two people will be happier than before, or that, in due course, new humans will be brought into the world. But let us also notice that what may transpire materially in the future can have further formal consequences. A piece of their behaviour may, for example, be classifiable as adultery.

Usually, or initially, we do the things which have formal consequences for the sake of some material results which may ensue. For example, I say 'I do' and achieve matrimony in order

---

[2] This distinction is an extension of J. L. Austin's distinction between the conventional ('illocutionary') and the real ('perlocutionary') consequences of speech-acts. See his *How to Do Things with Words* (Oxford, 1962), 98–132.

to be able to have (legitimate) children, or in order to become happier. But, once the initial formal deed is done, I may base the choice of my future material acts on the kind of further formal consequences they will have. Once I am married, I may, for example, refrain from a sexual involvement, without any thought as to how it might affect the happiness of people involved, but purely because it would constitute adultery. If I do that, my thinking would be deontological. And the moral philosopher who holds that this is the proper way of making moral decisions is a deontologist. We may add that, corresponding to the two kinds of consequences our actions may have, there are two kinds of values—material and formal. The difference between teleology and deontology can thus be viewed as the difference between which of these two kinds of values are looked upon as being the supreme values—in other words, the pursuit of which of them is held to be what is really important and makes life worth living. Mill, as a teleologist, said, in effect, that all formal values must, if necessary, be sacrificed for one single material value—happiness. We found his doctrine unconvincing. Kant, as a deontologist, went in the opposite direction. He said, in effect, that the uncompromising values are formal values. Let us continue our quest of whether his view is more plausible.

Let us take Kant's most convincing example—promising (*GR* 70–1). Suppose I say to myself that, whenever I see some selfish advantage in giving a false promise, I shall not hesitate to do so. Can this maxim become universal? The answer is, no. For, Kant claims, a deceitful promise is a kind of self-contradiction. In giving a deceitful promise I would be committing a kind of formal blunder. In saying 'I promise to do x', I imply, give it to be understood, that I intend to do x. But that implication is there only because promises that are given are, as a rule, sincere promises. You take my words, 'I promise to do x', seriously only because you feel comfortable with the assumption that, when I utter those words, I 'mean' them, that is, have the intention of doing x. But if it were known that everyone feels free to give deceitful promises, then, were you to say 'I promise to do x', I would or should *not* be comfortable with the assumption that you are in fact intending to do x. Then your promise would simply not come off; it would be empty, null and void. To make an insincere promise is morally forbidden because a world in which there is only a fifty–fifty chance that a promise is intended to be kept *and* in which there still is such a thing as promising is a logically impossible world.

When you come to think of it, very many actions presuppose rule-governed practices. Besides promising, examples are: getting married, signing a contract, mailing a letter, enrolling in a college, serving as a juror. Many of the things we do can therefore be declared illegitimate, just as some presumed plays and moves in a game can be declared illegitimate, on the ground that they violate the very rules that make them possible. I must not commit adultery or divulge a secret for the same kind of reason that I must put the proper stamp on my letter, or must not fail to say '*J'adoube*'. Similarly, I must not give a promise which I do not intend to keep, for that is not, you may say, part of the 'promising game'.

But now the basic weakness of Kant's position is evident. A violation of the constitutive rules of a game or practice in which humans happen to engage cannot be the basis on which we *morally* condemn an action. When we say that an action was morally wrong we cannot mean that it merely goes against the rules of how things happen to be done. It may indeed be true that, if everybody always felt free to act on the maxim that, should self-interest demand, he will give a deceitful promise, then giving promises, and breaking them for that matter, would no longer be possible. Giving promises is possible only in a world in which people more often than not keep their promises, just as playing soccer is possible only in a world in which players other than the goalkeeper do not, as a rule, touch the ball with their hands. But it is hard to see how the moral wrongness of a deceitful promise can lie in nothing more than the fact that it does not square with the business of promising. Let it be admitted that a deceitful promise goes against the very idea of what promising is. But that it is morally wrong to give a deceitful promise on that account must presuppose that it is morally obligatory to maintain the practice of promising to begin with. Similarly, that it is morally wrong to have sexual relations with someone other than your spouse presupposes the moral value of marriage. That such things as promising, marrying, entering a public office, joining the military forces, and so forth, by doing of which humans take it upon themselves to submit to and to honour certain rules, are morally worth endorsing and preserving cannot be determined a priori.

With regard to rule-governed practices the Categorical Imperative—as the law of universalization—can be looked upon also as the demand of avowability—an action is morally permissible only if the person who is about to perform it is willing to let it become public. In *On Perpetual Peace* Kant says that publicity is a test of the morality of civil legislation (*CPrR* 341). The immorality of giving a false promise could thus be looked upon as the fact that it is unavowable: you would spoil everything if you were to let others know that it is a false promise. Avowability or publicity *is* a formal, a priori, and necessary precondition of all co-operative as well as competitive rule-governed practices. A session of a court or of a parliament or of a stock market or a tennis tournament could not take place without the participants knowing the rules. Which, of course, and that was my point, is not in itself why, morally speaking, those things ought to be indulged in in the first place.

Kant's formalism is not totally without insight. It brings out the fact that, in a sense, or to some degree, there is wrongness in our actions simply in so far as they contradict the rules which constitute the formal conditions of their own possibility. In other words, there are actions which are 'wrong' simply because they are infelicitous. But Kant made too big a thing of this. Rampant promise-breaking leads to the demise of promising, rampant adultery to the demise of marriage, rampant cheating on income taxes to the demise of the internal revenue system, and so on. But none of these social institutions can be said to be necessary a priori, on the basis of the 'concepts of pure reason'. There are no rule-governed practices that rational beings *must* adopt. All there is are historical processes shaping human interactions into more or less fixed structures. To go against the rules of how things are done, particularly when those rules are sanctioned by society, custom, or some other authority, is, in a sense, wrong. But it cannot be said to be wrong absolutely, for we cannot assume that the accepted social practices, institutions, and their rules are themselves ethically justified. It may be that morality sometimes demands that those rules be broken or even that a whole social practice or institution be scrapped.

Moreover, many things humans do are not parts of institutionalized and rule-governed practices at all. There are helping others or not doing so, being industrious or wallowing in one's idleness, getting drunk, onanism, sodomy, making scandal, self-mutilation, using one's body or that of another merely for sexual pleasure—to mention some of the things Kant cites in his *Lectures* and in his *The Metaphysic of Morals*. In connection with these the Kantian formalistic argument cannot even get started.

Kant's formalism contains a mild truth. Untruthfulness *is* a kind of inconsistency. As Arnold Isenberg put it, 'A man who lies, in a sense, opposes himself: he denies what he affirms and affirms what he denies.'[3] Something has gone wrong when there is a lie. For, as Isenberg also points out, we do not ask why a man is telling the truth, but we do ask why he is telling a lie. Truth-telling is as natural as eating and sleeping, but lying is 'queer'. At the same time, the wrong of lying *as such* is not very great. There are lies which are trivial and innocent. In *The Metaphysic of Morals*, in a section called 'Casuistical Questions', Kant himself writes:

An author asks one of his readers, 'How do you like my work?' One could merely pretend to give an answer, by joking about the impropriety of such a question. But who has his wits always ready? The author will be insulted at the slightest hesitation with one's answer. May one, then, say what the author would like to hear? (*MM* 95)

Kant left that question unanswered, but not, I believe, because, according to him, lying may sometimes be morally right, but because it is sometimes inappropriate solemnly to label what one says a lie, although it goes against one's opinion. It is likely to be silly to call saying what someone likes to hear a lie, even though you have your reservations. Kant did not want to trivialize the word 'lie', but he was against the trivial application of it. He warned us against 'purism' and 'pedantry' in applying the moral law (*MM* 89). I think that Kant took *de minimis non curat lex* (the law does not concern itself with trifles) to be applicable also to morality. What makes saying what goes against your own belief a real lie—a thing of moral concern—is a variety of

---

[3] See his 'Deontology and the Ethics of Lying', in *Aesthetics and the Theory of Criticism* (Chicago and London, 1973), 245–64.

things. It is a matter of what one is talking about and its importance, the relationship of the speaker to his audience, and, most of all, the speaker's motive.

In the *Groundwork*, besides insincere promising, three more illustrations are given of how to apply the Categorical Imperative (GR 89–91). Suicide is to be condemned, Kant maintains, because it involves an inconsistency. This example is confusing and we must first clear it up. He wants us to consider a man who 'feels sick of life as the result of a series of misfortunes that has mounted to the point of despair' and who says to himself, 'From self love I make it my principle to shorten my life if its continuance threatens more evil than it promises pleasure' (*GR* 89). It seems that Kant, instead of just giving the maxim of that person, gives us, in the same breath, the motive from which that person adopts his maxim. However, when Kant speaks of self-love, he does not mean by it a blind instinct. He means by it another maxim or subjective principle of action. The state of mind Kant wants us to consider with regard to its coherence does not consist of a deliberate desire to serve a blind urge, it consists of two principles which the agent has adopted, one more general, the other more specific:

(*a*) I shall always further my life, that is, my pleasure and happiness, and

(*b*) Whenever my life threatens nothing but pain and unhappiness, I shall end it.

Clearly, there is no contradiction between (*a*) and (*b*) even if they were universalized. It is true that (*b*) does not follow from (*a*): I would not *further* my life of pleasure and happiness by making it cease. Suicide is absurd: you would not ameliorate your condition by suicide; after it you would not be in any condition whatsoever. But, I believe, Kant wanted to argue not just that there cannot be any good reason *for* killing yourself *from self-love*, but that there is actually a good reason against *ever* killing yourself. Part of that argument is Kant's thorny notion that man is an end in itself not only as a moral but also as a natural being. But that aspect of his moral doctrine is best discussed when we come to the second formulation of the Categorical Imperative.

Next, Kant takes up the case of idleness. Not to develop and to apply one's talents is morally wrong, says Kant, because the will of the idler, if made universal, contradicts itself. His maxim is, to paraphrase Kant's words, 'Since I find myself in comfortable circumstances, from the love of pleasure and leisure, I shall not bother to develop and exercise my talents' (*GR* 90). Kant's concern here does not seem to be with this complicated maxim or combination of maxims, but with the simple resolve 'I shall be an idler'. Where is the contradiction? Idleness, Kant himself admits, could exist as a universal order. The world of happy-go-lucky individuals is not like the world in which a given day both is and is not Tuesday. Nevertheless, Kant claims, we are 'unable to will' universal idleness. Perhaps he succumbed to the temptation to argue like this: in not lifting my finger I would be a parasite and making an arbitrary exception for myself because I myself want to live in a world which only human industry can provide. But, as a cultural anthropologist which he also was, he must have been aware of the fact that some people are content to live in a world of utmost simplicity if not in one which is just a heap of filth, misery, and ugliness. If you are a person like that, you would be perfectly consistent in willing your idleness to become a 'universal law of nature'. Still, as a child of the Enlightenment Kant urges that idleness is wrong: 'For as a rational being [man] necessarily wills that all his powers should be developed, since they serve him, and are given him, for all sorts of possible ends' (*GR* 90). This argument also is removed from the formal question of self-consistency of maxims. It too relies on Kant's notion of man as an end in himself which we shall discuss more fully later. Let me just point out that Kant gratuitously believed that reason itself has infused man with the desire for civilization and culture. The fact is that, to the extent to which humans have such a desire, it is a product of a fragile and equivocal process of history. If I am caught up in this historical movement and want a world in which there are conveniences, amenities, and refinements, I shall think that, when a talented person idles away his days, it is a shame. Something has gone wrong. It is 'only natural' that we 'do our best', or at least this is what our parents and teachers tell us. But to attribute absolute and objective moral wrongness to idleness borders on fanaticism.

Kant's last illustration of the application of the Categorical

Imperative as an a priori and purely formal supreme principle of morality is unconcern with the lot of others (*GR* 90–1). He says that pure reason tells me that it is my duty to help those in distress. But what, on purely formal grounds, is wrong with the maxim 'I shall neither harm nor help others'? Everyone looking out just for himself, Kant admitted, could exist as a universal order. As a matter of fact, he said, a world like that may be in some ways a better world than one full of prating do-gooders. Still, he maintained, I cannot *will* the maxim 'Let me look out only for myself' to become a universal law. For then my will 'would be in conflict with itself', since I would then have to deny myself 'the hope to receive help from others'. Is this just a lapse? As we have seen, according to Kant, prudence is not morality. But, I believe, Kant's argument here is prudential only in an extended sense. It would matter to the prudentialist proper whether or not my acting on the maxim 'I shall look out only for myself' would, *in fact*, increase the likelihood of others acting on the same maxim. That is a debatable question. Will others pay back my hard-heartedness with the same coin? They may not—because they may want to set a good example or because of their sentimental mercy. Kant, on the other hand, is here, just as in the case of deceitfulness, asking us to contemplate a purely speculative spectre. My selfishness permits the selfishness of others. Still, we may ask, why should I shirk from it? Kant's answer has to be that I am necessarily a vulnerable and non-self-sufficient being. This, again, involves the introduction of a non-formal facet into Kant's ethics. A full discussion of Kant's views of man as a social being would take us too far from our central concern, but we shall remark on it below when we shall mention what is sometimes called the third formulation of the Categorical Imperative—namely, that we are always to act as though we were members of a 'Kingdom of Ends'.

In so far as Kant's formalism is concerned, we must conclude that, with regard to the duty to help others, it does not take us beyond our mild, vague, and inconclusive common sense any more than it does with regard to the duties of telling the truth, of not committing suicide, and of being industrious. Indeed it is 'natural' for me to help others. But, as we pointed out while discussing Mill, there is also 'natural' rivalry and

Schadenfreude. All that can be said is that acts of benevolence are more likely to go unnoticed than acts of malevolence.

So it has become clear that Kant's formalism fails. This is a pity, because it is exactly in this feature of his doctrine that his originality lies and on which his fame is based. The universalizability-with-consistency argument, as we may call it, does not, unfortunately, get us anywhere. So far, anyhow, we must judge that Kant's thesis that there is an objective ground of morality which lies 'solely a priori in the concepts of pure reason' is a fantastic illusion.

Why did he espouse that view? Well, he believed that the alternative is too dismal. If the foundation of ethics is not reason, it must be the feelings of emotion, and he considered those blind and wayward. We have seen that Mill too denied any cognitive role to the emotions. He said that we must arrive at our decisions concerning what we ought to do by rationally calculating and weighing utilities. According to him, the emotions can serve merely as sanctions, that is, as psychological prods of morality. Kant had gone even farther. For him, not only are emotions cognitively blind, but even as incentives for moral conduct they are too shaky. No feeling is uniform and steadfast enough. Only pure practical reason will do. Our emotional make-up and fortitude depend on such factors as our upbringing and circumstances. But there are situations in which morality will have lost all its emotional appeal. Consider the wasteland of a prison, a concentration camp, a group of guerrillas fighting against vast odds. Is no incentive left in those situations for doing what is morally right? Kant could not believe that this is so. He believed that, no matter how crushing a human situation may be, there would still be our purely rational knowledge of the moral law with its own motivating force.

Here the faith and hope of a moralist again get the better of the moral philosopher. Mill, we saw, rushed into the belief that we all are, or can be, enlightened utilitarians. Kant believed in an even greater illusion—the already perfect pure practical reason.

Have we been fighting a straw man? Kant himself pointed out that moral laws require empirical judgements to determine the cases to which they apply. It is only the moral law itself—the foundation of morality—that is necessary, a priori and formal, not particular moral judgements. The situation, one may say, is parallel to the one in science. Science is impossible without mathematics, and, for Kant, mathematics is a priori. But this does not mean that we can know particular scientific facts without experience. According to Kant, besides the truths of mathematics, we also know a priori that every event must have a cause, but of course the knowledge of the particular causes of particular events must come from experience. Still, in Kant's view, all cognitive experience presupposes purely rational and a priori principles; without them, we could not think at all.

This is not the place to criticize the whole of the Kantian epistemology. But the parallelism between the structure of the knowledge of what goes on in nature and of the knowledge of what we ought to do is perhaps just a product of Kant's overly systematic mind. As to the former, unless you are an Einstein, you do not devise your own mathematics. The mathematics and logic of our scientific investigations is by and large given and not something on which you can improvise. But the kind of prior order which an acting subject can make use of and have confidence in may be more volatile. Perhaps, in the end, each of us has to develop the 'logic' of his moral quest as he goes along. The method through which our volitions develop may be subjective in a way in which logic and mathematics presumably are not. What is or is not consistent in our particular decisions and their maxims may be just a matter of what other, more general, commitments we have made. The rigour of particular ethical decisions may just lie in the fact we always have to live in the wake of our previous more far-reaching resolves. But there may not be any objective test—such as Mill's Principle of Utility or Kant's Categorical Imperative—which guarantees that we are living the right life.

11

Rule- and Act-deontology

A FURTHER problem stemming from Kant's formalism and apriorism is that his doctrine allows no exceptions to moral rules and consequently leads to conflicts of duties. Kant of course denies this. He believed that the Categorical Imperative, and the moral principles which are presumably derivable from it, provide without fail unequivocal answers to our moral problems. He said that a 'conflict of duties and obligations is inconceivable' (*MM* 23), for moral principles are necessary principles and two conflicting principles cannot both be necessary. An objective collision of duties, said Kant, is therefore 'unthinkable'.

But Kant is begging the question. *If* moral rules are objectively necessary rules, then indeed there cannot be two of them such that one of them tells us to do *x* while the other tells us to do not-*x*, nor can then any *one* of them, taken singly, produce in practice incompatible results. But, by the same token, if moral rules *are* capable of yielding contradictory results, the conclusion has to be that moral rules are not objectively necessary rules.

As one delves into the details, not to say trivia, of Kant's voluminous writings on ethics, one discovers that he made all sorts of distinctions between different kinds of duties. Some of our duties were said to be 'wide', others 'narrow'; some 'perfect', others 'imperfect'; some 'meritorious', some 'incumbent'. In doing this, Kant was not at his best. He had to do a great deal of teaching and he had to use (officially approved) textbooks in which such terms were used. So he had to use them also. But he never shaped them into any clear, consistent, and comprehensive nomenclature. It is best largely to ignore them, particularly because one may get the impression that, according to Kant, some moral principles are less rigorous than others in that they allow exceptions. This would be very far from the truth. According to Kant, a moral principle never has the form 'Do *x*, for the most part'. There are rules like that: for example, 'Students should not cut class.' If Margaret is absent once or twice during the term, she is not (seriously) violating that rule.[1] But such a rule, Kant would say, is not a true principle. Perhaps his view against exceptions in morality is best expressed in a short work which he wrote in response to a critic and called *On a Supposed Right to Lie from Altruistic Motives*:

All practical principles of right must contain rigorous truth, and the so-called 'mediating principles' can contain only the more accurate definition of their application to actual cases . . . but they can never contain exceptions from the former. Such exceptions would nullify their universality, and that is precisely the reason that they can be called principles. (*CPrR* 350)

What Kant held was not that some moral principles permit exceptions, but only that some of them involve a greater degree of difficulty in applying them, that is, in judging what is and what is not a case falling under them, than others. There arise therefore what Kant calls 'Casuistical Questions' (*MM passim*). But in the rare passages in which he discusses such questions he seems to take the stance that, if they are unanswerable, they are also trivial. I wish to argue that, to the contrary, a moral framework which consists of rules which are both exceptionless and objective produces dilemmas which cannot be written off as trivial. It produces questions which are far more serious than, for example, one which Kant poses and feels no need to answer: 'Can we at least justify, if not to extol, a use of wine bordering on intoxication, on the ground that it enlivens the company's conversation and combines it with frankness?' (*MM* 91).

The utilitarian does not have to worry about conflicts of duties so long as he does not take rule-utilitarianism too seriously. When two 'secondary rules', as Mill called them, say 'Always tell the truth' and 'Always protect innocent life', both are applicable to a given case, but one dictates doing x and the other doing not-x, the conflict is spurious for it can, in principle, be resolved by determining whether it is doing x or doing not-x which has greater utility. From Kant's point of view, on the other hand, one moral principle cannot yield to another since they are all

---

[1] Cf. R. M. Hare, *The Language of Morals* (Oxford, 1952), 50–3.

necessary principles. We saw earlier that Mill's difficulties stemmed from not being able to take moral principles seriously enough. Kant's difficulties stem from taking them too seriously. There is, first, said Kant, *the* moral law or *the* Categorical Imperative. But he believed that, as we detail the supreme and absolutely general moral law, we arrive at subsidiary moral laws or principles whose dictates are equally categorical. For Mill, you might say, moral rules come from below—they are, or correspond to, empirical hypotheses concerning the utility of kinds of acts. For Kant, they come, you might say, from above—*the* moral law dispenses subsidiary moral principles. Besides *the* four intermediary principles discussed in the *Groundwork*—not to commit suicide, to keep promises, to develop one's talents, and to help others—in his *Lectures* and *The Metaphysic of Morals* we are told that we also ought to sacrifice ourselves, curb our feelings, resist carnal lust, be moderate in the use of food and drink, and so on. Often Kant gives only a faint indication of how such rules and duties are derived from his supreme principle of morality. Today's reader may find several of them, if not objectionable, then at least quaint. The more important point is, however, that a logically consistent system of moral rules and duties is an idle dream. There is no guarantee that Kant's subsidiary moral imperatives never produce contradictions in practice.

The moral rule which always seems to come first in Kant's mind is the one against mendacity. A lie is always prohibited whatever its intention or consequence may be. But another plausible candidate for being an exceptionless moral rule is 'Always protect innocent life'. Oddly enough, Kant never mentions it explicitly, although it seems to be implicit in his principle to help others. At any rate, we would be appalled if Kant's system did not accommodate it. But it is not hard to see how the prohibition against lying and the prohibition against injuring another, or letting him be injured, can come into conflict with one another.

Benjamin Constant (who is better known for his novel *Adolphe*) had posed such a dilemma to 'a German philosopher' and Kant, believing it was he who was under attack, tried to resolve the dilemma in the polemical work already mentioned, *On a Supposed Right to Lie from Altruistic Motives* (*CPrR*

346–50). Constant's scenario is the following. A friend has taken refuge in my house from someone who is pursuing him with the intent to kill. The pursuer arrives and demands to know if my friend is inside. Should I lie? Constant says that I should. Kant says that I should not. The point I wish to make is not that Constant is right and Kant is wrong. It is rather that neither Constant nor Kant nor anyone else in the world (assuming that we have already buried the utilitarians) can *objectively* determine what is right and what is wrong in a case like this.

Let us take a look at what Kant says in favour of his stubbornness. It is to his credit that he does not resort to the legalistic distinctions that the duty not to lie is 'perfect' while the duty to help others is 'imperfect' in the sense that it is up to us to what lengths we should go in performing it. But his argument is legalistic just the same. The centre of it is the claim that, should my telling the truth lead to the murder of my friend, it would only be an 'accident' and I would not be culpable: '[in telling the truth I do] not do harm to him who suffers as a consequence; accident causes this harm' (*CPrR* 349). This is supported by two, or perhaps three, considerations.

First, the consequences of my telling the truth, says Kant, are 'unforeseen': my friend could slip out and neighbours could come to the rescue. This seems like fudging. The (real, material) consequences of our actions are never foreseen with perfect certainty. I cannot take it for granted that my friend is going to get away through the back door or that the neighbours are going to become aware of what is happening and rise to the occasion. It is true that, equally, I cannot take it for granted that, if I lie and tell the man who has murder on his mind that my friend is not in my house, he will just walk away and that my friend will be safe. For, as Kant points out, the villain, as he turns around, might spot my friend, who, in an attempt to escape, has run into the street, and shoot him. My friend, due to my having told a lie, falls dead in his tracks! Nevertheless, the conclusion has to be that, whether I tell the truth or lie, an accident can cause in *either* case a grim outcome. In this respect, it *seems*, there is nothing that makes my telling the truth right and my lying wrong. However, I think that Kant is correct in pointing out that, nevertheless, there is a significant difference between the two eventualities. For, he maintains rightly, while we cannot be held responsible for the 'accidents' which happen due to our doing what is right, we *can* be held responsible for 'accidents' which are due to our doing what is wrong. If, for example, a motorist driving on the *right* (correct) side of the road accidentally runs over a child who suddenly dashes in front of his car, he will be judged not guilty of anything; but if he is driving on the *wrong* side of the road and the same thing happens, he is in hot water even if his being on the wrong side of the road is not a 'contributary factor' for the accident to have happened. But, in the light of this, what follows is that, in the overall context of the argument, Kant is begging the question. For what is at stake is precisely whether or not, in the situation Constant described, it *is* the right thing to tell the truth.

Second, in addition to saying that if I tell the truth and my friend gets killed, it would only be an 'accident' because that consequence of my truthfulness would be 'unforeseen', Kant says that my friend's death would be an accident also because 'one is not at all free to choose' between truth-telling and lying, 'since truthfulness . . . is an unconditional duty' (*CPrR* 349). The phrase 'not being free to choose' is ambiguous, but, apparently, Kant meant by it, 'having, morally, no alternative' —and then it is immediately clear that Kant is again begging the question, for Constant had, evidently, claimed that we do have, morally, an alternative to telling the truth.

Third, although Kant actually did not point this out, part of what we mean when we say that something was an accident is that the agent did not intend or aim at that outcome of his act. It is this that frees him from being accountable. Kant could have said that, as I tell the truth about my friend's whereabouts, I do not intend or aim at his death and, should it nevertheless occur, I am not guilty of it.

The reason why I said that this idea is not really Kant's own is that it leads to the overthrow of deontological objectivism. Kant, we have said, was a rule-deontologist; in other words, he held that there are exceptionless subsidiary moral principles. But, since he also emphasized the importance of the role of subjective 'maxims' in deciding whether or not an act is morally right, we may want to revise his doctrine so that it becomes, let us call it, act-deontology. In doing so we would eliminate the problem of conflicts of duties. For Mill, as we saw, moral rules are, among other things, time-savers. In the thick of life we do not always have time to figure out the utility and disutility of particular actions. For the sake of efficiency we therefore use rules which tell in a general manner which acts are likely to promote human happiness and which acts work against it. But the rules of utility are, as Mill said, just 'signposts' and there may be circumstances in which one or another of them ought to be ignored. The ultimate arbitrator is always the Principle of Utility itself. A similar stance may be deemed appropriate by the deontologist. For the act-deontologist, 'Do not lie', 'Do not harm others', and the like, are not, to be sure, indices of utility, but guidelines for the discovery of the agent's intentions, aims, and motives, in other words of his maxims. They tell us that, by and large, when a person tells a lie, or harms another, his maxim cannot be made universal. But we must always be alert and realize that we may have to ignore such rules and go straight to the Categorical Imperative itself. To do this is called for when two rules seem to be equally applicable to a given case but dictate opposite actions. Even when there is no rivalry between two rules, it may be that just following a single rule will not do, it may give us incompatible results. Ordinary moral precepts cover only the garden-variety of cases. They are rules of thumb for applying the ultimate rule—the Categorical Imperative; they cannot usurp it. Ultimately, particular acts may have to be judged without any mediation. But, we have to realize, this leads to jettisoning the objectivity of moral right and wrong.

In order to see this, let us ask what is a full-dress act. It is the sort of thing which novelists and playwrights use their art and talents to portray. Suppose that Smith walks up to Jones and slaps him. In order to portray this act in a meaningful way, we have to go beyond just saying, 'Smith at time *T*, in place *P*, walked up to Jones and slapped him'. An entry in a mere chronicle is not morally revealing. But going beyond that calls for interpretation and conjecture. Even the fact that what happened was an intentional and voluntary act on Smith's part is open to caveats. The trajectory of Smith's hand might have been a spasm, or he might have been reaching for his cocktail, or he might have taken Jones for someone else, and so on. From here we reach an even more speculative ground. Was Smith's act deliberate and premeditated? If so, we shall want to know what was his aim, his motive or maxim, and, eventually, what sort of person he is—his whole mentality. We may not be totally satisfied until we know that, for example, as he swung his arm he said to himself 'I shall suffer no insult', that is, that his motive was vindictiveness and that he is a person of overweening pride.

Besides a bodily movement which is often part of an act (although which, as we shall see when we turn to Sartre, is itself not just a fact of pure physics since it involves the *human* body), a full-dress act includes an intention, a maxim or motive, and it ultimately emanates from a part or whole of a person's cast of mind. Let us not be confused by the words 'motive' and 'maxim'. In Kant's usage they come to the same thing. Both a 'motive' and a 'maxim' are a 'subjective principle' of action. We saw that, when in the *Groundwork* he asks if the maxim of a prospective suicide can become a universal law, he states the maxim of that person as being 'From self-love, I make it my principle to shorten life if its continuance threatens more evil than it promises pleasure' (*GR* 89). This, we pointed out, makes it appear as though the motive of an act could be part of its maxim. That would be confusing, for it appears that the thing to say is that I adopt a maxim because I *have* a motive. I may not even be aware of my motive. A woman may make it her maxim to watch her husband's every move, even though she may quite sincerely, although mistakenly, deny that she is doing it from jealousy. Also, I can decide on the same maxim from different motives. We saw that Kant himself was anxious to point this out when he discussed the 'true moral worth' of honesty, for an example. I may subscribe to the maxim never to lie, either from duty or from prudence. However, as I pointed out earlier, when Kant formulated the maxim of a prospective suicide as he did, his fault was merely that he did not make it clear that he was compressing two maxims into one. What *is* a motive? In the Millian tradition, it is an emotion construed as a blind feeling, or drive. But, according to Kant, what moves me as a rational being to action is not a blind feeling; it is an internalized rational principle, either 'hypothetical' or 'categorical'. A motive is never just an instinctual blind force or disposition over which I have no control; it is always a maxim, that is, a principle adopted by a rational being. It is just that maxims come in tiers. My maxim may be, for example, 'I shall brush my teeth twice daily'; and I can say that the motive behind it is a feeling, let us call it orthodontophilia. But to say that is no different from saying that the motive behind that maxim is the higher-order maxim 'I shall take care of my teeth'.

Now it may be said that this creates the problem of an infinite regress. The maxim 'I shall take care of my teeth' seems arbitrary unless it is itself adopted by force of a still higher maxim, say, 'I shall take care of my health'. But that maxim cannot be regarded as totally, that is, morally, final either. We recognize duties or demands which go beyond just worrying about our own health. Marie Curie continued her search for radium even though her hands became badly damaged. Why did she do that?

Kant's proposed solution to this problem was that, as we follow the hierarchy of maxims and/or motives to their ultimate limit of generality, we reach what he called *Gesinnung*, that is, our total mentality or cast of mind. The central point of Kant's ethics is that either my spirit is duty, or it is selfishness. In the former case, I am a morally good person and my life is worth living; in the latter, I am a morally bad person and my life is not worth living. What makes me into the one or the other? It is our free choice, says Kant. To anticipate what we shall discuss in the last chapter of Part Two, let me give this quotation:

[the] subjective ground [that is, the mentality which underlies all of our choices of subsidiary maxims and, eventually, all of our actions] . . . must itself always be an expression of our freedom . . . it can lie only in a rule made by the will . . . that is, in a maxim. (*RE* 16–7)

How is this to stop the infinite regress? Kant's idea was that the ultimate moral maxim—the moral law itself—although freely chosen, is the result of a choice based on, or is the same thing as, the *recognition* of ourselves as purely rational beings. There is nothing inevitable in choosing as our ultimate maxim Mill's Principle of Utility, he would have said. That is only the principle of an alienated man, a man who lets his desires get the better of him. The true man is the purely rational man, the man who recognizes, and hence freely chooses, as his ultimate maxim the Categorical Imperative as the law of pure practical reason. Reason is not bondage; it makes us free. How do we know that someone has made reason itself his maxim? We don't. At least not objectively. Kant says that 'the ultimate subjective ground of the adoption of moral maxims is inscrutable' (*RE* 17 n.).

We are now ready to draw our conclusion with regard to act-deontology, which, as an alternative to rule-deontology, promises to relieve the latter from the fatal embarrassment of generating conflicts of duties. Rule-deontology says that there are kinds of actions, for example, lying, which are without exception morally wrong. Act-deontology, on the other hand, says that, in order to assess an individual action morally, we cannot just subsume it under a rule; we may have to penetrate to its specific motive or maxim. It is in this way that act-deontology hopes to accommodate our intuitions and to enable us to say that, for example, telling a lie is morally justified or even obligatory, if it is prompted by, for example, the motive or maxim of protecting an innocent life. But this leads to subjectivism; 'a man's maxims are not observable', not even his own (*RE* 16). It would be a contradiction to say that I know objectively my subjective principles. When faced with a decision, knowing one's own mind is not a matter of standing back and taking a good look. My knowledge of my own motives and maxims lies in having decided—deliberately and reflectively—to act in a certain way. Thus it comes, so to speak, too late; it cannot *guide* my decision. My awareness of my motives and maxims lies in my very decisions to act in one way or another. My decision to act in a certain way in certain circumstances is what Hare has called a 'decision of principle': 'in order to act on principle it is not . . . to have a principle already, before you act; . . . to act in a certain way . . . is to subscribe to a principle of action . . .'[2] In retrospect, I may conclude that my motive was really evil and feel regret or even remorse. But that is just so much water over the dam. Others may, in an objective spirit, query my motives, criticize me, and give me advice. But then I must again decide, on my own, whether or not what they say is really true and anything I should pay attention to. In morality, as I have said already in the Introduction, others cannot make my decisions for me.[3]

---

[2] Hare, *The Language of Morals*, 59.

[3] Cf. Hare, *The Language of Morals*: 'As Kant points out in the important passage on the Autonomy of the Will (*GR* 88), we have to make our own decisions of principle. Other people cannot make them for us unless we have first decided to take their advice or obey their orders' (p. 70).

For the agent, there may always remain agonizing incertitudes. Therefore, as Sartre will put it, he finds himself in anguish. For example, a woman who is seeking divorce may not be sure whether her motive is the good of all concerned—herself, her husband, her children—or that, deep down, she just wants, at long last, to live 'her own life'.

The revisionist deontologist who wants to eliminate conflicts of duties that threaten the Kantian scheme, I have said, wishes to say that the subsidiary moral imperatives are really just rules of thumb. They are not truly categorical in the sense in which *the* Categorical Imperative, or *the* moral law itself, is categorical. They are just signposts for guiding us through the maze and mystery of human motives. We must not lie, kill, betray, deceive, harm, entrap, delude, dope, mock, scoff, ridicule, slander, and the like, because these are actions which are *likely* to be guided by bad motives, that is, ones that violate *the* Categorical Imperative. While to protect, aid, to be truthful and faithful, to forgive, to let bygones be bygones, and the like are kinds of actions which are *likely* to be guided by motives which *can* be the motives of everyone, and, hence, likely to accord with the supreme moral law. Just as Mill recommended that in the thick of life we should use the accepted moral rules in order to be more efficient in estimating what sorts of effects our acts will have on general human welfare, the revisionist Kantian recommends that those rules are to be used to make educated guesses with regard to the maxims of agents. But, as a consequence, he must write off Kant's own notion that there are any objectively valid moral rules, not even the one demanding honesty. While rule-deontology guarantees objectivism, it creates irresolvable conflicts of duties; act-deontology, while it provides for the resolution of conflicts of duties, leads to subjectivism.

12

Man as an End in Itself

By and large, our exposition and critique of the Kantian doctrine has been confined so far to matters connected with the first formula of the Categorical Imperative. But there is also the second formula, which, Kant claims, is equivalent to the first even though it sounds very different. As a matter of fact, it makes the Categorical Imperative sound like a teleologist or consequentialist principle, since it seems to say that the moral rightness of actions depends on their serving an end over and beyond morality. We shall see, however, that this is only a deceptive appearance. It says: 'Act in such a way that you always treat humanity, whether in your own person or in the person of any other, never simply as a means, but always at the same time as an end' (GR 96). Persons, says Kant, are radically different from mere 'things'. Only persons possess absolute worth, only they have 'dignity'. Everything else has a price, that is, can be equated with the value of something else. But there is nothing which is equal in value to a human being, not even another human being or any number of them. Here arithmetic just does not apply.

But it is not easy to tell what exactly Kant did mean by a 'person' and by 'humanity'. It is easy to get lost in the effulgence of those terms. Often it seems that a human being, according to Kant, has dignity solely because the moral law as the law of reason resides in him. For him, a person is not essentially a being capable of pleasures and joys, sufferings and frustrations. Man's essence is not his pathos, but his will and actions. There are many other places besides the *Groundwork* (GR 96) where Kant makes the point that by humanity he means not the sensuous but the moral and hence purely rational character of man, in other words, as we shall see in the next chapter, man in his autonomy and freedom. In the *Critique of Judgement* we read:

The value of life for us, if it is estimated by that *which we enjoy* (by the natural purpose of the sum of all inclinations, i.e., happiness) . . . sinks below zero . . . There remains then nothing but the value which we ourselves give our life, through what we cannot only do but do purposively in . . . independence of nature . . . (*CJ* 284n.)

In the same work it is claimed that only as a moral being, a being who is capable of a good will, is man the final end of creation (*CJ* 294). In *The Metaphysics of Morals* Kant writes:

Man in the system of nature . . . is a being of slight importance and shares with the rest of the animals . . . a common value. . . . But man regarded as a *person*—that is, as the subject of morally practical reason—is exalted above any price; for as such (homo noumenon) he is not to be valued as a mere means to the ends of others or even to his own ends, but as an end in himself. He possesses, in other words, a dignity (an absolute inner worth) . . . (*MM* 99)

But there is also a more broadly humanistic trend in Kant's thought. For example, in *Religion* a very different estimate is made of man's sensuous nature and his happiness:

Natural inclinations, *considered in themselves,* are *good,* that is, not a matter of reproach, and it is not only futile to want to extirpate them but to do so would also be harmful and blameworthy. Rather, let them be tamed and instead of clashing with one another they can be brought into harmony in a wholeness which is called happiness. (*RE* 51)

The fullest discussion of what it means to call man an end in itself is found in *The Metaphysic of Morals* (*MM* 45–54). There, the 'ends which are also duties' are summed up as *'one's own perfection* and the *happiness of others'*. Kant writes:

Since every man (by virtue of his *natural* impulses) has *his own happiness* as his end, it would be contradictory to consider this an obligatory end. What we will inevitably and spontaneously does not come under the concept of *duty,* which is a *necessitation* to an end we adopt reluctantly. (*MM* 44)

But, by the same token, the happiness of others *can* be an end which is a duty for us to promote, for, according to Kant, we have no 'natural impulse' to do so. When Kant said, in the second formulation of the Categorical Imperative, that we must treat humanity not only 'in our own person', but also 'in the person of any other' as an end, he therefore evidently meant that we must treat their *happiness* as an end. But, of course, from the fact that the happiness of others *can* be our duty to promote, it does not follow that it *is*. While discussing earlier the application of the first formulation of the Categorical Imperative to the case of beneficence towards others, I pointed out that Kant's argument smacks, curiously, of prudentialism. In his discussion of this example in terms of the second formulation, Kant does not do any better:

Now humanity could no doubt subsist if everybody contributed nothing to the happiness of others . . . This is, however, merely to agree negatively and not positively with *humanity as an end in itself* unless every one endeavours also . . . to further the ends of others. For the [in the *Metaphysic* it is added parenthetically 'permissible' (*MM* 47)] ends of a subject who is an end in himself must . . . be also . . . *my* ends. (*GR* 98)

This is just begging the question. For the issue is, *is* the other, *in his desire for happiness*, an end in itself? What we find in the *Metaphysic* is not an improvement either. Kant lapses again into a prudential argument: 'The proof that beneficence is a duty follows from the fact that our self-love [*sic*] cannot be divorced from our need of being loved by others (*i.e.* of receiving help from them when we are in need) . . .' (*MM* 53). Kant just pays lip-service to the intuitive, that is, the widespread subjective ideal of beneficence. Mill, you recall, argued that the happiness of others is our duty to pursue because the desire for the happiness of others is just a natural extension of our desire for our own happiness. We found that argument to be contrary to the facts of human consciousness. Kant would have agreed. But he would have found all this quite beside the point. As a deontologist he held that nothing can be our moral duty simply because we happen to have an inclination or desire to pursue it. Therefore, he tried to show that there is a purely rational necessity to regard the happiness of others as an end. If he could have shown that, deontology would have been saved. For then he would have been able to say—true to his non-consequentialist thinking—that, when we make the ends of others our ends, we are not acting from a direct inclination, but for the sake of duty. In other words, it would then remain true that morality is an end in itself. But, as I have pointed out, there is no purely rational necessity to make the ends of others our ends, that is, to help them.

When Kant speaks of what it means to consider 'humanity' as an end in itself in 'our own person', he is on firmer ground. Again, in order to avoid lapsing into consequentialism, he has to show that humanity is a purely rational end. Here he says that man is an end in itself not as he is, with his natural inclinations and desire for happiness, but as he ought to be. The end in itself is man's perfection. Since man's perfection is essentially his freedom and autonomy, 'it is contradictory' to consider the promotion of the perfection of *others* a duty. For the perfection of a person 'consists precisely in *his own* power to adopt his end in accordance with his own concept of duty' (*MM* 44–5). We can make another man happy but we cannot make him perfect any more than we can make him free. This comes remarkably close to Sartre's existentialism: another man can be an end in itself for us only in the negative sense—we must not interfere with his freedom. But we can make ourselves perfect and the duty to do so is twofold.

(*a*) We have a duty (*a1*) to increase our capacity of 'setting ends' together with (*a2*) the 'cultivation of [our] powers (or our natural capacities)' or skills which are necessary for the achievement of the ends.

(*b*) We have a duty to strengthen our good will as the capacity to act for the sake of duty.

Let us take (*a2*) first, just to get it out of the way. There is, according to Kant, a kind of human perfection which consists of being intelligent, clever, and adroit. Of this, Kant speaks also in the *Critique of Practical Reason*:

The concept of perfection in its practical meaning . . . is the fitness or sufficiency of a thing to any kind of ends. This perfection, as a characteristic of man . . . is nothing else than talent or skill, which strengthens or completes talent. (*CPrR* 151)

Now it may seem curious why then Kant said in the *Metaphysic* that we cannot foster the perfection of others. For the things he himself lists under the heading of developing talents and skills are: increasing 'understanding' (the ability to think in terms of general concepts), 'diminishing ignorance', and 'correcting errors'. These things, he himself says, are also the business of education. Surely, we *can* improve the 'skills' not only of ourselves but also of others.

However, Kant did not mean that the development of our ability to achieve whatever we want is a separate end in itself. Such development involves the learning of mere 'hypothetical imperatives', which, we saw earlier, deal only with means, not ends. 'Who wills the end', says Kant, 'wills (so far as reason has decisive influence on his actions) also the means which are indispensably necessary and in his power' (*GR* 84–5). I cannot be said to have chosen an end at all, as opposed to just wishing for something, if I do not have at least some idea of what are the means thereto and have not committed myself to them. In the *Critique of Practical Reason*, Kant wrote: 'Only if ends are already given can the concept of perfection *in relation to them* [my emphasis] . . . be the determining ground of the will' (*CPrR* 151).

To turn to (*a*1), part of our perfection which is our duty to promote is, according to Kant, our capacity to set goals, in other words, our purposiveness. However, these goals must be due to our 'humanity' and not our 'animality'. In other words, they must be reflective or deliberate ends, ends specified by maxims, and not just the objects of our drives and instincts such as, presumably, food, drink, and sex. At the same time, they need not be moral ends, that is, ends which are themselves duties. In other words, Kant seems to say that the Categorical Imperative in its second formulation tells us, in part, just to choose ends and to keep on choosing them, whatever they are. But, more explicitly than in the case of our duty to promote the happiness of others, Kant adds a proviso. Man is an end in itself, in part, because he is a naturally purposive being, but in this respect he is not an *unqualified* or final end in itself. Our non-moral humanity must be tempered by our moral humanity, it must be subordinated to what Kant calls 'wisdom':

wisdom consists in the harmony of the will of a being with his final end, and in the case of man this requires him first to remove the inner obstacle (an evil will actually present in him) and then to develop his inalienable and inherent disposition of good will. (*MM* 107)

The reason why the promotion of our own ability to set ends, any ends, is not an unqualified duty is that our (natural) humanity is capable of diminishing, even contradicting, itself. The 'evil will' present in us consists of vices, flaws, failing, and perversions. For example:

Man in a drunken condition is to be treated as a mere animal, not as a man; as a result of over indulgence . . . he is . . . incapacitated for such actions as would require adroitness (skill) and deliberation in the use of his powers. . . . The maxim of miserly avarice . . . is to get and keep all the means to good living, but *without regard to this enjoyment* (i.e., in such a way that one's end is only to possess the means, not to use them). (*MM* 90, 97)

Turning to (b), we must therefore understand the central concepts of the second formulation of the Categorical Imperative —'humanity' and 'personhood'—to mean, in the end, 'morality'. Our duty to promote our own perfection is, ultimately, the duty to cultivate our 'will to the purest attitude of virtue, in which the moral law is the motive as well as the norm for our actions and we obey it from duty' (*MM* 46). In the *Groundwork* (*GR* 110) Kant said that the concept of human perfection must presuppose the concept of morality. According to him, the truly perfect man is the morally perfect man. So, deontology is preserved, there is no ultimate end besides morality itself.

The second formulation of the Categorical Imperative introduces a mode of argumentation into Kant's scheme which is very different from the argumentation derivable from the first formulation. Even mendacity—which we have said is a case most fitted to be dealt with in terms of the pure formalism of the first formulation—often gets a different treatment. Kant is fond of saying such things as: 'By a lie a man throws away and, as it were, annihilates his dignity as a man [and] has even less worth than if he were a mere thing. . . . [When we lie we look upon ourselves as mere] speaking machines.' (*MM* 93–4). This mode of argumentation is connected with the notion of the 'purposes and ends of nature'. For example, in the *Groundwork*, while defending the claim that we have the duty to develop our talents and that idleness is wrong—which is the same as the duty specified in the *Metaphysic* as the duty to promote our perfection as the ability to set and pursue ends—Kant said that this just follows from 'nature's purpose in our own person' (*GR* 97–8).

The purposiveness of nature is one of Kant's most puzzling

doctrines. He expounds it at great length in various works. Without trying to do it full justice, let me indicate briefly what, for our discussion, is the upshot. Kant, of course, was not some kind of an animist who believes that all things possess a soul and a will. There are no purposes or ends inherent in things: 'the purposiveness of a thing . . . is no characteristic of the object itself . . .' (*CJ* 26). Nor, in agreement with Mill, is there any 'ought' in natural processes:

The understanding can know in nature only what is, what has been, or what will be. We cannot say that anything in nature *ought to be* . . . [in] the course of nature . . . *'ought'* has no meaning whatsoever. It is just as absurd to ask what ought to happen in the natural world as to ask what properties a circle ought to have. (*CPuR* 473)

Still, according to Kant, to think of nature *as if* it contained purposes and ends is no idle fancy. To do so is a 'maxim of reason' for it regulates and furthers, although it does not in itself constitute, knowledge (*CPuR* 547). The idea of a *'purposive unity of things'* spurs us on and leads to 'many discoveries' (*CPuR* 560). This does not mean that teleological thinking can replace thinking in terms of mechanistic principles (which, according to Kant, physical science and technology must ultimately aim at), nor that the two are incompatible. As a delightful example Kant gives the 'spheroidal flattening' of the shape of the earth. That fact, he points out, is a good thing because, in spite of the great unevenness of the earth's surface, it keeps its axis steady. 'And yet, wise as this arrangement is, we feel no scruples in explaining it from the equilibrium of the formerly fluid mass of the earth' (*CPuR* 560 n.). There is no reason to curb our teleological, or purpose-oriented, inquisitiveness about nature: 'For the worst that can happen would be that where we expected a teleological connection . . . we find only a mechanical or physical connection . . .' We can (and should) feel free to see a purpose in anything, just as we can (and should) feel free to see beauty in anything. While Kant had the reputation of a witty conversationalist and lecturer, his writings seldom contain humour. Still, I think, he meant to be amusing when he wrote: 'Thus some persons regard the tapeworm as given to the men or animals in whom it resides as a kind of set-off for some defect in their vital organs,' or when he reports his own 'discovery' that, while people complain about having dreamt too much when they wake up exhausted, they should be grateful for their dreams because dreams 'excite the vital organs by the medium of the imagination' and the activity of such organs is all the more desirable 'when the stomach is overloaded' (*CJ* 226–7).

Nevertheless, according to Kant, teleological thinking can go beyond its proper limit. We must distinguish between the 'internal' and the 'external' purposiveness of a thing. Any concrete thing may be looked upon as exhibiting internal purposiveness, even a blade of grass: its various structural elements work together to maintain it. But when we concern ourselves with the 'external' purposiveness of things, that is, ask about the purpose of the very existence of them, we sooner or later run into blind alleys. Kant is particularly anxious to point out that this happens when we reach man. 'Grass is needful for the ox, which is again needful for man as a means of existence, but then we do not see why it is necessary that men should exist . . .' (*CJ* 225). We could speak of the external purpose of man only if we could ask what man is good for, but man is an 'end itself'. Thinking that man has an (external) purpose would involve thinking of the whole universe as having its origin in the design or intention of a higher intelligence. But, says Kant, to assume such a thing would be 'presumptuous' (*CJ* 230). He makes the shrewd observation that, if we bring in God at this point, we may 'sound very humble' but our pious pronouncement is then really one 'by which we pretend to extol divine wisdom by ascribing to it designs [intentions] in the works of creation and preservation which are really meant to do honor to the private wisdom of the [subtle] reasoner' (*CJ* 230 n.). We know nothing of God's purpose in creating the world. When we speak of purposes in nature, we have nothing but our subjective reflections to guide us; the principle that 'everything in the world is some way good for something; nothing is vain in it' is a 'subjective principle or maxim' (*CJ* 225). When it comes to man as a natural being we can reflect only on his inner make-up. We saw earlier that, according to Kant, the *moral* world, since it contains the idea of the 'supreme or consummate good', leads to the 'postulation' of God. But, according to Kant, the *natural* world, even in its purposive order, does not. The difference in Kant's mind was, I believe, the following. While we know the laws of the moral world objectively, the teleological laws of the natural world are merely subjective. In the former case, the premiss—the moral law—is objective, although the conclusion—there is an omnipotent and just Being—is just a matter of faith and hope. In the latter, the starting-point—nature is a teleologically ordered whole—is itself subjective. The idea that there is a supreme 'Architect' merely flatters our own ingenuity and tickles our fancy. Therefore, Kant never asks what is nature's purpose *for* us. But, while trying to give support for his claims that certain things are our duties, he often asks, what is nature's purpose *in* us. However, we have already seen that reflections on that point yield only feeble results. Mendacity, suicide, idleness, not helping others, we said, are indeed 'unnatural' but only in that they surprise, astonish, perplex, or displease us. This is not enough to show that those things are objectively always and absolutely wrong. However, the alleged duty not to be idle but to aim at the fullest development of our capacity to choose and to accomplish ends may occupy a special place.

Kant's moral psychology distinguishes between three, not just two, things. There are, first, our sensuous appetites and instinctual drives. Above those—way above those—is our will as the faculty to act not just in accordance with, but for the sake of, purely rational principles which culminate in the moral law or the Categorical Imperative. But between those two there is the faculty of free choice. Kant does not dignify that faculty with the grand name 'free will'. Nevertheless, he regards it as something which already separates us from the brutes. Animals do not choose, at least not reflectively, by using concepts. But men do. Making deliberate choices is peculiar to humans. This faculty mediates between our pure animality and our supra-natural ability to be cognizant of, and to act from, the *purely* rational or a priori moral law. It is this faculty, which we have seen, besides our moral faculty, that Kant wishes to say is a part of our humanity and, as such, must be considered a part of man as an end in itself.

Man's aspirations and strivings, his intelligence and culture, have been extolled by many a poet. His visions and accomplishments fill us with admiration and awe. Kant would have to reject this way of thinking as overweeningly teleological. But, as a deontologist, perhaps he could say this. Man is an end in itself simply because without him there would not be any ends at all. I may reject any end that comes to mind, but I cannot reject as an end my ability of setting ends. The ability of setting ends cannot, without contradiction, set its own extinction as an end. But this too is unwarranted teleology. While it is perhaps true that I cannot want to be totally frustrated—I want to live a life—restraint or resignation does not make me irrational. It is indeed a shame when the human repertoire is arbitrarily thwarted. But anthropologists tell us that the world governed by 'work ethic' is of a rather later origin. There is no purely rational necessity that the world be full of high achievers.

As we have seen, Kant himself said that the whole way of thinking in terms of purposes of nature, including purposes of nature in man, is subjective. It is a response to a psychological need. It is depressing and anguishing to think that all human aspirations are just so much sound and fury. It is gratifying to think that in our endeavours and aspirations we are, somehow, answering a call, that in what we do we share in a wider and deeper meaning. Sartre, as we shall see, was adamantly opposed to such wide-eyed optimistic humanism. It is, for him, the result of our subjectivity gone wrong, guilty of 'bad faith', just flattering itself. This kind of humanism is overweening and silly. As I watch on my TV a spacecraft blast into space, I say to myself, vicariously taking credit for this accomplishment, 'Man is simply amazing.' But I had nothing to do with it and nor did 'humanity'. It was the feat of a small group of remarkable individuals (cf *EH* 54). Sartre pokes fun at the Promethean side of man:

That kind of humanism is absurd, for only the horse or the dog would be in a position to pronounce a general judgment upon man and declare that he is magnificent, which they have never been such fools as to do—at least, not as far as I know. (*EH* 55)

Let us now turn to Kant's concept of reverence or respect. He says: 'Duty is the necessity to act out of reverence for the law' (*GR* 68). By 'duty' is meant here the motive of duty and by 'law' the moral law. The 'object' of this feeling is the moral law itself, but, derivatively, also men because they can act from that law and, actually, are themselves authors of that law. Kant's idea that we owe respect to men as persons has had an enormous influence and has generated much enthusiasm. But Kant also throws cold water on that enthusiasm, just as, as we have seen, he throws cold water on the enthusiasm generated by the idea that man is an end in itself. For him, persons are not objects of respect because they are capable of pleasure and pain, being happy and unhappy. Nor are they really objects of respect because they can set themselves goals and pursue them through their skills and talents. The industrious and talented man deserves respect as a kind of example: 'Because we regard the development of our talents as a duty, we also see in a man of talent a sort of *example of the law* (the law of becoming like him by practice), and this is what constitutes our reverence for him' (*GR* 69 n.). But elsewhere we read that 'the common run of men give up their respect for a man [of talent] (e.g., Voltaire) when they think they have in some manner found the badness of his character . . .' (*CPrR* 185). The true example of the moral law, and hence the true object of respect, is to be found in a man, however humble, who exhibits moral virtue, that is, a good will:

Fontenelle says, 'I bow to a great man, but my mind does not bow.' I can add: to a humble plain man, in whom I perceive righteousness in a higher degree than I am conscious of in myself, *my mind bows* whether I choose or not . . . Why? His example holds a law before me which strikes down my self-conceit when I compare my own conduct with it . . . (*CPrR* 184)

Persons, for Kant, are, in the end, the true objects of respect and possess 'dignity' and 'absolute worth'—only because they, owing to their pure practical reason, are moral beings.

Why did Kant introduce this concept to begin with? Because morality must make a difference in practice, it must affect our actions, and, it seems, only feelings or emotions can do that. Still, says Kant, respect is a very special feeling. It only 'furthers' the influence of reason on the will. All feelings are 'passive' and 'externally caused' by their objects. Respect, however, is a 'rational feeling', it is 'spontaneous', has an 'intellectual cause'; it is determined by 'reason and the will itself' and the 'rational concept of law' (*CPrR* 181–2). But all this sounds like doubletalk, particularly if we consider what Kant himself said in his *Lectures*:

an intellectual inclination is a contradiction in terms; for a feeling for objects of the understanding is in itself an absurdity, so that a moral feeling resulting from an intellectual inclination is also an absurdity and is, therefore, impossible. A feeling . . . cannot belong to both our intellectual and to our sensuous nature . . . (*LE* 37)

It is true that Kant says that respect or reverence is not an inclination or fear but only 'analogous' to it (*GR* 69 n.). However, this is a nicety without any real consequence. If respect is just an offshoot of reason, it is redundant, it has no real job to do. We have seen that many precepts concerning what to do are, according to Kant, just 'technical' or 'pragmatic' imperatives. The moving force which leads us to follow them is provided by an inclination or the general desire for happiness. The principle of action is then a mere channel, so to speak, for already available psychic energy provided by our appetency. The Categorical Imperatives, on the other hand, must motivate us directly. The moral law as a law of pure practical reason has to be by itself the incentive for acting. But Kant had to confess that we cannot understand or explain how this is possible (*CPrR* 181). To solve this mystery, Kant cast about for something that could mediate between pure reason and actions. But his concept of respect is really a *deus ex machina*. This feeling as he describes it is a peculiar hybrid. It cannot be anything 'sensuous'. It is a mere 'consciousness of subordination' of our self-love to the moral law. It is neither an enjoyment nor a pain, but it nevertheless 'can be called' pain since the moral law rejects, checks, and thwarts all our inclination; it humiliates our self-love. Still, it is also a positive feeling, for it is the awareness of our personal worth (*GR* 69 n.). So Kant's concept of respect is a pure paradox. It is a desire to thwart all desire; it is both painful and pleasurable; it is part of both our humility and our pride.

All feelings and emotions are, according to Kant, mere blind subjective responses, either pleasurable or painful. They are not insights into the objects which call them forth, nor can they become part of such insights as sensations can. In *The Metaphysic of Morals* he writes:

we call the capacity for pleasure or pain at a representation *'feeling'* because both of these comprise what is *merely subjective* in the relation to our representation and contain no reference to an object which could give us knowledge of the object (or even knowledge of our own state).

Even sensations have, over and above the quality (of e.g. red or sweet) added to them by the subject's nature, a reference to an object, which is part of our knowledge of the object. (*MM* 7–8)

Of course, what calls forth a feeling or emotion can be a perception or cognition:

Feeling is the effect of the representation (which may be either sensuous or intellectual) on the subject, and it belongs to sensibility [receptivity, how we are affected], although the representation [of the object] itself may belong to understanding or reason. (*MM* 8 n.).

So one thing that can be meant by calling respect a 'rational feeling' is that it involves or is a response to a concept or a judgement. But there are other 'rational' feelings in this sense. Anger involves the judgement that there has been an uncalled-for injury to oneself or to others. Remorse involves the belief that what one did was wrong. And so on. It is true that what Kant maintains with regard to respect is something stronger. He claims that, in the case of *this* emotion, the concepts and judgements involved are a priori. But it is doubtful that what stems from our *pure* reason—such as the law of non-contradiction—can, as such, arouse in us any emotion at all.

Kant's conception of respect is clearly too narrow and rarefied. To respect someone is indeed distinct from simply liking him. It is to recognize his merits apart from whether we stand to gain anything from him. We can respect our enemies. But it is not true that therefore respect springs solely from the realization that someone's maxims are free from self-contradiction. The human attributes which command respect include qualities of emotional life as well. If a man shows courage, unselfishness, dedication, steadfastness, and the like, we respect him. We respect what is grand and splendid; we despise pettiness and meanness. But grandness and dignity can attach also to genuine humility. Perhaps what we respect in people, when it comes right down to it, is nothing but the indefinable thing called 'style'. Certainly, we respect people by virtue of their humanity. But perhaps 'humanity' defies definition. Perhaps we can learn less about it from philosophers than gain appreciation and a 'feel' for it through the great works of literature, or just by living.

On the other hand, Kant was certainly right in claiming that respecting persons entails non-interference with their freedom and autonomy. To respect something—a person, his character, his maxims, his works—is to leave it alone, to forbear meddling with it. Sartre, as we shall see, prefers the word 'generosity' to refer to the same sort of attitude. At any rate, Kant claims that mutual respect would, ideally, bring about a community of 'rational beings' which he calls 'the kingdom of ends'. It is in this idea that all the central concepts of his moral philosophy are united (*GR* 100–2). The kingdom of ends is a community in which every member is, at the same time, both a subject and a supreme legislator. It is, you might say, an ideal democracy. It is governed by the moral law. But that law is self-imposed; it is made by man himself. Therefore man, in recognizing it, remains autonomous. It is also exactly because of this that the moral law is categorical; there are no external conditions—such as rewards and punishments—as to why we should follow it. We carry it with us wherever we go, we cannot get away from it. But, if each member of the kingdom of ends is a lawgiver, how does it happen that there is only one law? Well, I am a member of that kingdom only because I am a being capable of pure practical reason—a being capable of appreciating the fact that only these actions are morally right, the maxims of which are fit to be universal laws. The law I give in that capacity is therefore universally valid. At the same time, the other members of that kingdom remain autonomous also. For they too are beings who possess pure practical reason and therefore freely recognize the validity of that law; they see in it nothing alien. I am not, as an individual with my particular desires and goals, the author of the moral law; the author of it is, so to speak, reason in me. The pure practical reason unites all men. It is because of this that in this kingdom everyone retains his autonomy, that it is a kingdom of ends (in themselves). Kant says that the idea of such a kingdom or realm affords a third formulation of the Categorical Imperative which unites the other two (*GR* 103–4). Departing from Kant's actual words, but, I believe, preserving his intent, I should like to put it as follows: 'Always act so that the maxim of your will can be considered a maxim of a potential member of a possible kingdom of ends.'

13

Freedom as Autonomy

AFTER we have understood what the moral law or the Categorical Imperative tells us, that is, which of our actions are morally right and which are morally wrong, there remains, says Kant, the question of how it can move us. No such problem, as we said earlier, arises with regard to hypothetical imperatives. If you have your wits about you, you will take the means necessary to achieve the end you happen to desire. But the bindingness of the Categorical Imperative cannot arise from the promptings of our desires. For that imperative does not tell us how our desires and needs are to be satisfied. How then is the moral law 'possible', Kant asks, that is, how can it furnish an effective law of conduct? In spite of his talk about 'respect' or 'reverence', Kant's answer boils down to 'Well, it just does'. The psychological impact of pure practical reason is, for Kant, totally mysterious, which, for him, meant that it cannot be explained through our desires, needs, inclinations, pleasures, and pains as causes. The moral law affects us simply, Kant says, in effect, because we *can* follow it, because our will is free.

Kant's discussion of the freedom of the will involves a great deal of metaphysics. It involves the distinction between what he calls 'causality of nature' or 'physical necessity', and what he calls 'causality of freedom' as well as the distinction between two orders of reality—the 'phenomenal' or empirical and the 'noumenal' or purely rational and 'intelligible'—and their (incomprehensible) unity in man (*GR* 114). For our purposes, we can skirt most of that. I believe that the whole convoluted issue of determinism versus indeterminism—whether our will and actions are free or causally determined—originates from the notion, quaint to the post-modern mind, that nature is a kind of wilful agent who lays down certain laws—the laws of nature —and through them exercises a kind of compulsion. I believe that that issue, whatever it may exactly be, and the problem of freedom as it is relevant for ethics, pass each other by. At any rate, what is, or should be, of greater interest to the moral philosopher is what Kant calls the 'positive' as opposed to the 'negative' conception of freedom, in other words autonomy (*GR* 114). The latter involves the idea that man is free *from* 'natural' or 'physical' necessity. The former shapes up as the distinction between two kinds of laws—laws of nature or scientific laws, on the one hand, and prescriptive laws or normative laws, of which the moral law constitutes a special case, on the other—as well as the distinction between causes and reasons.

According to the 'positive' conception of freedom, or autonomy, freedom is not lawlessness. It is just that the laws of freedom are of a radically different kind from laws of nature. The latter are descriptive and explanatory and deal with causes; the former are prescriptive and justificatory, and specify the legitimate reasons for actions. One of Kant's most important and original theses is that what happens in nature always happens merely in accordance with laws; humans can act for the sake of laws, because there is an imperative saying 'Do so-and-so'. Human actions are, of course, events in the world; they exhibit regularities and, within limits, they are predictable. But, as we pointed out in discussing Mill, they are also things to be justified, deemed either right or wrong; and, according to Kant, this is possible only because there are normative laws. From the point of view of a scientifically inquisitive spectator, we are satisfied when we have shown that the action in question is, or was, to be expected. But the moral agent is not concerned with that. What matters to him is whether or not there are good reasons for his action. Such reasons, if believed in by the agent, are of course themselves among the causal conditions for the occurrence of an action. Still, the agent does not think about that. He does not note a configuration of facts in order to predict his action; for him, that there are such and such facts is a reason for acting in this way or that. It is this that transports human conduct into the realm of freedom.

Now it is natural to *feel* that we are free to choose between alternatives. That, as we saw in discussing Mill, was enough for Sir William Hamilton to show that our will is free. However, Kant believed that such a feeling may be deceptive. He therefore wished for proof that freedom is not just an illusion. At the same time, he did not think that such a proof is possible. For in trying to give it, we should be going in a circle. From freedom follows morality and from morality follows freedom. But there is no independent ground to establish either. All Kant was confident about was that morality and freedom mutually presuppose one another. A free will and a will which comes under the moral law are one and the same thing (*GR* 114). On the other hand, we *are* subject to the moral law only if our will *is* free, that is, only if the moral law can effectively move us. But the only evidence we have for the freedom of the will is our awareness of the moral law. There is the possibility that the belief in that law is an illusion. Freedom and morality are two sides of the same coin; still, the whole thing may be counterfeit.

At the same time, in several places Kant makes an interesting move in order to get out of this impasse. In the *Groundwork*, he says:

every being who cannot act except under the *Idea of freedom*, is for that very reason, from the practical point of view, really free, that is, all the laws that are inextricably connected with freedom hold for him, just as if his will were declared free in itself and on the valid grounds of theoretical philosophy . . . (and) . . . every rational being who has a will also has the Idea of freedom and acts only under that Idea. (*GR* 15–16)

How are we to understand such an argument? What is it to act 'under the Idea of freedom'? It is to act in the belief that you are free. And that is the same as acting in the belief that your actions 'come under moral laws', that is, that those laws are applicable to your actions and that you can act from them and be motivated by them. Moreover, if you believe that your actions come under moral laws, that is, that such laws are applicable to your actions and that you can act from them and be motivated by them, then your actions *do* 'come under moral laws', that is, those laws *are* applicable to your actions and you *can* act from them and be motivated by them. If you *believe* that you are free, then, 'from the practical point of view', you *are* free.

This type of argumentation becomes plainer if we regard freedom as just a matter of acting from reasons. Reasons for acting will do their work only if we, so to speak, invite them in. It is taking reasons seriously that makes them serious. Only if we *believe* that they matter, *will* they matter and make a difference. To the conduct of a person who believed that with regard to his ultimate choices reasons are just rationalizations, mere shadows, that thinking of them is an empty shuffle, they would not, in fact, make any difference. If you do not put your faith in reasons, you will not be influenced by them, and you would, in effect, not be free. Freedom is hence not a theoretical, but a practical issue. For Kant, freedom in its 'positive' sense is not, so to speak, a super-fact about humans; it is an attitude with which we look upon ourselves and our actions.

This leads us to the so-called principle of '*ought* implies *can*' which is sometimes attributed to Kant. A slogan closer to what Kant actually says would be 'You ought, therefore you can'. Many philosophers today hold that '*ought* implies *can*' can be used to defeat not only attributions of legal but also of moral obligations and culpability if we can show that the party in question was not able, due to a lack of capacity or opportunity, to perform the act in question. They take the relation between 'ought' and 'can' to be entailment, so that, by contraposition, one can argue that, since the agent could not do the thing, it is false that he had the obligation to do it. But, I believe, Kant would have said that, although it is true that 'ought' entails 'can', the argument using contraposition can never be used in morality. When it comes to moral obligation, there is never an independent, that is, empirical, ground on which we can say that the agent could not have done the act which, on moral grounds, he ought to have done. For him, there could never be a factual discovery that he could not do what he, based on reasoning founded on the moral law, ought to do, and that therefore he had no obligation to do it. In other words, according to Kant, the hypothetical statement 'If one ought, one can' can never be turned into any other argument except 'A ought to do x, therefore A can do x'. It must not be looked upon as an inference licence which would permit the reverse argument: 'Since, as a matter of fact, A cannot do x, it is not the case that A ought to do x.' Kant said, as we have seen, that an 'ought' or an imperative is ambiguous. In one sense, I ought to do something if that is a means to an end I already have. In that case, 'ought' expresses a mere prescription for solving a technical or pragmatic problem and must therefore be within the realm of empirical possibility.

In another sense, there are things I ought to do *simpliciter*, that is, simply because they are my morally obligatory ends. Morality, according to Kant, thus gives rise to a kind of possibility or 'can' which is independent of any empirical conditions. In *To Perpetual Peace* he wrote:

morality is in itself practical, being the totality of unconditionally mandatory laws according to which we *ought* to act. It would obviously be absurd, after granting authority to the concept of duty, to pretend that we cannot do our duty, for in that case this concept would itself drop out of morality . . . (*CPrR* 331)

And in the *Critique of Practical Reason* we read: '[man] . . . judges that he can do something because he knows that he ought, and he recognizes that he is free—a fact which, without the moral law, would have remained unknown to him' (*CPrR* 141).

As I said in the beginning of this chapter, Kant's doctrine of freedom is steeped in metaphysics—it involves the division of reality into the realm of phenomena or appearances and the realm of noumena or 'things in themselves'—and this leads him to say some startling things, particularly in the *Critique of Pure Reason*:

The actions to which the *'ought'* applies must indeed be possible under natural conditions. These conditions, however, do not play any part in determining the will itself, but only in determining the effect and its consequences in the [field of] appearances . . . it may be that all that *has happened* in the course of nature . . . *ought not to have happened*. . . . The real morality of actions, their merit or guilt, even that of our own conduct, thus remains entirely hidden from us. . . . [Our moral merit] can never be determined; and upon it therefore no perfectly just judgments can be passed. (*CPrR* 473–4)

But in the same work a more down-to-earth point is also made. Kant says that, with regard to morality, experience is 'the mother of [deceptive] appearance' and that: 'Nothing is more reprehensible than to derive the laws prescribing what *ought to be done* from what *is done*, or *to impose on them the limits by which the latter is circumscribed* [my emphasis]' (*CPrR* 313). If the 'ought–can' principle were to be taken to lead to 'If, empirically speaking, I cannot do x, then it is not the case that I ought to do x', it can, in Kant's view, lead to all kinds of illusions concerning the limits of what we can do and would open the road to all kinds of rationalization and self-deception.

Let us look at what Kant himself has to say about self-deception or what he calls an 'inner lie'. As an example he gives a man 'who does not really believe in a future judge of the world' but who nevertheless 'professes' such a belief 'in the presence of the scrutinizer of hearts' for it 'could do no harm and might indeed be useful' (*MM* 94). But to try to deceive God is really self-deceit. There is also an inner lie when 'from self-love we take a wish for a deed because this wish has a good end in mind' (ibid.) and again 'when a lover's wish to find only good qualities in his beloved blinds him to her obvious faults' (ibid.). So, says Kant:

It is easy to show that man is, in fact, guilty of many *inner* lies, but to explain the possibility of an inner lie seems more difficult. For a lie requires a second person whom one intends to deceive, and intentionally to deceive oneself seems to contain a contradiction. (*MM* 93–4)

Kant observes that the same paradoxical structure is present in our conscience:

conscience has something peculiar about it: although its business is an affair of man with himself, man yet sees himself necessitated by his reason to carry it on as if at the bidding of *another person*. For this action is the bringing of a case before the court; and to think of the man *accused by* his conscience as *one and the same person* with the judge is an absurd way of representing a court of justice, since the prosecutor would always lose. (*MM* 104)

Kant mentions two ways of solving the paradox. First, 'the man who accuses and judges himself in conscience must think of himself as a twofold personage, a doubled self': one part of him being the purely rational and supra-sensible self which gives the moral law and judges in accordance with it, the other being man 'as a member of the sensible world' and the subject to whom the law is applied. Second, the 'other person' who either accuses or excuses is the 'knower of hearts', in other words, God. In either case, however, we are just projecting our subjectivity: according to Kant, we have no objective knowledge of the intercourse between us and God, or between our lower and higher selves. Both conscience and the inner lie remain inexplicable structures of our moral consciousness.

Sartre's concept of 'bad faith', that is, self-deception, which we shall discuss in Part Three clearly has its origin in what Kant says about not heeding our conscience:

Consciousness of an *inner court* in man ('before which his thoughts accuse or excuse one another') is *conscience*. Every man has a conscience and finds himself watched . . . by an inner judge; and this power watching over the law in him is not something that he himself (arbitrarily) *makes*, but something incorporated in his being. It follows him like a shadow when he plans to escape. He can indeed numb himself or put himself to sleep by pleasure and distractions, but he cannot avoid coming to himself or waking up from time to time; and when he does, he hears at once its fearful voice. (*MM* 103–4)

Sartre, as we shall see, says that one of the ruses of bad faith is distraction and likens it to letting ourselves fall asleep. Moreover, while Sartre will say that our only sin, as it were, is bad faith, Kant says that our moral innocence or guilt is totally a matter of having or not having listened to our conscience:

conscience is [pure] practical reason holding man's duty before him . . . with a view to either his acquittal or his condemnation. Thus it is not directed to an object but merely to the subject . . . And when we say: this man has no conscience, what we mean is: he pays no attention to its verdict . . . if someone is aware that he has acted with the approval of his conscience, then so far as guilt or innocence is concerned nothing more can be required of him. (*MM* 60–1)

If we ignore Kant's notion that conscience is pure practical reason (the foundation of *every* aspect of our moral consciousness, according to him, is pure practical reason—not only of conscience, but also of the good will, of the moral law, of the Categorical Imperative, of freedom), we can say that being in bad faith and acting without the approval of conscience are one and the same thing. Bad faith and bad conscience are both an inner lie.

While reading Kant's *Religion* (*RE* 30–3), it becomes clear that, for him, immorality—in the sense of moral guilt or blameworthiness—is nothing but a gigantic inner lie or self-deception. We are immoral when, against our own better judgement, we make self-love into our highest maxim. The sensuous nature of man, is, in itself, innocent, says Kant; it can make man merely animal-like, but not evil. Nor is the source of moral evil the 'corruption [depravity]' of reason. That would make man into a 'devilish being'. Immorality, as we pointed out earlier, is not saying to oneself 'Evil, thou be my good'. Nobody does that. Rather, man is evil to the extent he takes the maxims of self-love *'as in themselves wholly adequate* to the determination of the will [choice]', and makes them 'the condition of obedience to the moral law'. Moral evil is not devotion to what is wrong and bad, but a failure; it is 'the perversity [capriciousness] of the heart':

> the evil heart . . . arises from the frailty of human nature, the sufficient strength to follow out the principles it has chosen for itself, joined with its impurity, the failure to distinguish the incentives (even of well-intentioned actions) from each other by the guage of morality (*RE* 32–3)

Such frailty, capriciousness, and impurity may be just an 'unintentional guilt' but it can become 'deliberate guilt' when it is due to an 'insidiousness [cunning] of the human heart'. For then it is a 'dishonesty, by which we humbug ourselves and which thwarts the establishment of a true moral diposition [spirit] in us . . .' (*RE* 33).

This leads us to what Kant calls 'The First Command of All Duties to Oneself': know yourself. 'Know your heart— whether it is good or evil, whether the source of your actions is pure or impure' (*MM* 107). Now such knowledge of oneself cannot be ordinary knowledge, which, as Kant explains in the *Critique of Pure Reason*, and elsewhere, is always empirical. Through 'inner sense' we can know ourselves only as phenomena, as mere appearances or 'empirical selves' (*CPuR* 67). But the ultimate ground of morality is my noumenal self, the self as a 'thing in itself' or 'soul' of which empirical knowledge is impossible. Kant puts it also in this way: we can know only what the mind receives, but the activity of the mind itself eludes us (*CPuR* 88). In other words, I cannot, in the ordinary sense, *know* myself as freedom. Of myself as free I can only have an a priori 'Idea'. The only access I have to myself as freedom is my supra-sensible awareness of the Categorical Imperative. Consequently, I cannot know that the Idea I have of myself as free corresponds to reality. All I can do is to take a certain standpoint —look at myself as free—or think of myself *as if* I were free. I wish to suggest, therefore, that the foundation of morality is, for

Kant, not the factual reality of my freedom—whatever that may mean—but nothing more nor less than the assuming of a certain attitude on the part of the agent, or, to use a Sartrean word, his commitment. This is the attitude or standpoint of honesty towards oneself. To look at myself as a mere empirically deter-minable object governed by causal laws is self-deception or an inner lie; it is bad faith. The lucid and authentic attitude tells me instead that, once I have become aware of my moral obligation, it is disingenuous still to ask whether or not I can carry it out. Of course I cannot, for example, add at will a cubit to my height. But is there a situation in which I conceivably *ought* to do so? On the other hand, there is a myriad of instances where there is no hard and fast evidence concerning what I *can* do. A severe threat may make me revise my estimate of what I am capable of. Similarly, my conviction that I am morally bound to do a certain thing may be the very thing that summons up my power to do it.

The 'ought–can' principle as Kant conceived it, and with it freedom, is not a theoretical but a practical—in fact itself a moral—issue. When we profess that there is an empirical restriction, in ourselves or out, on what, in the face of a moral obligation, we *can* do, chances are that we are seeking phony excuses. Freedom is a subjective attitude of the moral man—the attitude of honesty as opposed to self-deceit. Let me paraphrase from the *Critique of Practical Reason*:

Suppose there is a man who under the threat of death is asked to bear false witness against an honourable man. That he will not, he is perhaps not ready to assure us. But without doubt, he will admit that it is possible for him to refuse. Hence he judges that he *can* do something simply because he recognizes that he ought to do it. Thus he acknowledges his freedom. (*CPrR* 141)

There is nothing fantastic or *outré* about thinking of freedom as the ability to act beyond what, on empirical evidence, appears possible. Just think of J. L. Austin's golfer (one that takes his game seriously). 'I could have holed the putt,' he says, while he did not.[1] True, he tried his hardest, the green was soggy, it was the fifth day of the tournament, it was the eighteenth hole, and so on. Still, he believes he could have sunk it—absolutely and

---

[1] J. L. Austin, 'Ifs and Cans', in *Philosophical Papers* (Oxford, 1979), 166 n.

not only if the conditions had been different and if he himself would have been a better golfer. If you believe in an unconditional demand, or make an unconditional commitment, you must believe in an unconditional *can*; in that case, in your eyes, the world submits to freedom.

PART THREE

Sartre and the Ethics of Subjective Commitment

JEAN-PAUL SARTRE (1905–84), after having taught philosophy for some years, became a man of letters in the French tradition. Not only did he produce philosophical treatises, but novels, plays, critical biographies, essays on literature, politics, and art, and he was a co-founder of a politico-literary journal. He was a political activist, an epitome of what he himself called an 'engaged' or committed thinker. He never married but maintained a remarkable lifelong relationship with Simone de Beauvoir, or 'Castor' as he called her. Coming from a somewhat tattered bourgeois family, he became a passionate fighter against the complacency, sham, and hypocrisy of contemporary Western society.

14

Some Comparisons and Conclusions

PHILOSOPHICAL theories of morality are not like the theories of the sciences. I said in the Introduction that there are what may be called the data of ethics—the historically given individual as well as collective attitudes and beliefs concerning the right and the good—and the moral philosopher tries to systematize them. But the systematization he may attempt does not consist in constructing empirical hypotheses. For, although moral philosophy is not exhortation, it still aims at choice and conduct, not mere theoretical understanding. If the data of ethics are to be brought together into a system, then this is to be done not in terms of explanatory laws but in terms of normative principles. Sartre differs from Mill and Kant in thinking that even this is impossible, and, since we have seen how both Mill and Kant failed in trying to develop systems of ethics, we may be disposed to share Sartre's belief that system-building in ethics is fundamentally wrong-headed.

For Sartre, there are no ready-made and objective norms to guide our lives and to give them meaning. There are only our personal commitments. Values are given neither in God's commandments, nor (as in Mill) in the empirical, nor (as in Kant) in the a priori nature of man. Sartre wants to make a totally new start. Man has no nature, or, if you prefer, man's nature is his freedom, that is, his open-endedness.

Of course, when Sartre says that there is no human nature, he does not mean that human life is just a succession of disjointed happenings. In what humans do, meaning both goes back to the past and reaches out to the future. But it is not anything given, it is constantly being created as well as revised. Therefore, the human sciences are really ill-suited for telling us what man in process is. The diversity and open-endedness of being human is often better illuminated through imaginative literature. The novelist does not try to *explain* human lives, but to portray them from the inside as configurations of subjectivity. Literary characters may impress and grip us, and the last thing we want then is an *explanation* of them through some motivational laws of psychology. The meaning of human existence is forever open just as art is. Neither Homer, nor Shakespeare, not even Joyce or Proust put an end to literature, any more than either Titian or Rembrandt, or even Cézanne or Picasso, put an end to what is possible in painting.

When Sartre said that man is free, he did not of course claim that, since I am free, I can make it false that two and two make four, or that I have a body, or that that body has a certain physical make-up, or that it is located at a mean distance of 9,290,000 miles from the sun. Nor did he deny that I am living in a historically rooted culture and economic system. Nor did he claim that humans have amazing powers ready to burst forth and to astonish everyone, or that science fiction is truer than one thinks. What he claimed was rather that man can falsify any generalization concerning the *ends* of his actions. Sartre says that there is a universality in man's aims simply because we are capable of understanding, seeing the point of, the endeavours of every other man everywhere and in all epochs of history, provided that we have enough information (*EH* 46–7). But such understanding is itself a subjective project of ours for which, in the end, all proposed universal and objective laws of human nature are useless.

In an important way Sartre is closer to Kant than to Mill. According to Mill, all we must do in order to determine the moral rightness or wrongness of an action is to assess its effects as those of just another event. For Kant, the first thing to realize about a human action is that it is not merely an event that happens, but a choice that is made, a case of spontaneity. With this Sartre agrees. We have already seen what an avid reader of Kant Sartre must have been. His criticism of Kantian ethics centres round Kant's idea that as a moral being man is transported into an abstract region of pure essences, that he is an end in itself not in his concrete desires and projects within a social, political, and historical milieu but as an embodiment of an abstract concept—a being who can act from the pure idea of a universal law. In his posthumous *Cahiers pour une morale* Sartre claims that Kant's imperative, 'Treat humanity as an end', says, from the practical point of view, nothing at all (*CM* 14). For it leads to irresolvable conflicts. There are situations in which I have to sacrifice one person to another (*EH* 36). Sartre denies that there can be any test by which our ultimate choices can be weighed and then certified as objectively right or wrong. It is true that our moral choices are implicitly universal, but this furnishes no other validation for them than how much confidence, resolve, and fortitude we show in abiding by them. Sartre agrees with Kant that, while the content of ethics is variable, its form is universal. However, the universality of its form does not make the validity of particular actions testable through cold logic. What universal humanity means is constantly tested and challenged by individual men.

When you make a moral choice, you cannot deny that it is always right for everybody to make that choice. For Kant, this was the foundation of ethics. But his conception of this requirement was both too ephemeral and too rigid. He took it to be a formal and disembodied principle, a principle which says no more than that we must be conceptually consistent. Mill saw the inadequacy of this idea and maintained that, if the principle of universalizability is to be of any use, it must be conceived as the Principle of Utility—that is, as the principle that bids us to ask about the *actual* universal consequences of our rules of conduct on human happiness (*UT* 4). Sartre's remedy against the barrenness of Kant's moral law is quite different. For him, the concern with universality is simply what he called the attitude of 'good faith' and the avoidance of self-deception. For Kant, an action is morally permissible if its maxim is, so to speak, part of a logically possible world. For Sartre, on the other hand, an ethically viable world is not merely a logically possible world, but a world which a person can envision and endorse and work for as someone already situated in an existing world with his own involvements and commitments.

Both Kant and Mill believed that we can assess a moral decision by using a general principle. Sartre's view is that, in moral thinking, we can do no more than to present telling examples. No ethical 'theory', that is, a grand generalization from which particular moral judgements can be deduced, will do. No formula can always hit the mark. What counts as a morally good will can be exhibited only by giving the full details of a particular choice which confronts a particular person in particular circumstances and against the background of his prior choices. As a matter of fact, we can never be certain that we have, so to speak, enough premiss material. A human decision *can* be made intelligible and be assessed, but that requires that we comprehend the whole particular story, and, moreover, that we comprehend it from the subject's own point of view. Only the grasp of all the ins and outs of a whole life, or at least a considerable segment of it, will give us enough data. To imagine, as Kant did, that we can always find a 'maxim' in the mind of the agent which sums up the whole affair and which we then test through our logical acumen is, from Sartre's point of view, totally unrealistic.

15

Subjectivity and Intersubjectivity

EXISTENCE, says Sartre, precedes essence (*EH* 26). This slogan expresses what he takes to be the fundamental truth about us and sums up existentialism. *That* we are is prior to *what* we are. As humans, we are not mere things. Sartre, perhaps misleadingly, for an artefact is not a 'mere thing', uses the letter opener to illustrate. First, the letter opener is produced from a blueprint. Second, it is made of certain materials. Third, certain methods, processes, and techniques go into making it. Fourth, it serves a purpose. All these factors determine what a particular letter opener will be like and therefore *its* essence is prior to its existence. Sartre's point is that philosophers have, in various ways, conceived of a human being along analogous lines. First, in the Judeo-Christian tradition, man is thought of as created by God 'after his own image'. Before humans existed, there was a blueprint in the divine mind. Second, for Kant, for example, to be human is just as determinate as to be a geometric figure —man is ultimately made of the purely intelligible stuff of reason; the rest in him is mere appearance. Third, the empiricists—Mill is an example—also think of humans in essentialistic terms, for to them humans are determinable by biology, psychology, sociology, and the rest. A human being, for them, just as anything else, is the product of certain processes and conditions. Fourth, in the Greek and Thomistic traditions, all beings, including man, serve a purpose. To be human is to fit into the universal functional order of things. Nowadays, the same idea, although conceived in relative terms, is found in sociology. An individual's essence is his societal and cultural role and status.

Now all these ways of conceiving man have furnished purported foundations of ethics. Our ultimate choices, if they are not to be arbitrary, must have a basis in what itself is not subject to choice, that is, in our nature. It matters little whether that nature is thought of as something fixed or evolving. The idea is that we can know what the good life is only if we are guided by a prior insight into what we are, and how we fit into the world as it is and its processes. Sartre, on the other hand, maintained that the final truth about ourselves is that there is no such thing as human nature, or an evolution of it, and therefore no objective knowledge to guide our conduct. Man simply exists, turns up, finds himself there, and then chooses what he will do and be.

I find myself existing, but my existence is not somehow a something. Cherishing paradox, Sartre says that I am nothing. I am a consciousness, but consciousness is not a thing with its own nature; it is a void. Thoughts, perceptions, memories have no substance of their own; they are pure transparency and lead us to external objects. Consciousness does not, as a rule, dwell on itself. It gives us the world, but it is not itself an object in the world. The 'I' and the world are like an eye and its visual field, said Wittgenstein. The eye is not itself an object in its own visual field and the 'I' is outside the world.[1] Acts of consciousness are what they are by virtue of what they are not. When Sartre says in several places that humans 'are not what they are and are what they are not', the point is not that human minds are difficult to penetrate, that a person may always deep down not be what he appears to be. Instead, what is meant is, for one thing, that consciousness is geared to action and the world in which action takes place; and in forming an intention to act I think of what is not yet the case. Therefore, in a sense, I already am my future. Man is 'ahead of himself'. My self-awareness is not that of an object with fixed properties and as an unalterable part of an unalterable world. It is an awareness of my challenges, opportunities, of my possible defeats or successes in an open world. To know myself is not to have the right description of an object. We are not mere observers of ourselves and the world. The self is the

---

[1] L. Wittgenstein, *Tractatus Logico-Philosophicus* (London, 1922), 151. In the earlier *Notebooks 1914–1916* (Oxford, 1961), 80, we find further 'existentialist' passages: 'The thinking subject is surely an illusion. But the willing subject exists.' 'If the will did not exist, neither would there be that centre of the world, which we call the I, and which is the bearer of ethics.' 'What is good and evil is essentially the I, not the world.' 'The I is not an object.' 'The I makes its appearance in [enters] philosophy through the world's being *my* world.'

lived self. As such, as I try to seize it, it escapes me. As I tell the story of my life to myself, it affects me. We never appear to ourselves as immutable. We saw that Kant, too, spoke of a form of self-knowledge which is different from the knowledge of the observable and predictable phenomena. To be conscious of the moral law in you is not to be conscious of one of your dispositions, for you can always decide to act against that law. Still, for Kant, self-knowledge was deemed to be knowledge of a kind of, albeit queer, object. For according to him, although the moral law is not a description of my 'phenomenal' self with its dispositions and wants, it is, or corresponds to, the description of my will as a 'noumenal' or purely rational entity, residing in the realm of pure essences. For Sartre, on the other hand, the point is not that the break we, as acting subjects, make with nature elevates us on to a higher plateau. We exist wholly in this world, but we exist in it not as objects but as subjects. We are in the world in the sense that we dwell there and not that we are, as it were, just part of its furniture.

In Sartre's view, in thinking about how, ultimately, we ought to act, it is impossible to go beyond subjectivity. In ethics there is no truth, only honesty and truthfulness. The truth of my beliefs does not depend on me. If what I believe to be so actually is so, then I have a true belief. If not, then my belief is false. The honesty or truthfulness of my belief, on the other hand, does depend on me, and me alone. My belief is untruthful if it is feigned. This is obvious as I communicate it to others—I may lie. But there is also mendacity towards oneself. I may make myself believe something which I know deep down is not so or I may refuse to spell out to myself the things that I know in my heart. My alleged belief may be a mere posturing even to myself, for I might not act on it when the chips are down. I may waver and change my mind. To believe is not merely to entertain a thought but to commit oneself, and the measure of my honesty and truthfulness is my conduct.

For Sartre, there are no norms of conduct other than our truthfulness and our constancy. For Mill, an action is right if the belief that it promotes human happiness is true. The quality of that belief—its firmness and honesty—is beside the point. If the contemplated action is *in fact* one that furthers human welfare, that action is morally right regardless of how firm or infirm is the agent's belief that it does; he may even believe that it does not. Kant, on the other hand, had already taken a step in Sartre's direction. What matters is what is internal to the will itself. Still, as we saw, Kant did not say that the moral rightness of an action is the same thing as its honesty and truthfulness, its having been done from a good will. Sartre, however, did exactly that. His view, in effect, obliterates the distinction between the moral rightness and the moral praiseworthiness of actions.

For Sartre, values and norms are created by our choices. This must not be taken to mean that what *ought* to be done reduces to what *is* done. That is the sociological or anthropological view of morality which we referred to earlier. That view makes value into an empirical and factual concept. Values are then relative to individuals or groups, but nevertheless objective—discoverable through empirical research. In that case, they could be quite indifferent to us, we could choose not to pay any attention to them. When Sartre says that value is 'consubstantial' with human life, he means something quite different (*BN* 145). Values stand and fall with the concrete choices an individual makes. *One* noble act proves as much about the value of nobility as thousands of such acts do.

Still, as Sartre puts it in his inimitable way, 'value haunts freedom' (*BN* 145). By that he means that, by the exercise of our free choice, we set up, or hold forth, or give an example of a norm intended for everyone and to endure forever. As I said when discussing Mill, I cannot desire something without implying that what I desire is good. Values are not fleeting figments of our imagination; they are anchored in our commitments with their universal import. Once they are decided upon, they have, so to speak, a life of their own; they continue to *be* through their own impetus. Moreover, I already find myself in a world of values. Values spring up all around me 'like partridges'; they are 'sown on my path as thousands of little real demands, like the signs which order us to keep off the grass' (*BN* 76–7). Values haunt us as physical objects do:

It is obvious that I remain free . . . to direct my attention on . . . values or to neglect them—exactly as it depends on me to look more closely at this table, my pen, or my package of tobacco. But whether they are the object of detailed attention or not, in any case they *are*. (*BN* 146)

However, when I ask about and reflect honestly on the foundation of values, I realize that the sole thing which makes them exist is my commitment to them.

It follows that my freedom is the unique foundation of values and that *nothing*, absolutely nothing, justifies me in adopting this or that particular scale of values. As a being by whom values exist, I am unjustifiable. My freedom is anguished at being the foundation of values while itself without foundation. (*BN* 76)

Nevertheless, in Sartre's view, we do not choose our ways of life willy-nilly. I am not the first person on earth. If I were constitutionally a Robinson Crusoe, living in a virgin environment, what I do would indeed be arbitrary. But I am not. I find myself in an already constituted human world. That world manifests itself in a whole civilization and culture. I am part of that world—contentedly or discontentedly. I did not have a hand in shaping it any more than I had a hand in shaping the trees and the mountains. Consequently, my actions cannot, as a rule, be arbitrary and whimsical. They have to fit into, or at least take into account, or be reactions against, the world as it is already constituted for me. There is the rub.

Sartre is particularly anxious to point out that my life-world includes other humans. My awareness of myself as different from the awareness of things with fixed essences is, at the same time, awareness of others as also different from mere things. This does not mean that I am aware of others, or even of myself, as pure noumena or intelligible beings. The community of humans, to the extent in which there is such a thing, is not anything like the Kantian kingdom of ends. I become aware of my fellow humans through concrete encounters. The argument is astonishingly simple. Sartre says that, while I look at you, you, unlike a rock or table, may look back at me (*BN* 340). I know therefore, right off, that there are other beings with consciousness and will around me. This may sound like a silly and pointless thing to say; just a case of belabouring the obvious. But, in philosophy, there is the rather persistent problem of the existence of other minds. Some philosophers have held that, when it comes to 'you', all I directly perceive is a body as a physical thing; I do not 'see' *you*, your thoughts, your intentions, and the like. Whether you are real as another mind is problematic. This doubt is reinforced by the argument that in my dreams I may have commerce with persons who do not really exist. How can I tell, while I am looking at 'you', that I am not dreaming. 'You' may be just a figment of my imagination. With the audacity of an Alexander the Great, who did not want to have any truck with mysteries, Sartre cut the Gordian knot. Since I can feel a look or gaze directed at me, you are real. Actually Sartre argues that, apart from the drama of reciprocal looks, concrete experience tells me that I exist in a world in which there are other consciousnesses and wills. Consider a walk in a park (*BN* 341–5). Another walker appears. This introduces 'an element of disintegration' into '*my* universe', that is, the lawn, the benches, the trees, the statue *as seen by me*. I see those things as being at certain distances from me, but *he* sees them at different distances from *him*. And,

This green [grass] turns toward the Other a face which escapes me. I apprehend the relation of the green to the Other as an objective relation, but I can not apprehend the green *as* it appears to the Other. Thus suddenly an object has appeared which has stolen the world from me. (*BN* 343)

But still the most important point is this. Not only may the other thing that moves in the park look at the grass, the trees, and so on from a different perspective; he may also look at me. I then become fully aware of him as a subject. For I have now become an object for him, and I cannot be an object for just another object.

   Without others, I would not, in important ways, even be aware of myself. The point is more radical than that, in order to come to know myself, I need feedback from others. Another example of Sartre's makes this clear (*BN* 347–54). Suppose, from jealousy, I am peeping through a keyhole. I am not aware of my jealousy, I am caught up in it, I do not reflect on it, I do not judge myself, I focus on the scene unfolding behind the door. Suddenly, I hear footsteps. 'Someone is looking at me!' Immediately, 'I see *myself* because *somebody* sees me.' I am presented to my own consciousness '*in so far as* [I am] *an object for the Other*'. In shame I become conscious of myself and my jealousy.

   My self-awareness depends on how others are aware of me. I

look at others and they look back at me. I exist in another person's eyes. It is 'the Other' who reveals to me what I am. I can judge myself only as others judge me. For example, I cannot determine that I am witty by telling jokes to myself and then see how hard I shall laugh. Of course, Sartre does not mean that we cannot know *anything* about ourselves except through others. All I have to do is to step on my bathroom scale to know that I am twenty pounds overweight. But the bathroom scale does not tell me that I am fat and ugly. Perhaps we can put it in this way: the meaning and the criteria of application of my 'moral predicates', in the widest possible sense of that term, are determined by others.

Before going on with our discussion of Sartre's idea that we live in an interpersonal world and its exigencies, two points must be mentioned, points which will be discussed more fully later. First, the self-revelations which the presence of 'the Other' forces upon ourselves are always in 'bad faith'. As I label myself—as others label me—as witty or intelligent or jealous or compassionate, or evil or righteous, I think of myself as consti- tuting an ego, a kind of object or thing. According to Sartre, however, as we have already seen, I *am* nothing, or I *am* my freedom. Second, while looking at me, 'the Other' sizes me up, judges me, regards me as an object; and, again in bad faith, I do the same with regard to him. The mutual 'look' is an epitome of the basic relationship between humans which Sartre charac- terizes as antagonism or mutual enslavement. Only occasionally does Sartre mention 'generosity' (cf. Kant's 'respect') as an attitude which allows for mutual freedom.

I live in an interpersonal world. Therefore, my choices, although inescapably subjective, have to struggle to fit into a wider whole. In fact, Sartre claims that, in choosing for myself, I choose for all others. My consciousness involves a network of ties to other humans. My choices have to be either for or against the choices of others. I and others may always run into a situation in which it is impossible to agree to disagree. This is obvious when I am a member of a militant party or union, or work for a corporation. But a moment's reflection shows that it is equally so when my decision is a so-called personal one. For example, says Sartre, when I choose to get married and to have children, I 'commit humanity as a whole to monogamy' (*EH* 30).

My decision presupposes, invokes, and endorses a human and potentially global institution.

For Mill and Kant, the ethical problem was how to transcend subjectivity. We start with our subjective desires, likes, and dislikes and try to rise up to a plane of objective validity. Subjectivity is something to be overcome. For Sartre, we start with objective demands and norms which are inherent in the public world. But the trouble is that these may be experienced by us as alien encroachments. Not subjectivity but objectivity is the threat. I am not just a specimen of humanity. From the impersonal world of objective norms, from the world of what 'one' does, I must make my way back to my own inwardness. At the same time, it is impossible to regain my subjectivity by just cutting myself off. To be a human is to interact with others and to exist with them in a common human world. So, from my own subjectivity, and with nothing else to rely on, when I make my choice, I implicitly choose also for all the others. Thus I carry the burden of the whole world on my shoulders (*EH* 30).

I have, in a preliminary way, tried to take some of the sting out of the commonly voiced criticism that if, as Sartre claims, morality is subjective, then it is arbitrary, a matter of personal predilections or even whims. This, I have tried to point out, is not so, because, in Sartre's view, in choosing for myself, I choose a certain kind of world. What we do matters not only to ourselves but, potentially or symbolically at least, to everyone else as well. As an aside, consider also this. There is no correlation between what is serious and important, and what is objective. When I say to Agnes, 'I love you, please marry me,' this is serious, but it is subjective. It is not a factual statement capable of being either true or false. It is a declaration, an entreaty. On the other hand, when I say to her, 'The sun is shining,' this is objective all right, but quite possibly trivial.

16

Freedom, Facts, and Values

'PHILOSOPHICAL freedom', as Sartre called it, is just the con-
stitution of consciousness, the indeterminacy of our responses to
what is 'out there'. What is 'given' is always already an interpretation. There are no bare data. Environmental input is
ambiguous; it always leaves room for different responses. Freedom 'in the philosophical sense', says Sartre, is just this 'gap' or
'distance' between consciousness and its object. But, beyond
this, there is acting from freedom. Every choice is free simply
because it is not unequivocally determined from the outside. But
not every choice is made for the sake of freedom. So, says Sartre,
it is not enough for the will to be free; we must *will* the will to be
free. In bad faith we hide our freedom from ourselves. We are
always free all right, but we do not necessarily value our
freedom.

So in the more directly ethical vein Sartre says that man is free
since he 'is nothing else but that which he makes of himself' (*EH*
28). This is not a claim to omnipotence. Sartre does not, of
course, mean that I can, if I choose, make myself ten feet tall.
The absolute freedom which he claims belongs to humans is not
the freedom to reach any goal they may set for themselves if
only they tried hard enough. To be free is not to possess
extraordinary powers. Freedom, for Sartre, is not freedom of
accomplishment, any more than it was for Kant. Working hard
in order to achieve a given goal, instead of being a manifestation
of freedom, may well be a mode of escaping from it. What Sartre
means in saying that we make ourselves into whatever we
choose is that we create the meaning of our lives, together with
the meaning of the world we live in. There are things in the
'universe' of which we are not even aware, so we cannot possibly
affect their meaning, but they are not part of the lived world.
Our environment does not unbeknownst to us determine our
choices. There is no fate, no invisible hand. Facts enter our lives

only as they constitute a difficulty, challenge, or opportunity, and they do that only because we have already decided upon certain goals.

Freedom is not just doing what we happen to fancy. I do not make choices in a vacuum. Facts do not count for everything, but they do count. The world is not a spectacle to be contemplated, nor a jigsaw puzzle to be put together, but a scene of action. The world as a vast thing, comprising everything which is just 'there', is actually an incoherent notion. There is a world only for a subject or subjects. At the same time, consciousness is not free to constitute the world in any way whatsoever. In all experience there is an ineluctable element. Pure facts are fictions. Still, facts are revealed to me as the resistance I encounter. In a sense, I am caught up in them; I do not start from scratch. They do not determine what I decide, but they do limit what is possible for me to achieve. I am not free from difficulties and limitations.

But this does not destroy my freedom. In fact, freedom requires that there be facts to contend with. I can form an intention, as opposed to a mere wish, only if I take into account what is factually possible. Freedom needs what Sartre calls a 'coefficient of adversity'. Without human limitations life would be like a dream in which the merely wished-for is not distinguishable from reality. In the dream world freedom is without a foothold. Freedom does not mean that we can annihilate facts, but only that it is we who endow them with meaning and that, within limits, we can modify them. In the *Critique of Pure Reason* Kant said that reason may be subject to the illusion that it does not have to recognize the limits which experience imposes on our knowledge, and uses the following image to make his point: 'The light dove, cleaving the air in free flight, and feeling its resistance, might imagine that its flight would be still easier in empty space' (*CPrR* 47). Sartre thought that this image is even more instructive with regard to freedom and morality: 'man thinks he would be *more* moral if he were relieved of the human condition, if he were God, if he were an angel; he does not realize that morality and its problems would vanish along with humanity'.[1]

---

[1] J.-P. Sartre, *The War Diaries*, trans. A. Hoare (New York, 1984), 108.

But are not facts sometimes fatal to our freedom? It is true that, although Mount Everest is steep and high, we do not have to climb it. It is perilous only if we set out to reach its summit. But, it would seem, a person is not in the same position with regard to the colour of his skin, for example. It seems an exaggeration to say that it is up to him what relevance it has for his life. Sartre himself came to say that it was outrageous of him to claim in *Being and Nothingness* that, for example, one can always, even in the face of torture, choose not to be a traitor. Still, that work, as well as *Existentialism and Humanism*, represents existentialism in its uncompromising purity. In these works he asked, rhetorically, in what sense is it a limitation on *me* that there are things that could be done only by a person whose circumstances and character are totally different from mine? If we say that circumstances may defeat our freedom, only God would be free. Therefore, he said, there are no situations in which a person is less free than he would be in any other (*BN* 702). Only a third person could compare my situation with that of someone else. If I tried to look at my own situation objectively, it would no longer be *my* situation. The situation confronting me is 'the single countenance which the world turns towards me for my unique and personal choice' (*BN* 703). In the same vein, he claimed that a slave is as free as the master. The conditions of a slave's life may be horrible, but he can still turn it into something magnificent. A slave is as free as anyone since he can always *attempt* to break his chains. His situation is 'to remain a slave or risk worse to escape servitude' (*BN* 703). To be free is not to be able to do what you want but to want to do what you can. A slave must choose *as* a slave and his slavery cannot therefore be an obstacle to *his* freedom. 'The life of a slave who revolts and dies in the course of revolt is a free life' (*BN* 703).

Again, Sartre argues, the kind of body I have cannot impose limitations on *my* freedom (*BN* 432), for it would be idle to compare my body with the body of another. The beauty or power of the body of another could never become the basis of *my* projects; nor could its ugliness and decrepitude. I could never act through the body of another. There is consequently a sense in which I choose to have the body I have, although I do not choose it in the sense in which I choose, say, my clothes. I choose the way in which I exist in my body. Both its beauty and it ugliness may be a burden. I may find a handicap an excuse for my failures, but I may also find it a challenge. Whatever my natural condition is, it is ambiguous. I may find it defeating or try to transcend it. Sartre says that there is even a sense in which it is true to say that I choose to have been born: I may curse the day of my birth, or bless it. There is really nothing mysterious in this. The words 'I choose to have been born' make sense, just as the words 'I choose to live in the country' do, even when said while I am already living there. They are very different from the words 'I choose to be born' or 'I chose to be born', which, admittedly, are without sense.

Freedom is not to have limitless opportunities. Only a finite and limited being *can* choose; only for him are there alternatives. For Sartre, just as for Kant, there are no degrees of freedom. To claim that all men are equally free, in the sense in question, is not like claiming that all men are equally wealthy. What Sartre says is simply that for all men in any of their circumstances there are *always some* alternatives. I may find that there is only beer available at a restaurant I have gone to and no wine. But if I then order beer, I have nevertheless chosen it, for I could have got up and gone to another restaurant or done without any beverage at all. I can make a choice only as this particular individual with my opportunities and powers, in my environment, and with my past. Freedom is not to have unlimited options, but to will to choose among the options you do have. Being free is therefore *believing*, believing in, and taking advantage of, your freedom. Thus Sartre's argument for freedom is simply that, to the extent men look at the world as a field of action, as an open world—in other words, take themselves to be free—they *are* free. We recall a similar argument in Kant: a rational being looks at himself as free and, consequently, 'from the practical point of view', *is* free.

I can always falsify, or at least try to falsify, a prediction concerning my conduct. When I am told that I shall fail the examination, I might study all the harder and pass it. When I am told that I shall cheat, I might decide, from sheer defiance perhaps, to be honest. It is true that I cannot falsify the prediction that I shall grow old and die. But growing old and dying and similar things are not things I do. Besides, my awareness of matters such as these may serve as the light in which I act. I did not choose to be mortal, but it is up to me whether my finitude fills me with eagerness or despondency, whether it will spur me on or paralyse me.

According to Sartre, freedom is incompatible not only with determinism but also with objective norms. To be free is just to take certain features of a situation we are in to be reasons for a certain course of action. There is nothing that certifies reasons as good reasons. In fact, reasons are subsequent to decisions. Such a view might seem to involve a conceptual muddle. By choice, it may be urged, we just *mean* something that is *guided* by reasons, not something that *produces* reasons. If there is nothing to determine beforehand what reasons are good reasons, there will be no reasons at all. Choices, if not arbitrary, are possible only if based on what is not subject to choice. If choices create reasons, then, in any serious sense, there are no choices. Thinking along these lines both Mill and Kant searched for the *foundation* of morality. But we have seen how this search in both instances failed. Curiously enough, Sartre was a kind of foundationalist himself. His inspiration came from psychoanalysis. One idea in psychoanalytic theory is that one's whole life is determined by some early experience or trauma. Sartre wanted to free psychoanalysis from its deterministic assumptions and advocated what he called 'existential psychoanalysis' (*BN* 712–34). In the place of what we undergo in our early life, he put what he called the 'original choice' or 'fundamental project' which we make in our early life. Our whole lives are a matter of coming to terms with it and its ramifications. In his account of his own early years, *The Words*,[2] he tells us how he came to make the decision to be a writer when he was about ten.

However, with regard to the problem of how choices are possible if there are no prior reasons for them, the idea of an original choice is useless. According to Sartre, all choices are made in a situation. But situations, he himself said, are not just facts. They are facts *vis-à-vis* our prior choices. Hence the first or original choice must be a situationless choice, in other words, no choice at all. The original choice is also an overblown idea. Perhaps an omniscient being can see how all the choices we actually make fit into a prefigured whole. But we have to work at

---

[2] J.-P. Sartre, *The Words*, trans. B. Frechtman (Greenwich, 1964).

the meaning of our lives piecemeal; we have to eke it out as we go. What binds me to my original project? As a psychological event, Sartre himself says, it is causally no more efficacious than any other event in my life. Nor does the original choice create an objectively binding norm for my subsequent choices. Each serious act of ours, says Sartre, either affirms or disaffirms the original choice and there is the possibility of abrogating it altogether and giving one's life a new fulcrum. Saulus may become Paulus. The truth of the matter is just that some of our decisions are more momentous than others and that we have to live in their wake. But we never start things from scratch, perhaps not even in the womb. Sartre's notion of the original choice is an exaggeration of the idea, correct enough, that reasons must come to an end. I push back the chain of reasons in order to reach rock-bottom. But I never reach it. At one point I must just decide and act.

When you listen to Mill and Kant, morality is supposed to spring from either of two kinds of magic hat—the Principle of Utility, or the Categorical Imperative. For Sartre, both of these notions are pure fabrications. But he resorts to a fabrication of his own—the original choice. He, too, felt a need for a nest, so to speak, where all the moral reasons and motives came home to roost. Sartre, in a curious way, no less than Mill and Kant, adhered to, or at least lapsed into, the philosopher's habit of believing that we can truly assess our beliefs and decisions only if we have an unchallengeable starting-point. Only in this case that starting-point was not the dogma of either empiricism or rationalism, but a dogma similar to that of psychoanalysis.

To be free is, then, for Sartre, to be free not only from causes but also from objective normative principles. A human choice may always go beyond, or against, any presumed values. But the resulting 'absurdity' of our choices is not that in the rational order of things there is suddenly a disruption, an emergence of a totally inexplicable and baffling event—a human choice—with regard to which we can only shrug our shoulders. It is just that morality has to be continuously reinvented; it is not given in one blow, in some grand overall view of man and his place in the universe.

Although a moral choice is always subjective, its meaning, says Sartre, is universal. Although there is no universal human nature, there is a universal 'human condition'—we all have to 'live, labour and die' (*EH* 46). Sartre agrees with Kant—the *intended* scope of moral judgements is universal; they are *addressed* to everybody, and their universal relevance is granted if they address the human condition. In my particular choice there is an implicit universal judgement. There are no objective universal ends. Still, in acting in a certain way I imply that it is the right way to act for all others as well. In choosing I give birth to value. Therefore, Sartre argues, I am responsible for all others. My freedom, instead of separating me from him, makes me my brother's keeper, and everyone is my brother.

But, in the absence of objective norms, is not then the exercise of my freedom just an attempt to dominate others, to make them see and do things in *my* way? Sartre says, no. In willing my own freedom I must will the freedom of all others. Why is this so? If I did succeed in enslaving others—making them submit to my will and carry out tasks which I ordain—I would in fact eventually become *their* slave. I myself would become dependent on them. In forcing another into total submission, I myself fall into servitude. My freedom is the freedom of *my* actions, I cannot act through others. My projects are free only in relation to the free projects of others. Genuine co-operation is also a rivalry. Challenges are needed for freedom to unfold. Therefore, willing my own freedom entails that I must will also the freedom of others, for only another free being can challenge me.

These, at least, are Sartre's arguments. At the same time, he seems to make the mutual recognition of freedom an impossibility. In *Being and Nothingness* Sartre says that the basic relation between humans is conflict (*BN* 475). I always attempt to constrain the freedom of others. I always try to incorporate the other into my projects. I do this even when I appear to be totally self-effacing. My modesty helps me to shine, my humility to conquer, my virtue to oppress, says Sartre. The sheer fact of my existence draws a boundary round other persons. Humans engage in mutual combat. Each of us tries to assert his own freedom in all sorts of ways, but they are, at the same time, ways of trying to deny the freedom of others. We are always bent on trying to turn others into mere objects, and they try to do the same with us. If Jones and Smith were mere objects, I could handle and manage them. But their freedom disquiets me. So I try to suppress it.

Just the same, I also want to preserve the freedom of others. A mere automaton would not intrigue me. The opinions and conduct of others are really of interest to me if they are not coerced. Love, says Sartre, incorporates the same paradox. In love I try 'to act upon the Other's freedom' (*BN* 477). At the same time, since love is different from mere physical desire, the lover 'wants to possess a freedom as freedom'; he 'demands a pledge, yet is irritated by a pledge' (*BN* 479). Someone may say that the lover does not want to '*act* on the Other's freedom' at all. He just wants to be there for the beloved, to offer himself, to be part of the world of the beloved. But with this offering of oneself, Sartre points out, comes the (silent) demand for exclusivity, of wanting to be the *whole* world for the beloved. With a loving presence comes inevitably a 'limiting, a gluing down, of the Other's freedom . . .' (*BN* 480).

For these reasons, love, the ideal of which is the unity of two freedoms, is liable to degenerate into either 'sadism' or 'masochism'. Both of these attitudes Sartre calls vices, for we know that they are bound to fail; vice is 'the love of failure' (*BN* 493). It might seem that the 'masochist' just wants to yield, to surrender. In reality he is bent on absorbing and dissolving the freedom of his lover. It is not that the 'masochist', as Sartre sees him, is insincere. Rather, to use again Kant's phrase, his will is in conflict with itself: he truly wishes to be a mere helpless victim, but only in order to *compel* the other's love (*BN* 493). But his strategy is futile. The more submissive he becomes, the less interest will his partner take in him. His submission is a perverted and futile assertion of his own freedom designed to destroy the freedom of the other.

A similar frustration awaits the 'sadist'. He wishes to *compel* the other to *choose* to do his will. As a 'sadist' I want my partner to be both free and, at the same time, my mere instrument (*BN* 522). But once I have succeeded in reducing him to a will-less thing, I lose interest in him. Actually, I believe, Sartre's purpose in discussing sadism is to demonstrate the invincibility of human freedom. Man's willingness to inflict pain and torture cannot be explained through the utilitarian theory of punishment, that is, that pain and torture, although, in themselves, regretful things, will deter or reform the evil doer. It is rather that we are bent on humiliating and forswearing our fellow man, in order to destroy the threat of his freedom. But, as an existentialist manifesto, one may say, Sartre points out that you cannot ever totally humiliate a man and destroy his freedom. For, although he has been hunted down and assaulted, there always remains the look of his body and eyes. No one, Sartre says, has shown this better than Faulkner in *Light in August*, from which he cites:

But the man on the floor had not moved. He just lay there, with his eyes open and empty of everything save consciousness and with something, a shadow, about his mouth. For a long moment he looked up at them with peaceful and unfathomable and unbearable eyes. Then his face, body, all, seemed to collapse, to fall upon itself and from the slashed garments about his hips and loins the pent black blood seemed to rush like a released breath. It seemed to rush out of his pale body like the rush of sparks from a rising rocket; upon that black blast the man seemed to rise soaring into their memories forever and ever. They are not to lose it, in whatever peaceful valleys, beside whatever placid and reassuring streams of old age, in the mirroring faces of whatever children they will contemplate old disasters and newer hopes. *It will be there, musing, quiet, steadfast,* not fading and *not particularly threatful, but of itself alone serene, of itself alone triumphant.* [Sartre's emphasis] (*BN* 576)

So, indubitably, human freedom is indestructible by forces without. But, as we shall see, it is, according to Sartre, constantly being gnawed at from within.

Can freedom be our conscious goal not only in ourselves but also in others. In the essay 'Why Write?'[3] Sartre states, just as he does in *Existentialism*, that my freedom 'is indissolubly linked to that of all other men'. This, he says, is exhibited in the relation between the writer and his public. The (good) writer is polite and generous; he does not manipulate his readers. Instead, he seeks to engage and challenge them. The (good) reader does the same. He is polite, he lends his ear and accepts the challenge. The author and the reader thus co-operate in good faith. Between them there is a mutual recognition of freedom. But is this possible outside art, outside the merely imaginary? Mutual recognition of freedom in real life, as we have seen, seems to be,

[3] In J.-P. Sartre, *What is Literature?*, trans. B. Frechtman (New York, 1965).

in Sartre's terms, a preordained impossibility. Were I to make the freedom of someone else my goal, by this very act I transcend and deny it.

This point, you recall, was already made by Kant. I cannot make another person free. Respect for the freedom of others must mean therefore solely that it is an end only negatively, that is, I must not undermine or sabotage it. Sartre forgets that Kant said this and is therefore suspicious of Kant's concept of mutual freedom. He implies that, according to Kant, to respect the freedom of others is to 'act for their benefit' and claims that this entails lording over them (*BN* 529–30). Sartre is more nearly on target when he criticizes the 'ethics of laissez-faire and tolerance'. He says that this removes from the individual 'on principle those free possibilities of courageous resistance, of perseverence, of self-assertion which he would have had the opportunity to develop in a world of intolerance'. He concludes that 'respect for the Other's freedom is an empty word . . .' (*BN* 531). In his view, man in relation to another man is always a kind of superfluity, a fatal nuisance. In a world where there are others, I am always *de trop* and hence guilty. This, says Sartre, is the meaning of original sin, of man's fall from grace, and the meaning of the words of the Genesis, 'They knew that they were naked' (*BN* 531).

Still, Sartre characterizes existentialism as optimistic. But it is optimism which is tough and without illusion. It is only in bad faith that we hope that others will do what we have failed to do. Existentialism, instead of being quietism, is activism. Sartre subscribes to the old adage, 'There is no need to hope in order to venture, no need to succeed, in order to persevere' (cf. *EH* 39–40).

The conclusion to be drawn is therefore this. Mutual antagonism cannot be overcome, and the co-operation of others cannot be taken for granted, but we can face all this in candour. We may, or we may not, avow to ourselves that it exists. The refusal to make this avowal is bad faith and self-deception: in that case we make ourselves believe that the primordial conflict among humans can be overcome, *either* by destroying the freedom of others through force and violence, *or* by other means such as a unilateral profession of non-violence and submission, *or* through mutual contract based on calculated self-interest, *or* just through the feeling of sympathy. In good faith, on the other hand, we face this predicament without fudging. Conflict between humans is inevitable. Still, mutual freedom can flourish when we face that fact. Sartre's ideal is not a world filled with peace and harmony in which the lamb and the lion lie down together. The freedom of another is a threat to me. Hence I embark on the effort to limit or even to destroy it. But I am bent on enslaving others only for the sake of the false ideal of my security and not for the sake of my own freedom. Freedom, let us say again, is not freedom from obstacles, hindrances, threats. I would not be free in a world in which everything without bother goes my way. To act for the sake of one's own freedom is not to seek to secure the automatic co-operation of others. It is rather to be willing to accept the challenge of their freedom. Deep down I realize that security is always a sham. To engage in action and to commit oneself entails relying on others. But such reliance is a leap into the dark and full of risks. Sartre says in *Existentialism* that 'as soon as there is commitment, I am obliged to will the liberty of others at the same time as mine' (*EH* 52). But this, together with the realization that no facts determine me and no objective values guide me, fills me not with peace and security but with anguish, forlornness, and despair.

17

Anguish, Forlornness, and Despair

WE have said that, for Sartre, freedom is basically just the indeterminacy of the mind. Consciousness is not like a camera, a computer, or a robot. Perception does not just faithfully reproduce what is 'out there', and volition does not just process the input. However, as we also said, ethical consciousness is not just free; it is consciousness conscious of its own freedom. Moral action, just as in Kant, is action for the sake of freedom. In order to be free in the ethical sense, we must come to see and face our freedom. According to Sartre, that is a matter of learning to live in anguish, with a sense of forlornness, and in despair. It is these feelings or moods which disclose to us the truth of our existence —namely that our freedom entails unlimited responsibility.

It might seem that, in order to be able to speak of responsibility, we must posit an objective order of right and wrong. To fulfil one's responsibility is to satisfy the demands of that order. Both Mill and Kant did that and their views therefore remained legalistic. Since, for them, there is an objective moral law—be it the Principle of Utility or the Categorical Imperative—moral responsibility has its limits. If what you did did not violate the law, then, whether you acted in good conscience or not, you are not legally guilty. The judge may deliver a sermon—give you a good talking-to—but he cannot get you. If there were also *objective moral* laws, then there would also be such a thing as being morally, not just legally, lily-white.

But can there be such a thing as total and objective *moral* justification of human acts? This very idea outraged Sartre. Moral responsibility and its extent are self-imposed. Hence, there is no objective way to tell where the liability to moral blame and guilt ends, nor where moral absolution or praise-worthiness begin. It is the awareness of this that engenders the feelings of anguish, forlornness, and despair.

It is through these moods that humans become aware of the

limitless moral burden of their existence. Of course I am not ordinarily in those moods when I go about my daily business. I hear the alarm, get up, go to work, keep appointments, remember to make phone calls, answer letters. I operate my car, pay attention to the traffic. I make sure that some piece of machinery I am operating is not breaking down and that I am operating it properly. I make plans for dinner, go to the cinema, watch television, and so on. 'The consciousness of man *in action* is non-reflective consciousness,' says Sartre (*BN* 74). But when there is a check, reverse, defeat, loss, I am led to ask about myself in relation to the things I engage in, as well as in relation to my past and future. In short, I then ask about the meaning of my life and raise the ethical question.

Anguish, forlornness, and despair are reflective emotions, which is not to say that they constitute idle brooding, the sort of thing which some unhappy temperaments, and the very young and the very old, are prone to. It is just that they, unlike ordinary emotions, do not have specific objects. Anger, for example, is anger at a someone for what he has done or has failed to do. Fear is fear of a particular danger. But anguish is not to be perturbed about anything in particular; to feel forlorn or abandoned is not to feel a particular loss; to feel despair is not just to feel the dashing of a particular hope. In them the whole world, and our own role in it, is put into question.

Anguish, which can also be called dread or anxiety, reveals to me that what I do is ultimately without any objective justification, that it is only I 'by whom values exist' (*BN* 76). It surges forth at moments when I disengage myself from the routine of my world. I then seek the ultimate reasons for my actions. But in the end I always confront the fact of my bare existence and the brute necessity to make decisions and to act without being given unequivocal pointers. What is around me does not offer me guidance or comfort. In fact, says Sartre, the world in itself is sinister. What happens may always defy any rational expectations. The belief in the regularity and intelligibility of nature or of human conduct is mere complacency. Some morning, when I open my mouth in front of the bathroom mirror, I might find that my tongue has turned into a centipede. In anguish I realize how easy it is for things of this sort to happen. The morning news may be that a plane carrying 250 holiday bound passengers has been shot down because of a mix-up in communications. Things and events do not obligingly adjust themselves to our powers of understanding.

Further, I am anguished because I am aware of my total responsibility in total solitude. I can rely on nothing and no one, but there is no getting away from the fact that others may hold me accountable. As we have said earlier, according to Sartre, in making a choice, I also choose for all others. My choices are implicitly universal; when I commit myself to something, I am 'thereby at the same time a legislator deciding for the whole of mankind'. I must always ask myself, 'What would happen if everyone did so?'

> I cannot escape from that disturbing thought except by a kind of self-deception. The man who lies in self-excuse, by saying 'Everyone will not do it' must be ill at ease in his conscience, for the act of lying implies the universal value which it denies. (*EH* 31)

All this sounds very Kantian indeed. However, when Kant spoke of how I must ask whether or not the maxim of my contemplated action can become a universal law, he was really telling me how to try to escape anguish. For all he meant by universalizability was logical self-consistency. The curious upshot of it all was, therefore, that, so long as I avoid doing what is not self-consistent, I am right, I have not gone against duty, and I am not to be blamed. For Sartre, on the other hand, whether or not a personal policy of mine is capable of becoming universal is a matter of my willingness or unwillingness to condone the idea that everyone adopts that policy. Condemning an action morally is not the result of going through a logical exercise. It is to express one's refusal and one's abhorrence. For Sartre, the question of whether what I am about to do is a morally right thing to do is not a question of whether or not it is logically conceivable that everyone might act in that way. It is a question of whether or not what I am about to do is the sort of thing I would be willing to live with if everyone were to do it. Thinking of my action as being universally adopted is the very same thing as anguish.

I am anguished because I must myself determine what in particular and concrete terms my universal responsibility really encompasses. To use an example from the *Cahiers*, a moral problem is not: ought one to rescue a drowning child? That is ridiculous. A moral problem is always individual and concrete, such as Luther's when he asked ought he or ought he not to abandon the peasants in their fight (*CM* 24). The fact that I can make an impact on the course of certain events need not be accompanied by a mandate to influence them in this direction or that. As a moral agent I am not duly elected, or appointed, or sworn in to perform a particular mission. I must choose my own calling. Hence my total responsibility is responsibility in total solitude.

Anguish is, finally, my awareness of the fragility of my choice. I am anguished because I know that I might always change my mind, that I might let myself and others down. It is the feeling of the reformed gambler who approaches the gambling table and feels his resolve melt away. Anguish is fear of what I myself might do. It is not a fear of what might happen, but of the abyss of what I may do or consent to. It is like vertigo. That feeling is not the fear of the yawning depth, but the fear that I might throw myself into it. Having made what I believe is the right choice, I also know that I may slide back, that I may always doubt, hesitate, ask too much, and destroy my own resolve.

My forlornness is, first, the awareness that there is no God on whom I can depend (*EH* 32). There is no omnipotent and benevolent being who guarantees that there will be cosmic justice and that the good will eventually triumph. Kant, as we have seen, found it necessary to postulate the existence of God. He could not tolerate the thought that there is no final justice and that virtue's labour may be forever lost. Sartre's attitude towards God was ambivalent, if not outright inconsistent. In a sense, he agreed with Kant that God's existence would be of tremendous moment. If God existed, there would be a basis for ultimate hope. He did not believe, as Mill did, in a purely secular morality of objective norms. For Sartre, if God does not exist, morality will lack all objective foundation. In *Existentialism* Sartre said:

The existentialist . . . finds it extremely embarrassing that God does not exist . . . Dostoevsky once wrote 'If God did not exist, everything would be permitted'; and that, for existentialism, is the starting point.

Everything is indeed permitted if God does not exist, and man is in consequence forlorn, for he cannot find anything to depend upon either within or outside himself. (*EH* 33–4)

But in the same lecture Sartre said also:

Existentialism is not atheist in the sense that it would exhaust itself in demonstrations of the non-existence of God. It declares, rather, that even if God existed that would make no difference from its point of view. . . . The real problem is not that of His existence; what man needs is to find himself again and to understand that nothing can save him from himself, not even a valid proof of the existence of God. (*EH* 56)

Six or so years earlier, in *The War Diaries*, Sartre had penned the same thought:

human reality is obliged to account only to itself for its morality. Dostoevsky used to write: 'If God does not not exist, all is permitted.' That's the great error of transcendence. Whether God exists or does not exist, morality is an affair 'between men' and God has no right to poke his nose in.[1]

Just the same, in *Being and Nothingness* he offers an abstract and rather obscure argument against God as a necessary being, a being who is 'its own foundation'. The gist of it, I believe, is this. God, it is assumed, is a conscious being. Now, since He is also His own foundation, He could 'not suffer the slightest discrepancy between what [He] is and what [He] conceives' to be possible for Himself to be (*BN* 127). God would perfectly coincide with what He perceives as His possibilities. He could not even think of what He *is* not. But the very nature of all consciousness is going beyond itself. No conscious being can coincide with itself; every conscious being also thinks of what he *is not* but *can* be. Consequently, 'In a word, God, if he exists, is contingent' (*BN* 129). But, less formidably, we can think of Sartre as arguing like this. The premiss is that, if there is a God, He would

---

[1] J.-P. Sartre, *The War Diaries*, trans. Q. Hoare (New York, 1984), 108. I believe that Sartre had in mind the following passages from Fyodor Dostoevsky, *The Brothers Karamazov*, trans. C. Garnett (New York, 1950):

if you were to destroy in mankind the belief in immortality [and God] . . . nothing then would be immoral, everything would be lawful, even cannibalism. . . . crime must [then] not only be permitted, but even recognized as the inevitable and the most rational outcome . . . for every infidel. (78–9) . . . For if there's no everlasting God, there's no such thing as virtue, and there's no need of it. (768)

be benevolent and omnipotent. Sartre did not contemplate the possibility of an irrational and unfathomable God. Consequently, if God did exist, we would not be forlorn. There would then be an omnipotent being looking out for us. At the same time, our candid experience tells us that we *are* forlorn. Therefore, in honesty, we must conclude that there is no God.

Someone may say that, even if a benevolent God does not exist, we are not forlorn because we have our emotions to rely on. We have seen that both Mill and Kant rejected the notion that the emotions can give us guidance. For both of them, the emotions have no cognitive power. While Mill allotted to them (or to some of them, if properly schooled) a role as incentives of morally right conduct, Kant thought that they were too fickle to serve even in that capacity. Sartre's misgivings concerning the emotions go even beyond Kant's. According to him, emotions sever us from reality. They transport us into the world of mere wish-fulfilment (*TE* 63). As a kind of soporific or hallucinogen, an emotion may, at least for a time, dissipate our anguish, forlornness, and despair. But it can never give us our realistic bearings. Reliance on an emotion is always reliance on 'magic' and constitutes a loss of reality (*TE* 63, 81).

What are Sartre's reasons for this seemingly rather eccentric view? First, he maintains that we cannot know what and how strong our emotions are until we have acted on them. The criterion of the genuiness of our feelings, not just for others but for ourselves as well, is our conduct. The emotions are not introspective episodes whose nature can be used as a test for the rightness or wrongness of conduct, for the touchstone of the strength and direction of an emotion is what we do (*EH* 37). Suppose that you are a young man attracted to two women between whom you must decide. You say to yourself, 'I'll choose the one I really love.' Have you then solved your problem? Not by a long shot! The trouble is that your emotions do not possess a reality ahead of your intentions and actions. Feelings of emotion are not data which we observe and collect and then use as evidence for deciding how we should act.

Second, for Sartre, feelings of emotion, instead of providing evidence for how we should choose, are themselves chosen. Part of what he means by this is that I undergo an emotion only because I have made a *prior* choice, I have already assessed something as being good or bad. I am therefore responsible for my passion (*EH* 34). A lion is coming at me through the bush. I am frightened only because I have already judged—no doubt in a flash—that the situation is dangerous. It is not that my fear *tells* me that the situation is dangerous. An emotion comes *after* I have made my judgement concerning the desirable and the undesirable. We can understand a person's reaction as an emotional reaction—as opposed to mere instinctive movements away from or towards something—only if we know the choice which he has already made.

We shall see eventually that there is enough reason to challenge such a view. Which comes first, the choice which posits, out of the blue, a value, or an emotion which is itself a judgement of value? Sartre never addressed himself explicitly to this issue. A passage in *Being and Nothingness* leaves us up in the air. In it he asks us to consider the case of my being offered a niggardly wage:

> If I accept a niggardly salary it is doubtless because of fear . . . of dying of starvation . . . and this fear is understood in turn only in relation to the *value which I* implicitly give to [my] life; that is, it is referred to that hierarchical system of ideal objects which are values. (*BN* 564)

I believe that a lot turns on the word 'implicitly' in that passage. Is the value of my life implicit in my fear, or is my fear implicit in the (already posited) value of my life? I shall eventually argue that the truth is the former.

There is another point in Sartre's theory concerning the role of emotions in relation to action. I shall, eventually, challenge it also. Sartre argues that an emotion cannot be my guide, not only because it itself is chosen in the sense that it comes in the wake of a prior choice of an end, but because it is a kind of chosen means to cope with a situation in which it is beyond us to employ rational and efficient means:

> consciousness can 'be-in-the-world' in two different ways. The world may appear before it as an organized complex of utilizable things, such that, if one wants to produce a predetermined effect, one must act upon the determinate elements of that complex . . . [Or it] tries . . . to modify these objects at no distance and with no means, by some absolute, massive modification of the world [into] . . . the *magical* world. Emotion can be called a sudden fall of consciousness into magic:

or, if you will, emotion arises when the world of the utililizable
vanishes abruptly and the world of magic appears in its place. (*TE* 90–1)

I see a lion in the bush and I faint from fear. That, of course, lacks
pragmatic value. At the same time, in a fashion, I *have* dealt with
the situation. I have taken 'magic action'. I have banned the
whole gruesome scenario. Sartre's view is that emotional agitations are always instances of bad faith. An emotion is just a
phoney substitute for the steps, often arduous, that are necessary for the realization of a goal. I feel an emotion when the
situation which, in part anyhow, I myself have created, proves
too much. The felt emotion is a magic escape from a situation
and what it would take to face it. It therefore constitutes no
excuse. We are not victims of our emotions; in their grip we are
not innocent sufferers.

An emotion is not a real solution, even if it is a solution really
believed in. If I faint from fear, I act on myself rather than my
environment. But, I myself do not look at it in that way. Others
can say, 'He fainted in order not to have to face the danger.' But I
cannot say, 'I shall faint in order not to have to face the danger.'
Or, while others can say, 'He flew into a rage because she was
getting the better of him in the argument,' I cannot say, 'I shall
fly into a rage so that she will not get the better of me in the
argument.' I could say such things only if my terror and my rage
were feigned. As I become self-consciously aware of my emotions, their spell is broken. A genuine emotion involves genuine
belief of having been carried or swept away. But, in truth, I bring
an emotion upon myself in order to escape responsibility and the
rigours of effective action. In feeling it I am therefore in bad
faith. Magic is a form of deception. Emotions are magic and
deception perpetrated on ourselves.

But can I not rely on the advice of my fellow men and
therefore not be forlorn? Here we are on the ground already
covered in our discussion of Mill's theory of qualified judges.
Sartre claims that there is no such thing as genuine advice, that
is, a definitive answer that someone else can give to my pressing
question, 'Well, what shall I do?' For we decide whose advice to
seek on the basis of our expectations concerning what his advice
will be (*EH* 137). Suppose a woman at a crossroads of her life has
to choose between her marriage and her career. Chances are that

she knows that, if she asks her mother—an unliberated woman —she will hear that marriage and children are the most reward- ing things in a woman's life. Were she to listen to her father—a free spirit—she knows that she will be told that she has a lot going for her and that she should take her chances in the world. Whichever way she turns, she will still feel forlorn. When we seek advice, the die is already cast (*EH* 37). For the opinions of others are just so many facts for me. I can always ignore them. Because of a judgement of others, I may feel shame. But I know that I can always shake it off, that I can always say to myself that I have been misunderstood. For others I am an object seen from their perspective, but I can never assume their perspective regarding myself. Seeking advice is a paradox. When I ask for advice, I am determined to remain free either to follow or not to follow the advice I shall receive. But, in the agony of my heart, I also want to be influenced by the advice I get so that it can serve as a justification of what I shall do. In that case, I seek to rid myself of or lighten the burden of my own responsibility. Asking for advice is really a ruse. In discussing Mill's theory of the qualified judges we said that, when we go to someone for advice, we do not necessarily go to someone who on the basis of some objective criteria is the most knowledgeable and wise. When seeking advice, we seek comfort, a bond, complicity.

Giving advice is equally paradoxical and disingenuous. I wish that the person advised would follow my advice but do so *freely* so that, if he does what I advise him to do, it would still be *his* decision. So I both do and do not wish my advice to be heeded. In order to give advice to someone, I must size him up. I have to ascertain that, being what he is, and his circumstances being where they are, doing such and such constitutes for him the right thing to do whether or not he himself can see it. But then I shall be denying him his freedom, taking the responsibility that belongs to him upon myself. So, in order to avoid this, I become of two minds—I wish my advice to make a real difference to him without really affecting him.

Despair, or lack of hope, is first of all the realization that what will happen as the consequence of my actions is uncertain (*EH* 39). The attainment of my goals is dependent on factors beyond my control. In every situation there is an element of ineliminable risk. I sent an important secret message by radio. How can I be certain that the enemy will not intercept it? Or, I have a serious illness. They give me a drug. It has worked in many cases. But will it work in mine? Planting crops is a gamble, as any farmer will tell you. In whatever I do, there has to be a synthesis of two orders—my freedom and the world—but I am never assured of this synthesis.

For Kant, we are free to engage in ultimate hope. For Sartre, it comes from shutting our eyes. In the midst of our frustrations we may make ourselves believe that there are powers which will make things turn out better than our own efforts warrant. Hope is nothing but an evasion of the terrifying truth that, when things go wrong, there is nothing else to do but to pick up the pieces. Reliance on God and Providence is a self-induced illusion. The same is true, in Sartre's view, of our reliance on our fellow beings. We cannot expect them to do what we have failed to do. To an extent it is in my power to ensure the co-operation of others. But what another person will do, just as what course nature will take, is, in the end, a matter of mere probabilities. On the other hand, there are situations in which nothing short of certainty will do. Perhaps not so much when I have everything to gain, but, when I have everything to lose, absolute assurance is the only thing that would put me at ease. Despair is the realization that I cannot always hedge my bets. It is also the realization that, while relying on others is risky, it is often necessary. Without counting on the loyalty of others, nothing gets done—on the battlefield, in industry, even in the family.

Sartre argues that despair does not lead to paralysis. Despair may be a source of strength; it may give us courage. It is the placidity of hope instead that will lead to inaction and resignation. Quietism is the attitude that others, or God, will do what I have left undone. Existentialism, to the contrary, is activism. It only denies us our illusions. There is no need to hope in order to venture, nor to succeed in order to persevere.

18

Sartre on the Emotions

ANGUISH, forlornness, and despair would disappear if there were objective knowledge of what is ultimately right, and we were always to do it. The emotions hold such a dual promise. If the emotions were the cognitive ground of morality, two birds would be killed by the same stone. Our knowledge of what is right would then also be our power to adhere to it. Mill, Kant, Sartre—all of them—have, however, denied us such a blessing. Mill and Kant did so because of their mistaken notion that emotions are just blind feelings; nothing is revealed to us through them. But why did Sartre? There are things that Sartre himself says about the emotions which make his dismissal of them quite surprising. All forms of consciousness, Sartre says over and over again, are directed at objects. Emotions are no exceptions. According to Sartre, emotions are not mere blind commotions. They are, he says, always forms of awareness of something, just as our thoughts and beliefs are (e.g. *TE* 56–7). Only if I idly reflect on my emotion can I separate it from what it is about and view it as it is in itself, as an inner perturbation exhausting itself in its own immanence. An emotion, normally, takes me beyond itself. It, just as sense perception, is 'consciousness *of* the world' (*TE* 56).

So, proceeding from his own premises, we are tempted to disagree with Sartre and maintain that the emotions are cognitive, that they can tell us, objectively, what is right and what is wrong. To apprehend the world emotionally is to see things and events as propitious or threatening, as pleasing or deplorable, and so on. It would seem that the emotions disclose reasons for actions. For example, in fear we apprehend something as to be avoided or fled from. My fear does not necessarily *make* me flee as a loud bang may *make* me take to my heels or a hideous roar may *make* me stand rooted on the spot. Within certain limits of its intensity anyhow, my fear presents considerations for acting.

I can neglect or ignore what it tells me or let it be outbalanced by what other modes of my consciousness present to me. But it is one of the sources that may lead to my intelligent decision.

Sartre, however, disagrees. When we say that a piece of behaviour was done for a reason, we mean that it was voluntary. According to Sartre, on the other hand, emotional behaviour, unless it is feigned, is involuntary (*TE* 75). But we must make a distinction. In some cases Sartre's claim is plausible enough. In the throes of overwhelming passion such as rage, it may indeed be true that we cannot help what we do. We foam at the mouth and strike out. In the case of some emotions, or some emotions in a certain degree of intensity, the intelligent choice becomes impossible. In rage we may just blush and shout. Sexual passion causes flushes and palpitations. Intense fear makes us tremble or faint. But even in those cases we do not look at emotional behaviour as just stemming from glandular secretions. It is characteristically true of the emotions that beliefs, memories, expectations, and so on are present in them. So why should we deny that emotional behaviour is intelligent behaviour?

In an emotion, Sartre maintains, however, 'consciousness transforms itself in order to transform the object' (*TE* 63). In fear, as we saw earlier, according to him, my behaviour becomes 'magical'; by fainting, for example, I 'obliterate' the feared object. In joy, as I break out into dancing and singing, my behaviour becomes 'symbolic', a magic 'incantation' (*TE* 72). In an emotion, says Sartre,

consciousness is caught in its own snare. Precisely because it is living in the new aspect of the world by *believing in* it, the consciousness is captured by its own belief, exactly as it is in dreams and hysteria. . . . We have to speak of a world of emotion as one speaks of a world of dreams or of worlds of madness. (*TE* 80–1)

Now, an emotion would indeed be incapable of giving guidance for action if it were, as Mill and Kant thought, a pure internally felt turmoil, having a causal impact on our actions, to be sure, but signifying nothing. For Sartre, an emotion cannot give guidance for action for the opposite reason: it is, as it were, over-sophisticated—a contrived excuse for lapsing into inaction, for taking inappropriate action, and for disclaiming responsibility. Sartre conceives an emotion to be a kind of self-induced temporary insanity. He wants us to believe that in all our emotions we create in ourselves a delusion in order not to have to confront a difficult situation through intelligent and volitional means. This, just as Mill's psychological hedonism, or Kant's rationalism, is an over-simplification. Again, too sweeping a claim is made and important distinctions are blurred. Rage, terror, and the like indeed may come over us like torrents, possess us, and may prompt actions which are ineffectual, disastrous, even criminal. These agitations occur when something is too much for us to handle. Emotional agitations are similar to being blinded by a too sudden and strong light, or to being deafened by a loud noise. Normally, however, our eyes and ears supply perceptions, that is, constitute sources of input which the rest of our organism can process and utilize in arriving at a controlled response. When the intensity of the input goes beyond the threshold, the sensory system is no longer able to cope with it, and the result is confusion. Similarly, there are emotional agitations which constitute a disruption of normal purposeful and organized behaviour. It is true, we must concede to Sartre, that even in such cases the manifested behaviour may still be 'chosen' in the sense of still being capable of being interpreted and understood in terms of some remote or, as it were, subterranean intentions, wishes, and the like. But the breakdown of, say, our visual apparatus can sometimes also be interpreted in these terms. May I not sometimes, to suit myself, see what is not really out there? I may, for example, take a face of a stranger in a crowd to be the face of a long lost friend.

On the other side of the issue, to say, as Sartre does (e.g. *EH* 34), that, although our emotions and the resultant behaviour are involuntary, we are always responsible for them, and that therefore they never constitute excuses, is odd. For, to take again the example of fear, to say that a person's intense fear and his consequent fainting were chosen, and to hold him responsible for them, is appropriate only when he is the kind of person who seeks to avoid all danger, even at the cost of great detriment to others or to the things he himself believes in; in other words, only if he is a coward. A person who faints from fear is blamable only if we can attribute it to a character flaw. But if his fear and resultant fainting is due to excessive stress, we do not blame him.

Sartre holds, paradoxically, that all our emotional behaviour is involuntary, but that we nevertheless are responsible for it. The more balanced view is that some such behaviour is involuntary and some voluntary and that we are responsible only for the latter. In a wide variety of cases, emotional behaviour, just as our behaviour guided by sense perceptions, memory, computations, and so on, is plainly voluntary and needs no special interpretation. Why, we must ask Sartre, cannot the emotions enable us to respond to the world through effective voluntary actions? Running away from a lion whom one encounters unexpectedly or shooting it may be prompted by fear just as much as remaining rooted on the spot and fainting might be. The latter are just symptoms of fear—not essentially different from, say, a heightened pulse rate or epinephrine flow. But if, due to our fear, we take to our heels or shoot, the situation is very different. Those pieces of behaviour may not be as deliberate as they would be if I had used, say, game theory, but in performing them I am still in control and performing with intelligence and purpose.

Sartre denies this. But his interpretation of flight as 'magical' behaviour is quite forced and arbitrary:

Flight, in active fear, is mistakenly supposed to be rational behaviour. It is thought to contain calculation—admittedly brief—by the subject who wants to put the greatest possible distance between the danger and himself. But that is a misunderstanding of this behaviour, which would reduce it to prudence. We do not take flight to reach shelter: we flee because we are unable to annihilate ourselves in unconsciousness. Flight is fainting away in action; it is magical behaviour which negates the dangerous object with one's whole body . . . (*TE* 67)

It would be an extreme form of rationalism to maintain that we always orient ourselves more appropriately in the world without the emotions. One might say, even if the snake is terribly poisonous and is about to strike, why *should* one be afraid, when it would be better coolly to shoot off its head? The answer is that it may just be our fear that will provide the needed impulse to get off the shot. It is true that an emotion may also slow us down or even incapacitate us altogether. But whether it does or not all depends on the kind of emotion one is having and the degree of its intensity.

Of course *one* point in favour of the emotions, why we should not want to do without them, is that lacking them our lives would be rather colourless. From that point of view, not ever to feel pity, regret, remorse, anger as well as joy, gratitude, and the like is clearly a human limitation. But the lack of emotions is a limitation not only of our sensibilities, but also of our sense. It is not just that, without emotions, we should be dull; we should also be stupid. The poverty of our emotions does not just limit our enjoyments and sufferings; it is also, like the dullness of the senses, a cognitive failing.

For Sartre, an emotion has the same structure and aim as what he calls 'bad faith' or self-deception. In both instances, the mind blinds itself, it falls away from reality, it makes a captive of itself. He likens both of them to falling asleep and dreaming (*TE* 78). One of the aims of bad faith is to escape responsibility. Similarly, says Sartre, an 'emotional crisis' may be 'an abandonment of responsibility, by means of a magical exaggeration of the difficulty of the world' (*TE* 70). In feeling an emotion I make myself a captive of the situation, a victim. I picture myself as 'passionate', as one who suffers and is carried away. It is all a kind of make-believe.

On the other hand, in *Being and Nothingness* Sartre himself says that not all emotionality is in bad faith. For example, he says that, while pride is bad faith, arrogance is not. This is so because in pride I am concerned with how *others* think of me; pride is just the other side of shame. But in arrogance I set my own standards and it is hence an 'affirmation of my freedom' (*BN* 386). As a matter of fact, according to Sartre, it is not the emotions themselves that constitute bad faith, but a certain way of looking at them. Emotions are bad faith only if combined with what he calls 'impure reflection', which produces the idea that our emotions constitute a psyche, that is, a mental self as a more or less fixed object (*BN* 223). In truth, our emotions are not mental entities, but ways of apprehending the world. They constitute forms of escape and provide false excuses only when they are dwelled on in their immanence and looked upon as constituting an inert spurious substance. In fact, what Sartre said about Maggie Tulliver in George Eliot's *The Mill on the Floss* and Sanseverina in Stendhal's *Chartreuse de Parme* clearly implies that to live by one's emotions may be a life in good faith, a life of courageous self-acceptance and purity of heart (*EH* 53).

Any emotion, just as any belief, we should say, can be either in good or in bad faith. It is in good faith if we are willing to draw the consequences in action. There are some emotions which tend to divorce themselves from all action and to demand no commitment or sacrifice. Pride and shame, for example, may easily be nothing more than idly wallowing either in one's glory or in one's guilt and involve no intentions and no resolves. But the emotions may also be motives and disclose reasons for action.

19

Emotions as Judgements

LET us take a somewhat more systematic look at the emotions and the possibility that they constitute the cognitive as well as motivational foundation of ethics. The problem of moral knowledge is that, if there is such knowledge, it must be practical—capable of determining not only our intellect but also our will. It must have a direct bearing on our conduct. Moral knowledge, if it exists, must be not only an insight but also a moving force. Therefore, it appears that it must be intimately bound up with the emotions. But can emotions constitute cognitions? There is ample reason for trying to come up with an affirmative answer. For, if we are successful, we should be able to avoid the impasse of both Mill's and Kant's intellectualism. Moreover, we should then also be able to avoid Sartre's position, unpalatable to many, that our decisions, commitments, and actions have, ultimately, nothing objective to guide them. But the reader must be warned that there will be a let-down. A good case can indeed be made that the emotions are not blind, that in them values are revealed. But such values are not ethical, that is, ultimate values. The conclusion we shall eventually have to draw is that, although Sartre's view of the emotions is lopsided, his overall position will have to stand—there is no objective cognitive foundation of ethics, not even in the emotions.

Let us clarify the idea that moral knowledge must be practical knowledge. It is a logical point. My realization that I ought to pay my gambling debts, say, may be causally connected with all sorts of behaviour of mine. It may cause me to beat my children. Or it may make me grow morose and listless to the point that I stop doing anything. The thought that I ought to do a certain thing may even be exactly what makes me *not* do it. Nevertheless, while my knowledge that I ought to go into the jungle to help eradicate leprosy may cause me to go camping in Saskatchewan, it is only by going where the lepers are and working with them that I would be exercising that knowledge. Cognitive certainty in ethics is certainty concerning what to do. To know the good is to have made up one's mind. Whenever someone tells us that he knows he ought to do such and such, and then does not do it, he owes us an explanation or an excuse.

Moral knowledge, if it exists, must constitute an incentive. The emotions patently do possess the power to move us to action, but do they also possess cognitive power? Perhaps we can settle the matter by considering to what extent there is an analogy between feelings of emotion and sense perceptions. In other words, let us consider the hypothesis that, while through sense experiences we may become cognizant of facts, through emotions we may become cognizant of values.

When I say that I see that this table is brown, I do not describe my visual experience. I attribute a property to an object. Similarly, when I say that I despise Jones, I do not make a report on my feelings. I make a judgement about Jones's behaviour. The claim that emotions are judgements has perhaps an odd ring. Judging, we are accustomed to think, is the prerogative of the intellect. Actually, judging is not the function of any one mental faculty. Seeing, hearing, smelling, touching, and tasting may be mere experiences complete in themselves, mere sensations with their own feel. As such, they exhaust themselves in their own immanence and point to nothing beyond. But they can also amount to judgements and lead to beliefs. Similarly, our emotions may be just experiences lived through with their own feeling tone. But they may also amount to judgements that lead to the formulation of intentions and the performance of actions. The emotions are not, so to speak, epiphenomenal vibrations set off by our intellectual judgements of good and evil; they do not just provide the thrills in our lives but mean nothing. Experiences, emotional or otherwise, amount to judgements when in them we aim to answer a question; and the questions which confront us concern either what is the case or what to do. In the former event, in the end, I rely on my sense perceptions in order to reach a state of factual belief. In the latter, I rely on my emotions in order to reach a state of volition.

There might appear to be a hitch. Judgements of fact, and beliefs that something is the case, are either true or false. We judge correctly and the resulting belief is true if what we judge and believe to be so really is so. Emotions and intentions, on the other hand, seem to be capable of neither truth nor falsity, but only truthfulness or insincerity. In other words, they seem to be purely subjective. If I say 'I despise Jones' and have no appropriate feelings and do not behave appropriately, I have been insincere. But, besides the sincerity of an emotion, there is also the question of whether it is right or wrong, appropriate or inappropriate. For example, when I despise Jones quite sincerely, there is the question of whether my despising him is justified. What does this question come to?

When I pass a factual judgement, the facts may or may not bear me out—and this is the whole question. This is not so in the case of an emotion. Of course, what the facts are is relevant. Suppose I honestly despise Jones, but it turns out that Jones did not really tell what I took to be a selfish lie. Or your aunt dies. I express to you my sympathy. But you tell me gleefully that she left you a fortune. However, in cases such as these, the emotion itself was not a mistake, it was *based* on a mistake, a mistake in belief. Is this the only way in which our emotions can go wrong? Can the emotions themselves and not just the factual judgements which they presuppose be mistaken? Well, our emotions may be disproportionate. Suppose I, after having sighted common house spiders in the basement, am too frightened to go down there again. This seems to be a cause of a mistaken emotion. It posits a danger which really does not exist. So we may wish to say that, just as factual judgements are mistaken when they are not borne out by facts, emotions are mistaken when they are not borne out by values.

But how do we determine whether or not our emotions are borne out by, fit, or are proportional to, values? Well, how do we determine whether or not our perceptual judgements fit facts? Not all sense perceptions are veridical. But we can, as a rule, single out the ones that are. It is widely held, for example, that, when two people are asked to judge the colour of an object, then, if neither of them is colour blind, wears coloured glasses, suffers from jaundice, is viewing the object under a coloured light, and so on, they must agree. If they do not, their disagreement must be merely a verbal one. In other words, one often holds that, when there are no interfering factors present, our sense perceptions are veridical. On the other hand, it is also frequently supposed that this is not so with regard to our emotions. With regard to them, there is a tendency to believe that meaningful disagreement may always persist.

But what is it to say that with regard to, say, colour, the disagreement, if it persists beyond a certain point, *must* be merely verbal? Is it not just that, in most instances, after an effort has been made to eliminate the interfering factors, we simply *will* agree. If we still do not, then we *decide* that communication has broken down. Is not the situation at least sometimes the same when it comes to emotions and values? For example, is it so erratic how people feel about throwing an unwanted baby into a well? If someone said that the idea of doing such a thing delights him, we would not quite know what to make of it. It is perhaps true that, with regard to such things as colour, the point at which we would decide that we have ceased to communicate would be reached rather quickly while with regard to values the situation is more complicated and stubborn. But even with colours there is no absolute point at which the decision that the limits of meaningful disagreement have been exceeded follows with logical necessity. What *is* the colour of the sun at sunset? When we do stop looking for further possible interfering factors and declare that the disagreement with regard to qualities perceived through the sense is merely verbal, then it is because we no longer know, or do not care, what further checks to perform. Of course, the example of colour is a rather artificial one. We are not asked to identify through our sense of sight only colours and such but also physical objects, plants, animals, people, anatomical tissues, wines and foods, faces and voices, musical chords, works of art and their authors or dates, and so on and so forth. In general, it is not at all clear at what point in making sensory discriminations we must say that two people who, on the face of it, disagree are merely embroiled in a verbal confusion. It may be that one of the parties has reached a higher level of discernment.

From all this no one would wish to infer that the distinction between correctness and incorrectness has no application to knowledge claims based on sense experience. It is just that the distinction cannot be specified once and for all. All we can do in order to reach objectivity is try to purify the subjectivity of the perceiver from noxious influences. We cannot say with complete assurance and at all times what such influences might be. There are many obvious precautions to take, but beyond that, no necessary and sufficient conditions can be stated for being in a good condition or position to perceive something through our senses. Still, we believe that respectable degrees of veridicalness or objectivity in our sense perceptions are achievable.

If we realize that there are no ironclad conditions which a perceptual act of the senses must satisfy before we grant that it is objectively correct, it appears no longer so implausible that degrees of objectivity can be reached also in our emotions as they disclose values. Perhaps too often, when the emotive reactions of two people differ, we hastily conclude that one has reached a dead end. Reaching agreement in our emotions seems indeed to be a much more involved and hazardous matter than reaching agreement in our sense perceptions. But it does not follow that the emotions do not ever allow a degree of objectivity.

The reliability of sense perceptions may be impaired by the condition of the perceiver and by his relation to the object perceived. If sight is to be reliable, the eye must be normal, and perhaps trained, and the object must stand in plain sight and be sufficiently illuminated. With regard to the emotions, the situation is broadly analogous. A person's own condition and his relation to the matter at hand can adversely affect the reliability of his feelings. A person's emotions may mislead him when he possesses some character defect, is prejudiced, or is under stress. His emotions may also be impaired when he is not conversant or familiar with the situation at hand. He may lack the sorts of intimacy and contact with the objects of his emotions which may come through work, through enjoyments and sufferings, through acting in social contexts, creating and enjoying art, playing games, and so forth.

Just the same, things that impair our emotions may be chronic, stem from our whole life history and the social conditions under which we happen to live. I cannot rid myself of them in the same way in which I can get rid of my bad vision by buying a pair of glasses. The upshot of our critique of Mill's theory of the qualified judges was that the ranking of our emotional preferences must be, in the end, subjective.

Perhaps the greatest and the most ineradicable obstacle to our emotions providing a cognitive ground for ethics is self-deception. We do not have to agree with Sartre that all our emotions are 'degraded' or 'debased' forms of consciousness (*TE* 78, 85). Still, they may easily be manifestations of such things as haste, laziness, vanity, and cowardice and hence forms of bad faith. For example, I have been working hard but am still getting bad grades. My vanity may then turn into hatred towards all intellectual pursuits. I may sneer at such things as academic degrees and honours without realizing that it is a case of sour grapes.

We argued that the emotions need not constitute a magic escape from reality as Sartre would have it. They can constitute judgements of value. We also argued that such emotional judgements of value need not be just clouds of subjectivity. As judgements of value, emotions can serve as reliable guides for right action *if* they are in order. However, it may be extremely difficult, nay impossible, to put our emotional life in order. Moreover, the kinds of feelings which may be deemed to have relevance for ethical, that is, ultimate, values seem to be constitutionally wayward. Feelings like mercy, compassion, devotion, forgiveness, loyalty, and self-sacrifice lack proper limits. They are like love. The object of that feeling, says Sartre, echoing Kant, is transformed. When I love someone, I judge him lovable. But that is a mere projection of my love. What can I possibly say to a person who dearly loves his cat although the creature is mean, is liable to scratch out your eyes, and has mange? Or if I feel that nothing whatever can harm me because my God is a 'mighty fortress', who could challenge me? Or who could challenge my feeling that I either am or am not ready for my grave? There are feelings inspired just by the sight of the tufted mountains illuminated by the eastern sky; there is the feeling that one has found and done due homage to the little and forgotten places. I may love the little stars for the sunset may be for me God's call to them, who each answer 'Here I am'. The varieties and objects of love are totally free and capricious. This is also true of many other emotions, especially when they reach the deeper layers of our lives. Emotions may be feelings of immense calm, of immeasurable confidence, of unspeakable tenderness, as well as of bottomless despair. They may be prompted by who knows what. A deep emotion cannot be deemed either proportionate or disproportionate with regard to its object.

We have considered the idea that which of our feelings of emotion, just as which of our sense perceptions, are reliable can be gauged by testing how competent and well placed is the perceiver. But from the ethical, that is ultimate, point of view, there are no criteria of emotional competence. Now, as we proceed with our comparison, competence is not the only criterion of the veridicalness of sense perceptions. We also insist on the agreement of our perceptual claims with other such claims. Empirical knowledge is system-building. What we take to be so on the basis of a sense perception may be challenged if it does not agree—across theory—with other deliverances of our senses. In other words, the second criterion of the veridicalness of our sense perceptions is coherence.

Is there anything similar to systematic coherence with regard to the emotions? Here even more severe doubts arise concerning the possibility of gaining moral knowledge from the emotions. They concern the place of generalizations in ethics. We pointed out earlier that asking, *à la* Kant, whether or not the agent's subjective principle or maxim can be adopted by everyone is inadequate to provide a basis for ethics. This is so for the same reason that universalizability, by itself, cannot generate science. For this requirement amounts to nothing more than that words are to be used consistently. If two things are qualitatively the same, then, if one of them has a certain property, then the other must have it also. If a given compound is soluble in water, then any exactly similar compound must be soluble in water also. But this does not tell us which compounds *are* soluble in water. The logical requirement that predicates have to be applied across the board has its place in science only because in science it operates together with substantive generalizations gained from observation and experiment. But this method, we have already seen, is of no avail in ethics. Observation and experiment can yield only descriptive laws, while the relevant generalizations in ethics would have to be normative. With regard to the latter, one instance of conformity to them is as decisive in giving credence to them as any number of such instances are.

I do seek order and consistency in my life. But this order is one that I myself create through my more far-reaching commitments. The only sense in which we can speak of experimental discovery in ethics is that my present choices may make explicit my prior commitments. Seeking to see what I should do in the light of my past, my culture, my involvements with others, and the like, may be looked upon as a kind of experiment. But it is not an experiment the upshot of which is decided by the statistics. In science we speak of discovery since the laws of nature are confirmed or disconfirmed by what in fact happens. But, we have learned from Kant, the normative rules which can be confirmed or disconfirmed by experience can be nothing more than hypothetical imperatives, spelling out the means of realizing aims already decided upon.

Our particular emotive responses do not build up evidence for general judgements of value in the way in which our particular sense perceptions build up evidence for laws of nature. It is possible for me to believe, for example, that all crows are black without being bothered by the fact that it is impossible for me to set my eyes on all the crows that are, have been, and will be. But I cannot be convinced of the inherent worth of all men without experiencing a love or respect encompassing at once all of mankind. The particular instances of love or respect felt for particular humans do not constitute piecemeal evidence for the worth of humanity. In ethics there are no hypotheses.

Particular sense perceptions are related to one another through empirical generalizations. The connection between them is external. But my various feelings of emotion are connected internally. Their relationships to one another are not understood in terms of empirical laws but in terms of the deeper layers of my own subjectivity, in other words, in terms of my own deeper and more basic emotional attitudes. The latter constitute the *meaning* of my particular desires and aversions in a way in which causal laws do not constitute the *meaning* of my particular sense perceptions. In ethics, as opposed to science, the difference between the particular and the universal vanishes. In choosing and urging choices on others, we posit ends of actions. In making a particular choice, I set a precedent or an example. Decisions to act, as we saw earlier, are characteristically decisions to adopt policies of action. But policies of actions are not hypotheses for the rightness of which particular decisions provide cumulative evidence.

For determining facts, there is the criterion of impersonal theory. But when it comes to value, everything depends on and is at the mercy of unaided concrete passions. Systematic coherence is totally irrelevant for judging the reliability of the emotions. All we can rely on here are our deeper feelings, choices, and commitments. But none of them has a natural priority. Compassion and love are sometimes held to be the bedrocks of morality. But such feelings are limitless and they may run into conflict with what is felt to be just and fair. We all feel that justice should be tempered with charity. But the question is, to what extent? Perhaps capital punishment is the case where the attempt to strike the right balance in our emotions most markedly flounders.

20

The Existentialist Ethics

S A R T R E, we must conclude, was right. If a person honestly and in full realization of his situation chooses a life which, according to all accepted notions and sentiments, is a life of moral depravity and turpitude, there is nothing we can do to prove him wrong. If someone does not believe that the sun will rise tomorrow, we can teach him astronomy. But to instruct him in the prevailing values of his society, or even in the time-honoured traditions of human civilization, would not prove to him the moral wrong-ness of his ways. Nor would he have been taught a necessarily good and relevant moral lesson if we point out to him that his feelings and actions are at odds with Mill's Principle of Utility or with Kant's Categorical Imperative. It will be equally futile to remind him of the values which he himself has professed and done homage to in the past. His freedom may make all these things crumble. It is true that I cannot change my past. But my past does not speak to me in and of itself any more than any other facts do. There are times at which things coalesce in such a way that they will have tremendous implications for our future. But these implications often become clear only after we have tried to live with them. This, I believe, is what should be taken to be the upshot of Sartre's analogy between living a life and creating a work of art (*EH* 46). Every new brush stroke has to fit in with what is already there on the canvas, and it also portends what colour, what line, what shape is to be fashioned next. But there are no rules which tell us how to do it right. You might have found your style. Or you might have formed your overall intention of your work—the direction of your artistic search. But unless you have become a mere hack, each work of yours requires new visions and revisions.

For Sartre, ethics—that is, what is ultimately right or wrong in our conduct, and what gives meaning to our lives—is subjec-tive. Now this may be easily confused with radical relativism

—the view that the right way of acting and living depends on the kind of individual one is and the kinds of personal circumstances in which one finds oneself. If you recall what was said in the Introduction, you immediately realize that this is not subjectivism at all, but a degenerate form of objectivism. What that view denies is not the objectivity, but the universality, of ethics. It says that what is morally right or wrong is objective but relative to individuals and their circumstances. It is a view which trivializes human life. It says, in effect, that there is no difference in kind between moral precepts and, for example, a piece of medical advice that, if you have diabetes, you should be on a sugarless diet.

Existentialism is an entirely different view. It denies that what is ultimately right and good, or what makes life worth living and makes it meaningful, is relative. The only thing on which the existentialist agrees with the relativist is that there are no *objective* universal rules. His view is, as we have already seen, subjective universalism. His central thesis is that our subjective choices have a universal import. The rightness of my ultimate choices is not relative to my 'psychological profile'. What matters instead is how I choose to stand in the world. The choices I make are made in view of their universal meaning. We understand and judge what we do, and what others do, because we share in the universal human condition. Nevertheless, the universality of the human condition gives us no answer to the question of what we should do in the concreteness of our individual lives. It merely lends seriousness to that question.

What gives life meaning and makes it worth living? This, we said at the outset, is the ethical question. According to Sartre, there is no answer—at any rate, no answer contained in a formula. There is no such thing as a supreme moral principle or highest intrinsic value which is constitutive of the good life. A value or norm is always an 'individual being', says Sartre. It is the synthesis of an individual's freedom and his concrete situation. Sartre writes: 'whenever a man chooses his purpose and his commitment in all clearness and in all sincerity, whatever that purpose may be it is impossible to prefer another for him' (*EH* 50). It is impossible, objectively, to pass moral judgements on others. All I can do is to condemn an act of another *for my part*. Beyond that, I can also challenge the other person's sincerity, lucidity, consistency, and resoluteness. I can take it upon myself to tell him, 'You are in bad faith, deceiving yourself, trying to have it both ways.' But if he says, 'So what!', all I can do is walk away.

The ethical imperative is simply 'Be honest, be true to yourself, and act for the sake of freedom'. We go wrong morally when we indulge in self-deception or bad faith. Bad faith is a wilful error. In self-deception I am a deceiver who deceives himself. I then take my false motives to be genuine while knowing that they are not. Bad faith is an inconsistency or a lack of lucidity. How can we tell whether someone is in bad faith? There is no litmus test. There are just sundry indications. For example, a man in bad faith self-consciously plays a role. Take Sartre's famous waiter:

His movement is quick and forward, a little too precise, a little too rapid. He comes toward the patrons with a step a little too quick. He bends forward a little too eagerly; his voice, his eyes express an interest a little too solicitous for the order of the customer. Finally there he returns, trying to imitate in his walk the inflexible stiffness of some kind of automaton while carrying his tray with the recklessness of a tight-rope walker by putting it in a perpetually unstable, perpetually broken equilibrium which he perpetually re-establishes by a slight movement of the arm and hand. (*BN* 101)

He is not just doing the job of a waiter, he is playing at being a paragon of a waiter; he is pretending not just to others, but to himself, that he is nothing but a waiter. He knows that he cannot *be* a waiter, 'in the sense that this inkwell *is* an inkwell' (*BN* 102). For, to dramatize a little, he knows that he can always throw the soup into the patron's lap.

So what must the waiter do? What must all the workers, tradesmen, grocers, tailors, auctioneers, do? What must all the students, teachers, professors, researchers, politicians, officials, do? What must, for that matter, all the parents, husbands, wives, relatives, even lovers, do? Must they all revolt, or quit? For on all of them are what Sartre calls 'public demands' to perform a 'ceremony' or to do a 'dance' (*BN* 102). In a way, I think, this *is* what Sartre was proposing. But he also offered, I believe, what may be called a 'consolation of philosophy'. Instead of taking precipitous action, we can, if we are philosophically astute, reach a more lucid attitude towards ourselves. I, as a waiter or whatever, can come to realize that 'I am a waiter [or whatever] in the mode of *being what I am not*' (*BN* 103). Sartre is speaking to us as humans who are caught up in civilization—a condition which sets all sorts of traps to our spontaneity. We are no longer hunters who just go after prey or gatherers who just go after nuts and roots, and who instinctually procreate. For us, there are ideologically—that is, self-consciously or reflectively—imposed goals as well as restraints in all aspects of our lives. In order that our spontaneity or freedom be not smothered by them, resentment and revolt—which are still reactions of a relatively primitive sort—are not necessarily called for. They might lead to other forms of oppression of freedom. For the revolutionary still exhibit the 'spirit of seriousness', that is, the idea that there just *are* certain goals, norms, values, although not yet realized. The evil which consciousness has brought upon itself can be relieved only by further reflection of consciousness upon itself towards a greater lucidity in understanding itself.

Sartre is adamant that this clarity and understanding cannot be brought about through scientific or objective means. Freedom must lift itself up by its own bootstraps. Subjectivity must elucidate itself, that is, decide whether or not it is engaged in bad faith or self-deception. When you go to the theatre to see *Hamlet*, you know that Sir Lawrence *is* not Hamlet, no matter how marvellous a 'Hamlet' he is. But whether or not François is just honestly doing his job as opposed to posturing as *being* 'a waiter', or whether or not John genuinely and spontaneously loves you and your children as opposed to just playing the role of a husband and a father out of duty or whatever, is a judgement-call. The bottom line is whether or not you are prepared to accept John as your husband and the father of your children, as opposed to whether or not he is, objectively, fit to be one.

The agent himself is in an even more precarious position to judge the authenticity of his life. The self-deceiver is not an impostor. He sincerely believes that he is the character he is playing. What he needs is not more objective knowledge about himself but a (philosophical) conversion. Good faith or honesty towards oneself is the awareness and the acceptance of the fact that I cannot *be* anything, that I neither possess nor can create in me a fixed essence. As humans we inhabit a kind of no man's land. Since we have a body, since we are 'flesh', we share in the meaningless and contingent existence of mere things. We may, on the other hand, aspire, with Kant, to the status of a 'purely intelligible being'. This ambivalence between contingency and rational necessity afflicting us is disquieting and we wish to have matters settled. We seek either to reduce ourselves to a mere contingent thing such as a cauliflower, or a rhinoceros, or to rise to the level of self-contained intelligibility. Both of these attempts involve double-mindedness. While engaged in the latter, I try to identify myself with and submerge in a larger whole—a family, a country, a race, a tradition and a culture, a cause, or, with Kant, the universal community of rational beings. While engaged in the former, I wish to think of myself as just a thing of nature in its own kind of splendid self-sufficiency. However, both of these efforts are doomed to failure. Neither one of them is a living option. While I want to be a member of a group or movement or of humanity as such, I also want to retain my individuality. I want to play the tune, but in my own way. Or if I wish to be a kind of cabbage, I still wish to possess consciousness and will. In either case, I want to have it both ways. But I can come to realize that, while I am not just a thing, I cannot be anything higher either, such as a father, or an American, or a Westerner, or a Protestant, or a Catholic, or a Jew, or even just a rational being. For I know that I can always repudiate any of those affiliations.

In good faith I accept the consequence of my freedom. I then admit to myself that the conflict between my freedom and my facticity can never be overcome. In bad faith I attempt to negate either the one or the other. I think of myself either as untouched by facts or as determined by them. In the former event I think of myself as being identical with what I could be, or could have been, regardless of the circumstances; in the latter, I think of myself as nothing but what the circumstances make me to be. In bad faith, I either maintain that I am really something more than what I appear to be, or see myself as the mere sum of what influences me. In bad faith, I am either a self-righteous stinker or a miserable coward who fabricates excuses (*EH* 52). Sartre spends more time on criticizing the stinker than the coward. The latter, you might say, is, for him, beyond contempt. But he is fascinated by the stinker. Suppose I am in love with Agnes. As a stinker, I shall then believe that she has all sorts of lovable qualities, and that, therefore, my love of her is objectively justified. As a stinker I may also practice humility. But, as Kant said, 'the man who tries to equal or surpass others in humility, believing that in this way he will also acquire a greater inner worth, is guilty of pride . . . and hypocrisy . . .' (*MM* 100–1).

The big difference between Kant and Sartre is this. While Kant believed that it is only our 'lower nature'—our feelings and appetites—that leads us to believe in spurious objective values, while our reason delivers *genuine* instances of them, for Sartre, *all* belief in objective values is the fabrication of the stinker. Genuine morality, says Sartre in the *Cahiers*, must be pure spontaneity—in it I must give myself over completely to the task at hand, without any concern with whether or not I am objectively justified in performing it. I must give someone a drink in order to alleviate his thirst and not because of my concern with my righteousness. The point is to practise charity, not to *be* charitable. Morality is choosing a certain kind of world and not to endeavour to possess a certain kind of inviolate inner self (*CM* 11).

The stinker is not a mere cheat or opportunist. He is genuinely concerned with his integrity and his own worth. But he wants to be more than it is possible for us to be—a fully justified being. On the other hand, if a man considers himself determined by forces outside himself—his passions, upbringing, character, social conditions, and so on—he is a coward. The origins of this persona are even more clearly Kantian. The biggest inner lie, as we saw, is, according to Kant, to hide one's freedom from oneself by believing that all of our motivations come from our sensible or 'lower' nature. The stinker believes that he is splendidly meritorious, the coward, that he has wholesale excuses. Both are deceiving themselves. The stinker realizes deep down that he is merely fabricating his ideals and principles to suit himself. The coward believes in an even more patent absurdity—that it is possible to choose not to choose.

Sartre claims that his doctrine is a kind of humanism (*EH* 54–5). But he is anxious to change what is to be meant by humanism. The traditional form of it, as we saw while discussing Mill, is that there is human nature incorporating what is lower and what is higher and that the ultimate principles of action are to be based on that distinction. We saw that traces of this view are present in Kant, for the unfolding of our higher nature, or reason, is, according to him, an end in itself. Sartre, on the other hand, argues that value can never attach to human beings, or their 'higher nature', as a kind of original endowment. A conscious being who *has* value, such as what Kant called 'dignity', is, according to him, a contradiction. To have value is to be complete, but man is never complete. Man is the sum of his deeds but to act is perpetually to go beyond anything already reached.

It follows then that the question of ethics as we have formulated it has, in Sartre's view, no answer. 'What gives life meaning and makes it worth living?' The answer is, nothing. We can only live life as meaningful and worth living as our ongoing work. The kind of experience which, as we said in the introduction, seems to assure us that the ethical question is not asked in vain—the experience that I am absolutely safe, that nothing can harm me, that I may hope—turns out to be indeed an illusion. For those feelings, Sartre substitutes the feelings of anguish, forlornness, and despair. In them, I recognize my freedom and that all values rest on my own shoulders.

In the *Cahiers* Sartre said (freely translated): 'The dilemma of morality: if the end is already given, it is just another fact and not a value; if the end is not given, then it is gratuitous and capricious' (*CM* 464). I believe that, for Sartre, this dilemma was really illusory. While it is true that human ends are not given, it does not follow that they are arbitrary and gratuitous. What follows instead is just that 'an end must be willed in order to be' and that there is no end except 'for a freedom which wants itself to be free'. This is very far from saying that our ends are arbitrary or gratuitous. For (again in my free translation) he also said:

the very existence of man as a free and transcendent project necessarily poses the question of the end in the sense that in its own being it puts the universe into question. And in its emergence freedom also puts itself into question, or rather, 'it is itself put into question'. Therefore there is only the original emergence not of ends but of questions. The answers are not given. There are no answers at all: they are not to be *found*, they must be invented and willed. (*CM* 464)

Subjectivity is transcendence, it holds the absolute within it. In the last year of Sartre's life he was again reminded of Dostoievski's words. Simone de Beauvoir tells us about the following exchange between her and Sartre:

DE BEAUVOIR: . . . as Dostoievski says, 'If God does not exist, everything is allowed.' You don't think that, do you?
SARTRE: In a way I clearly see what he means, and abstractly it is true; but in another I clearly see that killing a man is wrong. Is directly, absolutely wrong; is wrong for another man; is doubtless not wrong for an eagle or a lion, but is wrong for a man. It might be said that I look upon man's morals and moral activity as an absolute in the midst of the relative . . . which is man in the world and his problems within it. And then there is the absolute, which is the *decision* [my emphasis] which he takes with regard to other men in reference to these problems, which in its turn is therefore an absolute that arises *in him* [my emphasis] . . .[1]

_____

[1] Reported in S. de Beauvoir, *Adieux*, trans. P. O'Brien (London, 1984), 439.

FURTHER READING

ATWELL, J. E., *Ends and Principles in Kant's Moral Thought* (Dordrecht, Boston, Lancaster, 1986).

BEAUVOIR, S. de, *The Ethics of Ambiguity*, trans. B. Frechtman (Secaucus, 1975).

FINGARETTE, H., *Self-deception* (London, 1969).

GOSLING, J. C. B., *Pleasure and Desire* (Oxford, 1969).

KENNY, A., *Action, Emotion, and Will* (London and New York, 1963).

KLEMKE, E. D. (ed.), *The Meaning of Life* (New York and Oxford, 1981).

SCHEFFLER, S. (ed.), *Consequentialism and its Critics* (Oxford, 1988).

SMART, J. J. C., and WILLIAMS, B., *Utilitarianism for and against* (Cambridge, 1973).

SOLOMON, R. C., *The Passions* (Garden City, 1977).

——(ed.), *Existentialism* (New York, 1974).

INDEX